Days of Rain

Days of Rain

by ENZO TAYAR

YAD VASHEM AND
THE HOLOCAUST SURVIVORS' MEMOIRS PROJECT
New York • Jerusalem

Originally published as *1943: i giorni della pioggia*
© 2001 Edizioni Polistampa Firenze, Via S. Maria, 27/r, Firenze

This book is published by Yad Vashem, the Holocaust Martyrs' and Heroes' Remembrance Authority, c/o American Society for Yad Vashem, 500 Fifth Avenue, 42nd floor, New York, New York 10110-4299, and P.O.B. 3477, Jerusalem 91034, Israel

www.yadvashem.org

and

The Holocaust Survivors' Memoirs Project of the World Jewish Congress, 501 Madison Avenue, New York, New York 10022

in association with the World Federation of Bergen-Belsen Associations, Inc.

The Holocaust Survivors' Memoirs Project, an initiative of Nobel Peace Prize laureate Elie Wiesel, was launched through a generous grant from Random House Inc., New York, New York.

Cover photo and all other photographs courtesy of Enzo Tayar.

Library of Congress Cataloging-in-Publication Data
Tayar, Enzo, 1922–
    [1943 i giorni della pioggia. English]
    Days of rain
        p.   cm.
    ISBN 0-9760739-0-0 (pbk.)
    1. Tayar, Enzo, 1922– 2. Jews—Italy—Florence—Biography. 3. Holocaust, Jewish
(1939–1945)—Italy—Personal narratives. 4. Florence (Italy)—Biography. I. Title.
    DS135.I9T3913 2004
    940.53'18'092—dc22

2004059633

Printed in the United States of America.

DEDICATION

To my children
Peggy, Jane, Michael, Pamela, Richard

All this is come upon us; yet have we not forgotten thee . . .
—Psalm 44:18

CONTENTS

CHAPTER 1

Why I Was Born in Florence

I got my first look at this strange, difficult, marvelous world on November 24, 1922, in Florence. A few weeks earlier, unbeknownst to me and definitely without my consent, Mussolini and his men had made the "march on Rome," with the sanction of King Vittorio Emanuele. They were already putting in place the Voluntary Troops for the National Security and the secret service, or Opera Vigilanza Repressione Antifascismo (OVRA). While I was having my first taste of healthy, warm maternal milk, other events destined to have a bearing on my future existence were taking place here and there. With the knowledge of hindsight, I will note that at this time Jewish immigration to Palestine was becoming more intense; that the League of Nations authorized Great Britain to send troops to the western area of Jordan and to keep an eye on foreign policy, law, and internal politics there and on the Holy Land; that Stalin became the secretary general of the Soviet Communist Party; and above all that in Germany the monster Adolf Hitler, already the head of the National Socialist German Workers' Party, began to show signs of his virulent, perilous insanity, forming the Sturmabteilungen and preparing for that Bavarian putsch doomed to fail but also to commence the prelude to one of the most inhumane catastrophes known to man. In other words, I made my entrance into this world at a time that was anything but stagnant and tranquil.

My father, Ugo Salomone Tayar, a native of the island of Malta, had come to Florence in 1913, at the age of 27, and was hired by the Italian office of a large international transport company, Eyre & Humbert. The Tuscan city in those times was an important center of commercial activity as well as one of cultural ferment that made it a European attraction—which in the beginning could only have been an uncomfortable environment for a young man accustomed to the tranquillity and the typical limitations of an island. But he made the adjustment by the simple, firm decision to dedicate himself completely to learning the work assigned to him, and nearly every day put in more hours at work than the job required. As a result he won the respect of his superiors at Eyre & Humbert, who promoted him to head of the department and assigned him a private secretary.

By now he could feel permanently established in the business, and he began to go out with other young Maltese immigrants. Among these were two in particular: one a young pharmacist by the name of De Martino and another a brilliant merchant named Zammit. They spent some of their weekends together, often recalling the times when they went fishing off Valletta and yearning for the limpid sea and blue sky of Malta. But the lure of his real objectives in work brought my father quickly back to reality, and he would again plunge into the work piling up on his desk.

He lived with a Florentine family who gave him a clean bed to sleep in and a good breakfast in the morning. In the evenings, in a local establishment, he would have a supper of fried or hardboiled eggs and big cups of coffee and milk. Suppers were necessarily frugal, since the directors, although continuing to reassure him of their respect as one of the firm's most able employees, did not accompany their words of praise with concrete deeds, that is, with an adequate salary.

My father complained to his friends about his situation and they encouraged him to find a job that would give him greater autonomy and more money. Being shy and afraid of overreaching himself, my father delayed any decision for many months, which did nothing to better the tenor of his life, true enough, but at least he had the tranquillity of a secure position, and that was a desirable goal in those times.

One day a customer of Eyre & Humbert decided to open his own office in Florence and offered my father the position as director. The economic aspect was not exciting, but the offer was appealing just the same. The position offered greater prestige as director of a small office with total autonomy, and with it the concrete prospect of expansion that promised greater financial rewards. He put aside his fears and took the big step.

This new job required frequent trips abroad and meetings with interesting people.

My father was happy about it, and now that he was personally responsible, he worked without letup and was gratified by the results. He had grown used to Florentine customs and cooking, but now that he was also receiving better compensation for his work, he began to feel the need for other than male friendships. At first sight, unfortunately, it did not seem to him that Florence had much to offer in the Jewish sector, but it was there he went on his quest, because his parents, my grandparents, were very religious and a mixed marriage was unthinkable. He finally managed to meet Dora, a 21-year-old Jewish girl from a good family, eight years younger than he, whom he liked on first sight. Hers was a simple, healthy beauty, with slightly curly hair and large dark eyes that revealed her sweet nature and fine intelligence. She had recently graduated from the University of Bologna with full honors in mathematics and was also a talented artist. She played the piano well and loved beautiful music—an important affinity with my father, who loved music and studied voice.

Dora's parents were from different backgrounds: her mother came from an old family of Livornese Jews, the Friedmans, and her father, Maurizio Markbreiter, was a native of Vienna. Therefore they were of Ashkenazi extraction, while my father was Sephardic. There were moments when my father wondered if his way of thinking was not too unlike Dora's. With such confusing doubts, he decided not to see Dora for a while to find out if the separation would cool his feelings for her.

He threw himself headlong into his work. The paperwork on his desk grew steadily because my father hoped to expand his responsibility and, consequently, his earnings, especially now that Dora had entered his life. Things progressed favorably and the experiment proved that his feelings for the young Bolognese had not diminished. So the relationship resumed, until Signora Evelina, a very severe woman with very narrow ideas in regard to her daughter's friendships, agreed to accompany Dora to Florence one weekend.

Dora was the second of the family's four daughters. None of the other daughters had ever been courted or engaged, so Signora Evelina viewed my father's initial approach with suspicion. Who was this transplanted young Jew from Malta now in Florence in search of his fortune? There was no limit to the prudence required. Signora Evelina made this abundantly clear to my father without dousing his ardor. During that weekend visit, he put on the most elegant clothes contained in his sparse wardrobe. Pocketing all the money he had managed to put aside, he invited Dora and her strict mother to dinner in the most elegant restaurant in the city and took them on a tour of the city in a carriage as far as Piazzale Michelangelo.

My father was in an agitated state the entire weekend. His mind was seething with a thousand questions: "Have I made a good impression on Signora Evelina?" "What do I have to do now to let Dora know how I feel about her?"

My father was a very nervous man. His character was reflected to a large degree in his physical appearance. Short and lean, he was certainly not an athletic type to instantly attract a beautiful, still very young Emilian. After using up all his funds, he could not afford another trip to Bologna, at least for a few weeks, but he did not want Dora to think he had gone into hiding after meeting her mother. One evening in his office he got up his courage. After completing the umpteenth paper for exports to Turkey, he took a piece of stationery with the firm's letterhead and wrote Dora about his love for her and his plans for their future together.

On rereading his first declaration of love, he shuddered when he noticed the words: "Attention to the Department Head" on the stationery. With his pen he scratched out the words that certainly would have put Signora Evelina out of sorts. The letter was sent and my father began the wait for a reply. It arrived in the form of an official invitation from Signor Maurizio to spend a weekend in Bologna as the guest of the Markbreiter family. Evidently my father's limited means had not been lost on Signora Evelina.

Preparations for the visit to Bologna and for an official request for Dora's hand were feverish but exhilarating at the same time. My father prepared a little speech to make to his future in-laws and, because his Italian was good but not perfect (his native tongue was Maltese, which has its roots in a North African Arabic dialect), he memorized most of it.

He asked his faithful friends De Martino and Zammit for advice about the sort of gifts he should bring Dora and her mother; it was not easy to coordinate his desires with his meager finances. In the end, he bought a silk scarf for Dora and a nice little bunch of flowers for Signora Evelina.

The meeting in Bologna went better than expected. Dora was very sweet and looked happy. It was the first time the subject of marriage had been brought up in the Markbreiter household, and it was happening now to her!

Little linguistic uncertainties plagued my father's "official" announcement, but

Signor Maurizio helped him out because he was Viennese and had his own problems with speaking Italian perfectly. To this confraternity was joined his great good nature that counterbalanced his wife's stiffness.

The wedding followed the customary engagement period. Dora, my mother, moved to Florence, and my father left his furnished room to rent a small apartment at Poggio Imperiale, where he began his married life. In 1918 my sister Liliana was born, and in 1920 my brother Franco. It was my turn in 1922. The family was complete and by now my father and mother were definitely settled in Florence, creating for themselves a circle of good friends and leading a pleasant and comfortable life.

Something unforeseen happened to disturb that tranquil happiness, just when my mother was expecting the birth of my brother. My father had to have an operation on his eyes for glaucoma. In those days ophthalmological surgery was very primitive, and the operation had unfortunate results. His sight was so diminished that he could no longer read, and the images of the world around him became blurred shadows.

It was a disaster for my parents. With one baby barely two years old and another one on its way, my parents' future had overnight become tragically dark. My father was terrified by the fear of losing his job and becoming incapable of supporting his family. Fortunately that did not happen: he kept his position as director of the Florence office and continued to dispatch his work with great courage and ability. He had a faithful secretary who read him his mail and wrote his letters; she was an impeccably honest woman and my father could trust her completely. He also had learned to act with confidence in the presence of strangers, and very often those who did not know of this problem with his sight were not aware of anything. In spite of that, my father was quite disturbed by it and began to worry that his work contacts might cheat him.

Mother was terrified every time my father left the house or returned from the office. She was afraid that one day he would have an accident. My father could not afford a car, which was a real luxury in those times, so he always rode the streetcar that left him practically at his office door.

This grave impairment seriously undermined my father's fragile character. For the rest of his days he lived in terror of being unable to give his family a happy and comfortable life. Work had become the sole aim of his existence, and although my mother and we children never lacked for anything, he deprived himself of all but the most necessary things, and he was obsessed by the necessity of putting aside money "for a rainy day."

As with everything in this world, we adapted to the situation: we prayed for our father's safety, and my mother, following his example, was as thrifty as possible.

CHAPTER 2

We Three Children

I remember that we three dressed in costume at carnival time, and, for many years, always in the same costumes. Liliana and Franco masqueraded as Pierrette and Pierrot, wearing white rayon trousers and jackets with large fake buttons made of black cardboard. On their heads each wore a kind of skullcap with a pheasant feather stuck in front, their faces covered with white flour making them look like two ghosts. Liliana also wore a large beauty spot on one cheek. Franco pretended to play something resembling a mandolin, supposedly serenading Liliana.

I masqueraded as Charlie Chaplin, or "Charlot," as he was universally known. Mother fixed up an old pair of long black trousers and a jacket, each more worn than the other. Charlot was a poor man and it was logical that I should be dressed like one! Completing my costume were an old pair of papa's shoes, twice too big; a shirt with a small black tie and a black bowler hat (the only accessory they bought me, which they set at an angle on my head); and a kind of walking stick made with a bamboo cane. As a finishing touch they drew a mustache with a burnt cork. I made every effort to walk with my feet turned out and twirl the bamboo cane at the same time. Whatever the result, my getup was much funnier than those of Pierrot and Pierrette.

Mother would invite a dozen other children our age to come to our home in costume for a little party with confetti and streamers. At every carnival time they took a photograph of all of us in costume, looking rather ridiculous.

We took a vacation every summer. At the end of the school year the ritual would begin: if we went to the seaside my father would call the owner of the Villino Nelli, a two-story building with a little garden in front, on Via del Fortino, the main street of Lido di Camaiore. They would agree on the rental price for July and August, and my mother would arrange with one of her sisters (who in the meantime had married and had two children about our same ages) to spend the summer with us. If, on the other hand, the decision was to go to the mountains, the choice would fall on Maresca, in the Pistoiese Apennines, where we would routinely rent a house from a local family, the Filoni. Our cousins from Milan would spend the summer with us. These vacations were always fun, especially because we were with our cousins with whom we had such affectionate ties.

Departure was always an exciting time for me. We had two large wooden trunks covered in green canvas and lined with flowered paper. It was my job to carry the drawers from various bedrooms to the entrance hall where mother would fill the trunks with their contents. She would then telephone the man who transported our things to Lido di Camaiore or Maresca. The next day I would joyfully watch the luggage being hauled away, with the thought that it would soon be our turn to leave.

When we spent the summer in Maresca, my father would come on Saturdays and return to Florence Sunday evenings. He took the train that went from Florence to Bologna by way of Porrettana. It was a narrow-gauge train that wound through the beautiful Apennine valleys. At every curve (and there were many), the wheels of the little train let out a shrill squeal that echoed over those oak and chestnut woods.

At nightfall, as our father's arrival time grew near, we listened for those squeals, which could be heard from quite a distance. As soon as we began to hear them we would dash from the house to meet him. This was the special train of "commuting fathers," and other children were also waiting for the arrival of their fathers. Then the crowd would separate into small groups that moved slowly down the narrow mountain roads to the various houses.

When we stayed at Lido di Camaiore we went to the town piazza every Saturday afternoon to wait for the streetcar from Viareggio, which my father took after he arrived by train from Florence. He always brought a ring-shaped cake called *buccellato* that he bought at the Lucca station where he changed trains for Viareggio.

Sunday mornings we went to the beach: we children and our mother were as brown as berries, but our poor father was very white! We rented a twin-hulled boat and climbed aboard, while my father took the oars and intoned one of his favorite arias, "Cielo e mar," undoubtedly inspired by the surroundings.

During the week, while papa was working in Florence, the rule was that we could rent the boat only once and only for an hour. The three of us and mother would get on it and take turns rowing. Liliana and Franco knew how to swim, and when we went out where the water was deep they would jump in with mother while I, not yet a swimmer, stayed with the oars and slowly followed them.

The most fun for me was going out in the boat. However, I felt very limited by being able to go out only one hour a week and then having to share it with my mother and siblings. I decided to help the bathing attendant at the end of every day, when all the vacationers had gone, to take up all the deck chairs and umbrellas that were then stored until the following day. After that I would help rake the beach clean. As compensation for my services, I would ask Signor Gemignani to let me use the little children's boat for an hour every morning before the vacationers came to the beach. He agreed. I was happy not only because I now had a way to use the boat every day, but also because the physical work as the attendant's helper would help develop my chest!

Our life passed serenely. The three of us children went to public schools. Each to a different one—so much for simplifying our mother's life! Liliana went to Regina Margherita, Franco to another, while I went to Cesare Battisti, which had the advantage of being near home. In the mornings mother would prepare three little baskets for us with little aluminum boxes inside with screw-on covers, each containing an omelette, bread, and a piece of fruit. This was our noon meal. All of us walked to and from our respective schools all by ourselves.

None of us ever got the highest marks in school. Liliana and I barely managed to make average grades. Franco had to take remedial classes a couple of times. However, none of us ever had to repeat a year. One summer at Lido di Camaiore, when Franco had to make up his drawing class, he spent the summer drawing some dumb laurel leaves.

I remember vividly the very words that my father said to me while I was getting ready for my first day of school:

> Enzo, I want to talk to you before you begin elementary school. Sometimes things will happen that you aren't accustomed to because of the

fact that you are Jewish, while the school you are going to follows the rules of the Catholic faith. You are not obliged to conform to these rules, and you mustn't feel different from the other children in your class, or much less feel ashamed and inferior, because you are Jewish and they are Catholic. And because they are Catholic I might as well tell you that if one of your classmates should say something ugly to you because you are Jewish, you must never let it continue. You must face up to him and tell him he'd better stop if he doesn't want me to go and talk to the teacher. I realize it could be unpleasant for you and maybe you are too young to do it. However, you might as well learn now how you will have to behave in life.

It was the first time my father had had a serious talk with me. I was not at all frightened by the prospect he outlined. Instead, I was proud, and I am still grateful to him for making me responsible for taking care of myself at such a tender age. It was a sign of the great faith he had in me.

Father's warning was not long in becoming a reality. In fact, the very first morning the teacher told us all to rise and recite the "Our Father." I knew this was something I had never learned, so I thought immediately it had something to do with religion. I did not know what to do: surely the teacher would not notice the fact that I was not reciting it. I could pretend by moving my lips slightly. However, the problem remained that I did not know if it was right to stay seated while the others stood. I chose a compromise that seemed a good solution: I rose from my desk, but I did not stand straight, I bent forward with my elbows propped on my desk.

The teacher promptly noticed my unusual posture and pointing at me, she said: "What is your name?"

"Enzo Tayar, ma'am."

"Fine. Now will you tell me why you are bent over with your elbows propped on the desk? Do you have a backache?"

Her voice was kind and unthreatening, so taking courage I decided to grab the bull by the horns and said: "I am a Jewish boy and my father told me I don't have to do anything Jews don't do." I saw my classmates turn in my direction, perhaps to see who was this strange creature who called himself a "Jew," and who did not have to recite the "Our Father." Their expressions were full of curiosity and incredulity—not hostility, fortunately.

The teacher stood thinking for a second or two that seemed an eternity to me. Finally she said, "All right, Tayar, if you wish, you may remain seated," and with a smile she motioned for me to sit down. I felt happy and proud about what I had done, and most of all I would have liked to hug the teacher for showing compassion for me. I could not wait to tell my father. He patted me on the head, saying: "Bravo, you did the right thing."

After that episode I never had to face the question of my Jewishness, perhaps because my classmates were still so young they had not had time to become prejudiced against us. However, it made me want to know more about Jews and Catholics. I began to ask my father and mother questions, and I gradually became aware of what I was, and frankly I was not sorry to be a little different from the other children. I felt special. I learned the names of our holidays and their significance.

When we went to the temple, I tried to understand what was going on, and every once in awhile my father would explain the meaning of certain prayers and tell me about the ceremony unfolding before my eyes. I was fascinated by those beautiful silver ornaments that decorated the *sefarim* and by the long rolls of parchment handwritten in such unfamiliar characters. When I sat next to father while the hazan (cantor) read the Torah, my gaze wandered from one place to another of the temple. High over the *aron ha-kodesh*[1] were the law tablets. I tried to read silently those ten small groups of letters in Hebrew that represent the Creator's commandments to His people, commandments which the Jews have obeyed for thousands of years. I was in awe at the thought that such simple rules had been the foundation for the existence of an entire people and that parts of those same rules, because of their greatness, had subsequently been adopted by other peoples of different faiths. Every time I thought about these things I promised myself to observe the Lord's laws as long as I lived.

But the thing that touched me the most profoundly was the chorus alternating with the Torah reading. The great organ at the back of the temple filled the dome with sound, and the choir followed. My father joined in with some of the songs, but I noticed he did not know them all. I would have liked to join in the chorus, too,

---

1. The ark where the handwritten rolls of parchment of the Torah (Pentateuch) are kept.

but my father said: "Be patient. You'll know them by the time of your bar mitzvah."[2]

Going to the temple was an important event: mother dressed Liliana and Franco in sailor suits that were worn on special occasions. As the smallest, I was always dressed in Franco's hand-me-downs, which showed obvious signs of wear.

My mother wore her most elegant dress, a veiled hat, and pointed, high-heel shoes. She put on Coty cologne that I loved for its clean smell; mamma kept it in a beautiful little glass bottle the shape of a ball studded with stars, the deep blue color of a night sky.

My father dressed in one of his everyday office suits. He always had to be dressed properly and in fact some of his things were rather elegant: in the summer he wore a straw hat with a straight brim and two-toned shoes. He always wore a vest that had two small pockets. A gold chain attached to his watch in one pocket went to the other where he kept his gold fountain pen. In the winter he wore a light gray Homburg and felt spats over his shoes that were the same color as his hat.

At that time Florence had two synagogues: a beautiful one on Via Farini and smaller one on the second floor of a small building on Via delle Oche. During our religious holidays we would go to the big synagogue in the morning and in the evening to the one on Via delle Oche; it was close to my father's office so he did not have to cross the streets of Florence in the dark with all the inherent dangers. Although the synagogue on Via delle Oche was simpler and much smaller than the one on Via Farini, I felt good there and I liked the fact that after the services father would take us to Donnini, one of the best pastry shops in town, to buy sweet rolls.

In my family, Jewishness was never a question of religious orthodoxy in all its manifestations as much as a question of substance. We were not raised to observe the dietary rules of the kashruth[3] or to go to synagogue or abstain from any activity on Saturdays. Our father brought us to the temple for Passover, Rosh Hashana, Yom Kippur, and Sukkoth,[4] and if he was not busy with work, for some of the other holidays.

On the other hand, what has remained deeply rooted in us is an attachment to our faith, a pride in being Jewish, and a moral conduct consonant with the Lord's

---

2. The celebration for the Jewish boy when he becomes an adult from the religious point of view.

3. Jewish dietary laws.

4. Four of the most important Jewish holy days and festivals.

commandments. As a child I greatly admired those who knew how to read our prayer books, but as I grew up I realized that even though they knew how to pronounce correctly what they read, very few understood the meaning of it. This was disappointing.

In our temple I loved to follow our liturgy, even though I did not always understand its meaning. I found it simple and basic, full of beautiful symbolism. The sound of the shofar[5] repeated at the end of the service fascinated me. I made a bet with myself how long the hazan would be able to hold the last note. But the most moving part of all the ceremonies was and still is the *birkat kohanim*.[6] While father held his wide tallith[7] over our mother and us, I physically felt the intensity of the blessing that the rabbis and, in a special way, our father were giving us.

I wondered if my paternal grandparents had been more religious than we were. My paternal grandmother's name was Corinna Coen, and I thought that with such a last name she had to come from a very religious family. I would have liked to have known my father's parents. In his bedroom papa kept a large photograph of grandfather Cesare showing only his handsome face and long black beard. He had a large, full-length portrait of grandmother Corinna. Her bearing was very regal. She was tall and slender and with such a narrow waist I wondered how she could breathe. I am sorry to say my desire to know them could not be realized; they both died when I was still small.

The same was not true of my maternal grandparents. Grandmother Evelina, whom we all feared because of her strong character, came to visit us often. She did it to be near her daughter, whom she missed, and to see Liliana, her first granddaughter and the most favored of all her grandchildren. Liliana could do as she pleased: grandmother pampered her and let her have whatever she wanted. Toward Franco and me, on the other hand, she was very strict and never missed an opportunity "to straighten us up," as she would typically say.

If we ever contradicted something she or mother said, Grandmother Evelina would tell us: "If I say it is nighttime and the sun is shining outside, you must agree that it is nighttime. Children have no right to contradict what an adult says!"

---

5. A ram's horn on which the hazan blows repeatedly, making a very loud sound.

6. The blessing that is given by the high priests *(kohanim)*.

7. Prayer shawl.

One day when she was with us in Florence, I saw her take from a little blue box a kind of little black ball that to me looked like licorice. I went up to her and said: "Grandmother, would you please give me one, too?" She opened the little box and without a word gave me one of those little pills. I thanked her happily and put the presumed licorice in my mouth, but with a snort of disgust I had to spit it out immediately. It was more bitter than poison. I began to cry in mortification for having been tricked, but she showed no signs of distress. She only said: "And now you'll learn not to ask for things." The damned little pill was liver medicine called Boldina. I sulked around grandmother until the day she went back to Bologna, and even then I did not want to tell her good-bye.

Not that my father harbored a great deal of affection for his mother-in-law. He was very courteous, but he kept his distance. I noticed that every time grandmother went back to Bologna, father's good humor returned and he began joking again. I think perhaps he was also a little jealous of the attention grandmother gave Liliana, who was also his pet.

There were also brief periods in which father had some impulses of cordiality toward Grandmother Evelina. Then, he would ask mother to accompany him on the piano while he sang one or two opera arias for grandmother. There was one aria in particular that always moved her: "Una furtiva lacrima." Papa put all his interpretive ability into it and often grandmother would shed a tear of her own.

During the long periods when grandmother stayed in Bologna, a heavy correspondence went back and forth between her and my mother. Every day they exchanged a postcard, and I wondered what they had to tell each other every day that was so important, especially since I happened to notice that Grandmother Evelina's cards were filled on both sides and even crosswise if she saw a free space. I thought it was pure insanity, because often my poor mother could not decipher either what was written crosswise or on the regular lines.

The only other occasions when I saw Grandmother Evelina were during the Christmas holidays when we would go to Bologna. I played from morning to night with my cousin Bruno, with whom I had excellent relations. When we woke up in the morning our grandmother fixed wonderful breakfasts of chocolate and milk and crisp fresh bread with tons of butter and quince marmalade.

One of my favorite things to do in Bologna was to visit Aunt Matilde, my mother's younger sister who, along with Grandfather Maurizio, had a nice store, the Schostal, under the arcades of Via Rizzoli. I seemed to be dreaming when I went into that store full of wonderful clothing for men and women. Raincoats, overcoats, shirts, ties, gloves, scarves—all sorts of things, and all of the best quality. As long as we were children our visits to the Schostal were limited to playing in Aunt Matilde's office in the back of the store. When we reached the right age, Aunt Matilde would give us little gifts: a tie or a sweater or a pair of gloves. She was always very generous.

There was a clerk in the store that Bruno and I liked to make fun of. He was a nice looking, tall man who carried himself well, by the name of Sassoli. He was the English majordomo type. His manner of greeting customers was impeccable and he spoke with the typical Bolognese dialect, with the "salted *S*," as they call it there. That is, for *Signore,* he would say *Scignore. Cashmere* he pronounced as *casimiro,* and when he showed the ties, he said, according to the design: "Here I am in stripes" or "Here I am in little dots," and we would laugh like crazy.

Then there was Uncle Guido, Grandmother Evelina's brother, who entertained us by taking us on rides in his Fiat 509, which was considered a luxury at that time. Uncle Guido worked in the insurance business. He was a jovial man. Everyone knew him, and before dinner you could meet him at the bar under the Pavaglione having an aperitif.

He was a ladies' man and liked to court the beautiful young girls, even though he did not have the build of an Adonis. He was very corpulent, with a protruding stomach, but he considered this the ideal shape for a successful businessman.

Aunt Berta, his wife, was well aware of his escapades, but pretended not to notice. She was born in England and spoke Italian with a slight Anglo-Saxon accent that made her even more distinguished. When Uncle Guido wanted to be sweet to her he would call her "My Bertuccia."

Uncle Guido, unfortunately, also liked to gamble, and he never could get free from the habit, despite the pleas of his sister Evelina and Aunt Berta. It was a real sickness. Often on the weekends he would go to Venice or some other city in the north where there was a casino and try his luck. Sometimes he would come home happy, bringing a nice gift for his wife, a sign that it had gone well for him. But most of the time it did not go well and everyone paid the price of his bad mood. One Sunday evening he returned to Bologna very distraught. He told Aunt Berta that he had eaten something that did not agree with him and the next day he decided to stay in bed until he felt better. He waited until his wife went out to do her shopping and asked her not to waken him in case he was asleep when she came home. Aunt Berta did her errands and when she came home she found her husband fast asleep. She left him alone. It came dinner time and Uncle Guido was still asleep. It seemed odd to his wife, who decided to awaken him. She went cautiously into the bedroom and gently touched his face, but he did not move because he was dead.

Guido had swallowed a strong dose of sleeping pills. He had lost a lot of money gambling that weekend, and in trying to recoup his losses he had made debts he could not honor. For a man of his character, the shame would have been unbearable.

It was an enormous misfortune for all of us. Aunt Berta and Grandmother Evelina were destroyed by sorrow and by the shame of such a tragic end for their husband and brother. We nephews lost a great friend. Our visits to our grandparents in Bologna were never again so happy and carefree.

Our life in Florence ran smoothly. Mother very capably supervised the household with the help of a maid. She was also a good cook and changed our menu every day. The only menu she never changed was father's. I do not know why, but for some reason he got it into his head that he could not eat rich food. He was thin by nature, but I was sure that if he had a more abundant and varied diet he would put on weight. In any event, his dinner consisted of rice with butter and cheese, a very small veal steak cooked in butter, boiled vegetables with oil, and cooked fruit.

Every Sunday morning father took streetcar Number Three as far as the Logge del Porcellino and from there he went by foot to his office on Piazza Strozzi. The aim of this Sunday outing was to get the mail from his box at the central post office and pass by the bar Donnini to buy sweet rolls on the way home. Franco and I would go along to help him open the mail and to read aloud the names on the letterheads. Then papa would let us go see the showrooms where samples of every kind were on display: ceramics, alabaster from Volterra, glass from Murano, decorated Florentine boxes, leather goods, and other things. We were especially interested in the samples from toy manufacturers that papa allowed us to touch and play with a little.

Papa's offices were very large and beautiful. They occupied a floor of the building on Piazza Strozzi 5, and the room where he worked was on a corner between the piazza and Via Strozzi, with a fine view of Palazzo Strozzi. He had 30 people working for his export business, which was considered one of the best in Florence.

After the visit to his office, we would go toward the Logge del Porcellino to take the streetcar home, and on the way, besides the stop at Donnini's, we would make another obligatory stop at the newspaper stand under the arcades of the post office to buy the *Corrierino dei Piccoli,* a children's magazine.

We moved often. Father had a "bug for flakes of dry plaster," as they say in Florence, and every once in awhile he would go looking for something bigger and better for his wife and three children. On Sundays in the fall he would go in search of new apartments being built, along with mamma and those of us who wanted to go. He would climb up rough stairs full, precisely, of flaking plaster to look at apartments with barely finished exterior walls. My mother, whose patience was infinite, followed in papa's footsteps—mainly, I think, to keep him from hurting himself, because he could not see well where to put his feet.

CHAPTER 3

Our House

We always had a house in a good residential area in Florence, with nice large, sunny rooms. Franco and I slept in the same bedroom, while Liliana had one to herself. Our furniture was an eclectic conglomeration. The bedroom Franco and I shared was furnished with anonymous, ugly furniture of an inferior quality that my father bought secondhand. We had two beds that remained standing by a miracle. They were composed of a headboard and footboard held together by two side boards. Often when Franco and I jumped around on the two beds the supports would give way and the springs and mattresses, sheets and pillows would end up on the floor. Mother had to try to put everything back together with a screwdriver and hammer, but that only lasted a short while. We each had a bedside table. In my drawer I kept all the "treasures" I had collected over time. The most important piece in the bedroom was a wardrobe where Franco and I hung our clothes, with three drawers below where we kept sweaters, shirts, and underwear, and a large center door with a mirror. This door was a constant danger, because the hinge was worn, and often when we opened it to get our things it would fall off. I have always wondered what kind fate kept that mirror in one piece.

The other rooms were furnished with antiques, some of them valuable, the happy result of papa's scouring antique and secondhand stores; others were the less happy outcome of that hobby of his that made us all apprehensive when we saw papa come home with one of his new acquisitions.

It was a heterogeneous collection of various styles and epochs. Because not every piece blended well with the others, our house had the appearance of an antique shop. Father often exchanged one piece of furniture for another. I remember a period when Liliana's bedroom was pure Empire style. Then papa decided he did not like it and exchanged it for the inlaid furniture of the 1700s in Maggiolini style.

Among the finest pieces were a beautiful strongbox belonging to the Medici family and an ebony wood boulle piano completely covered by the characteristic bronze and tortoiseshell inlay. There were a Maggiolini-type writing desk, with very beautiful inlay, that my mother kept in her room, a splendid Venetian desk in briarwood, and two semicircular corner cupboards with inlay work and marble tops. We also had some nice paintings by different artists, such as Eugenio Zampighi and Frederic Soulacroix.

Once in a while papa, with mamma's help, would move everything around to suit himself. Often we would go somewhere in the house expecting to find a table and find a chair instead.

Another one of his hobbies was the birds that he kept in a cage in the entryway. He had all kinds: parrots of every color, canaries, goldfinches, hummingbirds, and others.

One day he felt the need to give his birds a more imposing habitat, and he came home with an enormous cage the shape of a cathedral with a large dome. This, too, was acquired from a secondhand dealer, and before moving the birds to their new home, we had to clean the "new" cage of all the dust and dirt that had accumulated over the years. Then we had to transfer the birds from one cage to the other, which was not a simple task because first we had to catch them one by one. During the operation two canaries got away and began flying around the house, forcing us on a chase that the little canaries won, because we finally had to open the living room windows to let them fly to their freedom forever.

Given the great size of the new cage, father began to buy other birds, until there were about 30. They made such an infernal racket that if we wanted some peace in the living room in the evening we had to cover the cage with a large dark canvas that stopped the twittering like a charm.

In the afternoons mother devoted herself completely to helping us with our history, geography, and mathematics homework, or to listening to the poetry we had to memorize, going from one of us to the other. Franco and I could dispatch it well enough by ourselves. Liliana needed more help than we did, so mother did the research for her in the encyclopedia or textbooks so Liliana could make a good impression with her essays. At times they stayed up late to finish her homework.

When I was still little, I would wait for my father to return from the office, and as soon as I heard his ring I would run to open the door. He would take me on his shoulders and carry me to his room, where he put on his house jacket, took off his spats and shoes, and put on his slippers. Then he usually went to the living room to listen to classical or opera records while the maid fixed supper. After supper we had little choice of what to do. Television did not exist even as a word. The only evening entertainment was to listen to a play on the radio, which did not occur more than two or three times a week. Our radio was in the living room, one of those beautiful, highly polished pieces of furniture that had the radio below and the record player on top. It was papa's pride and joy. We all gathered near it, some on the floor, some on the divan, and we enjoyed what the national station had to offer us.

When there was no play, I went to my father's room and begged him to tell one of his hunting stories. He would settle in his leather armchair, and I would climb on his lap to hear his stories for the umpteenth time. Often I would go to sleep while he talked, and he would lay me down on his bed where I continued to sleep tranquilly. When the time came for my parents to go to bed, they would carry me to my room and I continued my slumber undisturbed.

Mother played the piano well and was constantly extending her repertoire. She played Chopin, Scarlatti, Debussy, Bach, and Beethoven particularly well. Sometimes one of her friends would come to play works for four hands. When two of them were playing that poor piano thundered through the house.

This was mother's greatest pastime and, God bless her, she continued to play four-hand pieces with her friends until the venerable age of 90. Having heard her for such a long time, I knew by memory all the waltzes, the nocturnes, and Chopin's études. I knew the passages that required great finger dexterity and the passages where mother's fingers regularly stumbled. She played passages I loved very much, and even now when I hear them played by famous pianists, but without mother's hesitations, I think of her and the wonderful hours I spent listening to her play.

The piano was her best friend, she said, and that was true. She encouraged me to study it, and I did my best to please her. I took lessons from an elderly spinster who came to our house twice a week. I went through all the Czerny and Hanon exercises. I liked some of them for a certain harmony that made me forget the monotony of the exercises themselves. On Saturday and Sunday afternoons, when I did not have school work, I would practice for hours until Franco or Liliana screamed for mercy. Mother would run to my aid, saying I was her only child who really loved music, so they should leave me alone. Thus I could calmly continue to torment them with my pounding.

I kept taking lessons until my school work became too demanding and I was unable to manage both. I was obliged to give up the piano. Never mind. I had learned something and consoled myself with the thought that I could continue to pound anytime I so desired, which I did.

My father, on the other hand, had studied voice since a young man. He was an excellent light tenor, like Tito Schipa. He knew all the most beautiful opera arias and sang them often, accompanied by mother at the piano. A day did not go by in our house without music, either from the phonograph or my mother at the piano or my papa singing. Of the three of us children, I was the one who inherited the greatest proportion our parents' musical ability. I am grateful to them for having taught me to love all kinds of music.

Often when American buyers came to acquire things for their shops, father would invite them home for supper. We went through a regular routine with only slight variations, depending upon the guest.

It went more or less like this: mother worked with the maid all afternoon in the kitchen preparing the food and decorating the dining room table. We had a beautiful antique table in solid walnut, a very long and rather narrow trestle-type.

Papa would come home at the usual time, check to see that everything was in its place, and then tell us how to conduct ourselves according to whom the guest might be.

Usually the supper went by pleasantly. Mother was an excellent cook and the guests always made a fuss over her delicious delicacies. The American guests were especially nice with us children and praised us for our good behavior and for how well we spoke English, which was an exaggeration, if not a downright lie.

After the fruit was served and the supper was over, father would regularly offer to entertain the guests with his singing virtuosity, and mamma would, without delay, sit at her beloved piano and play a few thundering arpeggios (almost as a call for silence in the room), and then begin to play the first aria.

A few measures on the piano would come first, and then at her nod, papa would give full rein to his vocal cords. Ordinarily he sang only three or four arias, and of course we knew perfectly well which they would be and murmured the words under our breath as he sang.

The evening was not yet over. After the musical interlude, papa would ask his guests if they would like to see some old costumes of the Goldoni epoch. Naturally the response was always positive, and at this point he would head for the Medici strongbox where the costumes were jealously guarded. Under the guests' admiring glances he would turn the lock with the large, ancient key, raise the heavy lid, and take out three beautiful men's jackets of elegant brocade with gold and silver threads.

One jacket was a golden color, one red, and one green, all of rather small size to fit the men at that time. Papa would put one on so the guests could get a better look at it. And with this *défilé* the evening was considered to have come definitely and splendidly to an end.

CHAPTER 4

The World around Us

In the outside world things were going along "normally," we might say. Mussolini and his Fascist movement kept increasing in strength. In the public schools we attended they stuffed our heads with Fascist ideology and with Mussolini's famous sayings, which were then written in block letters on the front of houses, such as "He who stops is lost," or "It's the plow that cuts the furrow and it's the sword that defends it," or (the most famous): "Believe! Obey! Fight!"

So all three of us had to enroll in a Fascist youth organization. Lilian became a "Giovane italiana." Franco became a "Balilla aquilotto" (eaglet) that imitated the Alpine Corps. They went around dressed as members of the Fascist youth movement with the ridiculous little cord tied in an odd way that hung from a snap hook on their belt. Every Sunday they went on long walks through the Florentine hills dressed in that manner, singing Fascist hymns and mountain songs.

I became a member of the "Balilla Moschettieri," which in its creator's fantasy was meant to emulate the image of the Duce's Musketeers: a herd of fanatics organized for the job (purely theoretical as history would later show) of defending Mussolini's life at the risk of their own.

I wore the Balilla uniform and in addition had a kind of toy ammunition pouch and a rifle, also a toy, even furnished with a bayonet. We three went to the weekly assemblies where they had us march up and down the street. I remember that our group was led by a Jewish lieutenant, Eugenio Genazzani, who was always very nice to me.

At school they instituted a subject I hated with heart and soul. It was called

"Military Culture," or something like that. We had to become familiar with and memorize everything to do with the Italian military structure: the armies, the platoons, all the ranks from simple soldier to the grand general of the army corps, the weapons that the different divisions used, and other things I had no interest in. Perhaps my reaction stemmed from the fact that news had begun to come in from abroad that did not bode well.

It was 1933 and Adolf Hitler took power in Germany, spreading his insane theories about the purity of the Aryan race and its superiority over all others. My father was very worried about what was happening. Mother predicted that the Nazi plague would have ominous repercussions on Italian Fascism, which, up to that time, like everything else that happened in Italy, was more an outward manifestation of folklore, without any real content. Something, in other words, totally different from what Nazism appeared to be.

A period of great uncertainty began for all of us. We had hoped that in monarchic Italy, the king would try to keep the Nazi ideology out. We tried, in other words, to convince ourselves that nothing would change and that Mussolini would not follow Hitler in his crazed obsession.

In 1935 Mussolini invaded the Ethiopia of Emperor Haile Selassie to "liberate" it. He had an easy victory, sending his brave legionnaires in with rifles, guns, armored tanks, and airplanes to fight those poor blacks armed with little more than spears and shields. In 1936 Mussolini made his triumphal entry into Addis Ababa on a white horse. The Italians went wild with nationalistic joy and Vittorio Emanuele was proclaimed emperor.

The world turned against Italy for this aggressive action and economic sanctions were enacted against it by the League of Nations. It was a very awkward time for my family. We had British citizenship from Malta, a country which, along with the other members of the League of Nations, had decreed the sanctions. The press and radio stirred up the Italians' hate against "vile Albion." Papa began to fear that as British subjects we might be subject to restrictive measures.

Papa's worry was that he might be forced to close his office or that they might let him go and put a non-Jewish, Italian collaborator in his place. Making a decision definitely against his will, and one that no one in the family liked, he wrote a letter to the mayor of Florence, I think it was, condemning the economic sanctions imposed on Italy and asking for the "honor" of becoming an Italian citizen.

Through all this ferment I was immersed body and soul in the preparations for my bar mitzvah. I took Hebrew lessons from an elderly woman by the name of Corcos who lived near Piazza Oberdan. She was very tiny, and when she walked she took funny little hopping steps. For good or ill she managed to teach me to read Hebrew, to memorize certain *brachot*,[8] and to familiarize myself with the passage from the Torah that I would have to read in the temple during the ceremony. The part regarding Jewish history and everything pertaining to Judaism either as faith or as philosophy of life was taught by Rabbi Uzielli, who was the chief rabbi in Florence at the time.

When the day of the ceremony arrived, I was very excited and felt well prepared for the task ahead of me. I was the center of the family's attention and this made me proud. Grandmother Evelina came to Florence for the occasion. Mother bought me a new suit with a single-breasted jacket and long trousers. For the first time I put on a tie.

According to Hebrew law, the bar mitzvah signals the moment when a boy becomes a man, and as such, his presence in the synagogue is sufficient reason for forming a minyan.[9] I hoped that reaching this "maturity" also meant I would not have to wear Franco's old hand-me-downs any more. I received many beautiful gifts: a watch, a fountain pen, a pair of shoes, a box with a compass, drawing pens, and other assorted items.

I wanted my mother to give me her gold, oval-shaped *Shadai*,[10] engraved with her name and birth date. She kept it in a small box in her *secrétaire*, and I had always hoped to have one like it some day. So I asked her to give me hers and she put it around my neck, giving me a big hug with her blessing. From that moment I have always kept it with me, and have always felt that this little medallion carried my mother's blessing.

After this very short period of mystical-religious involvement was over, we fell back into a state of uncertainty and fear aroused by the political events in Germany and Italy.

Another crisis erupted in Europe in 1936 with the civil war in Spain between

---

8. Different kinds of benedictions.

9. A group of ten Jewish adults, the minimum number necessary for celebrating any public religious function.

10. A small medallion with the Hebrew letter s*hin* inscribed, the initial of the divine name *Shadai* (Omnipotent).

General Francisco Franco and the Republican government of the recently elected Popular Front presided over by the Socialist Francisco Largo Caballero. The Franco-ist revolt began in Morocco and continued on Spanish territory, with the support of Mussolini and Hitler who sent their troops and air forces to help, while the Republican troops lined up international volunteer brigades. After terrible and bloody engagements on both sides, the conflict ended two years later with the victory of Franco's Falangists, which was also a victory for the Fascists and Nazis. Mussolini's propaganda machine made a great hurrah over this victory on the radio and in the newspapers, singing the praises of the "heroic troops of Fascist Italy."

In the meantime, the economic sanctions against Italy were having their negative effects. Industries and retailers profited by increasing their prices, and many imported products were boycotted by the government in retaliation against the countries imposing the sanctions on us.

Eventually overcoming his confusion and dismay, papa recovered his old serenity and worked even harder to increase his business with his American customers—not an easy task considering Italy's growing unpopularity with Anglo-Saxon countries.

Mother tried to make greater cuts in expenses. We had to be prepared for the possibility that one day papa might be left without work, and then we would have to live on whatever mamma had been able to put aside. Unfortunately, we could see only clouds on the horizon because of the ever closer relationship of Hitler and Mussolini, first under the aegis of the Rome-Berlin Alliance and then the Anti-Cominterm Pact, along with the support of Japan. We asked ourselves why pacts of that kind were necessary, considering that Germany and Italy were already united by nearly identical ideologies. Evidently such an agreement aimed at keeping Mussolini, the less trustworthy of the two, from the temptation of spinning away from Germany into the orbit of other countries.

Every once in a while the Great Council of Fascism would meet in Rome and whatever decisions they made would be broadcast over the radio. I remember that we all held our breath, fearing that new hardships for Jews or foreign citizens residing in Italy might be announced. Any decision automatically became law, and there was no possibility that the king might intervene; he, too, had become a puppet who said and did whatever Mussolini told him to.

We got by. We studied to the best of our ability since that was the only way we could help our parents. Liliana and I went to the Liceo Ginnasio Dante in Piazza della Vittoria. It was considered one of the best middle schools/high schools in classical subjects, with excellent teachers. Franco went to Galileo Galilei, a high school specializing in scientific subjects.

I was lucky to be in a class of nice boys and girls and we all got along well, helping each other as much as possible with our school work. Some of the girls were cute and I tried very timidly to make friends with one of them who particularly appealed to me. Her beautiful blond hair flowed to her shoulders, her eyes were blue, and she was tall and slender. You could tell she came from an excellent family by her manner. Her name was Laura Carcasson. My attempts to establish a closer friendship failed miserably, perhaps because of my shyness, and I gave up. There would no doubt be other opportunities.

Among the boys, I was good friends with Giacomo de Sabata, who came from Milan, the nephew of the orchestra conductor Victor de Sabata. Giacomo and I shared a desk and he often helped me if I had trouble with my Greek or Latin translations. He was a good student and I envied the ease in which he grasped every subject. We spent almost every afternoon together either doing homework or playing. He had a younger brother, Victor, who was also brilliant. He was learning to play the mandolin, but I do not remember if he had any talent or not.

Sadly, Giacomo left Florence after two years. His family moved to Padua where his father's work took him. After a few months I went to visit him in Padua for several days. From that time on we lost contact, and our lives went in very different directions. Memories of Giacomo, however, stayed with me and every once in a while I would look in the phone books of Padua and surrounding towns hoping to find his name. No luck. In 1999 I finally found him in the Milan phone book; I was able to contact him and shortly afterward I went to see him. We caught up on what had happened in our lives from the time we had lost touch with each other. As one would expect, Giacomo had had a very full and successful life in his work and in his navy career. He was the only one among my old schoolmates I ever sought out, and I am glad I did so.

In October 1940, Hitler and Mussolini planned to meet in Italy. Why not make it Florence? Immediately the Fascist party planned enormous gatherings that involved both the military and the Fascist organizations of every kind, including the youth ones, to which we had the misfortune of belonging.

Mussolini wanted to show the *Führer* what the Italians were made of! I had to put up with it all day, dressed as a Musketeer, with that ridiculous rifle that became heavier with the passing hours. Because the historic encounter between the two dictators was to take place at the Palazzo Pitti, we had assembled in the Piazza Pitti, which was crowded with every kind of Fascist and military rank.

It was chaotic. No one knew what would happen next. At a certain moment a window in Palazzo Pitti opened and the two jolly friends looked out. The piazza exploded in a delirious shout. The two of them gave the Fascist salute, each in his own fashion until, satisfied by their bath in the ecstatic response, they went inside and the window was closed. That was it. We imagined they left Palazzo Pitti in an open automobile that took them directly to the station.

The next day at school we were told to write an essay in class describing our impressions of the historic meeting in Florence. I have entirely forgotten what I wrote; I have completely wiped out the episode.

CHAPTER 5

The Racial Laws

The last year of middle school was considerably more difficult because we had to prepare for the exams to enter high school. I was very nervous about it because, although I had not failed anything, my grades were only average. I prepared as well as I could. For the Greek translations I had a dictionary called *Ghemol,* which was particularly useful because it contained many phrases translated from the best-known Greek texts. For the Latin translation I bought a grammar book printed on very fine paper in very small letters; I had it bound in the middle of the dictionary so I could casually consult it without the examination proctor noticing anything.

Thanks to this clever expedient, and thanks to a dose of good luck, I was admitted to high school with a better than average score. And to think that the examinations began on Friday the 17th, a day that Italians consider unlucky! I was very relieved and happy to have obtained such splendid results at school. My father gave me 20 lire as a reward. They were four silver coins of 5 lire, which I promptly put in the little wooden box where I kept my savings. I thought that if I ever reached the conspicuous figure of a thousand lire, I would open a savings account at the Cassa di Risparmio di Firenze.

Once again it was July and mother began the ritual of packing the trunks with all the necessary things for spending the two summer months by the sea. We three children helped her pack what we considered essential, and mother had to struggle to get everything into two trunks which, as we grew older, had become increasingly inadequate. Franco and I sat on the trunks so mother could close the locks.

We went to Lido di Camaiore. For several years we had not rented Villino Nelli because my cousins from Milan, who had moved to Cernobbio on Lake Como, spent their summer vacations elsewhere. We took three bedrooms in a boarding house on the boardwalk. Settling in quickly, we took our clothes to our own rooms. Franco and I slept in the same room, as we did at home.

One day followed another without incident until Mussolini took it upon himself to wake us from our summer torpor with the 1,000th Grand Council of Fascism, and this time their decisions fell on us like a ton of bricks. From the Grand Council came what was defined as the "Racial Laws." For Italian Jews something was beginning that the unfortunate German Jews had undergone for many years. Mussolini had stopped behaving like the buffoon who strutted and boasted from the Palazzo Venezia balcony and had adopted a behavior more in line with Hitler's.

The same day those cursed laws were issued, papa hurried to Lido di Camaiore to discuss the situation with mother. Our lives were brought into question—not so much from the point of view of our safety, but of our economic situation, our studies, and in general of our living in a world that had pointed a finger at us and was taking away our most elementary rights.

Among other things, the racial laws prohibited Jews from frequenting elegant vacation spots, such as Lido di Camaiore. What should we do? Papa was in favor of returning to Florence at once. Mamma, on the other hand, was in favor of staying to the end of our planned vacation and then packing up. Mamma's proposal prevailed, naturally supported by the three of us.

And so we remained at Lido. The days were not as carefree as before. It is true that no one we had contact with knew we were Jews, so there was no danger that we might find ourselves in an embarrassing situation. The fact remains that it was enough that we knew it for our spirits to be shaken.

We finally returned to Florence. Each of us had to face his own situation in relation to the laws in force. Luckily the greatest danger, that is, that papa might lose his position, did not materialize. In fact, he received a phone call from his boss (Charles Roditi, a Jew living in Paris), who expressed his solidarity regarding the Fascist laws and reassured him that he could continue to direct the office in Florence and that no one would replace him. This news gave us new hope.

As anticipated, mamma had to let the maid go. She was a good Slav by the name of Zora who loved us all. The separation was very painful. Zora could not understand why she was being dismissed. Mamma tried to explain to her in simple words what was happening, but Zora could not understand how decent people like us had to suffer harsh treatment of that sort solely for being Jews rather than Christians. She worked by the hour for other families and visited us often to see that everything was all right.

As for our schooling, the Jewish community of Florence immediately organized a Jewish school in which all the Jewish teachers of the public schools who found themselves without jobs could teach. Unfortunately there was an oversupply.

Elementary, middle, and high schools had to be established. All Jewish children could enroll at once so that they did not miss any of the school year. Liliana, who had finished high school, could not continue her studies, so she decided to enroll in the Berlitz School to improve her English. Then, wanting do something else after a time, she enrolled in an Olivetti typewriting class, and for some time audited a class at the University of Florence.

Franco, still at the scientific high school, was not overly enthusiastic about continuing his studies in Florence and took a decisive step that was to influence his entire life. He decided to continue his studies at an excellent university in Malta. He traveled to Naples, where he embarked for Malta.

I was sorry to see my brother go so far from his family at such an uncertain time for our future and, more generally, for the future of the entire world. It was certainly a courageous act on his part, because he was leaving his familiar surroundings for the first time to face the world without being able to count on his parents and siblings. Luckily, he had a herd of aunts, uncles, and cousins he could count on. But the hardest part for him must have been to attend a university where the spoken language was English and not Italian.

Preparations for Franco's departure were very swift so that he would not miss an academic year. My parents suffered a great deal seeing him go away like that, all alone. For their son's good they braved this first separation and tried to make the best of it. As for me, I had lost a roommate. My sorrow was compensated by the pleasure of having the bedroom all to myself. We no longer had to argue over which of us would get to sit at the desk first to do our homework or when to turn off the light at night.

I was very sorry not to be able to continue my high school studies at Dante and afterward at the university to satisfy my aspiration to be a surgeon. To attend Jewish schools would have been a solution, but I had the strange feeling that the situation was worsening in Italy and I would not be able to reach my objective.

It was then I decided that the best thing for me would be to go to work in papa's office. I had very special memories of the Sunday visits to his office as a boy. I loved to sit at one of the typewriters and type all those neat, even letters on the white paper. I liked the large, shiny desks, the chairs that spun around and could be raised or lowered as necessary, and all the samples that my father kept in his office to show American buyers. I liked the smell of the wood furniture and the mixture of odors that were left in the cups of espresso that the office employees drank continually. Besides, maybe my father would be pleased to have me by his side at the office. I talked to him about it, and to my joy he said yes. I would begin the first of October, if papa got permission from his boss in Paris. I waited in fear and trepidation. Authorization came quickly in the form of a telegram, and on the first of October 1938 I began what would become my life's work.

Every morning I got up early in order to take the Number 3 streetcar to the office with papa. I was in the "general office," which was a very large room, with ten other employees. They gave me a small table with a typewriter and a chair: this was my workplace. My job was to type the letters in Italian and English that Signor Roberto Anforti, vice-director of the office, wrote by hand. Luckily he had small but very clear handwriting that was easy to decipher. Father's secretary taught me how a commercial letter should be written, which then had to be recopied (a ridiculous system that was soon replaced by carbon copies), and finally put into the addressed envelope.

In the beginning I was very slow because I did not want to make any errors. In addition I did not know how to type, so I enrolled in the same Olivetti course that Liliana had attended. Things got better quickly. I was happy to breathe the atmosphere of an office like papa's. I felt important and was learning about work I enjoyed doing. At the end of every month I went to the bookkeeper to get my pay check, 50 lire, which seemed like a lot to me, but in effect was a relatively low salary.

I understood that my father wanted to avoid criticism and that I was working there primarily because I was his son and not because I was needed. I had them pay me the 50 lire in ten 5-lire coins that I could put in my money box. After several months of work I decided to put my savings in the bank and opened an account at the Cassa di Risparmio di Firenze.

We heard regularly from Franco. He had learned English very quickly and was happy to be studying in Malta.

In the meanwhile, on different occasions, the Fascist Great Council unveiled new laws that further restricted the Jews' freedom in every aspect. I was very angry about what was happening, and to counteract this discrimination that was segregating us more and more, I decided to exclude non-Jews as friends. This policy served a dual purpose: the first, to show myself and others that I could meet all my aspirations within the Jewish community; the second, to avoid unpleasant situations with people in the Catholic world who nourished feelings of dislike toward me or Jews in general. It turned out to be a good decision. I had close friendships with many Jewish young people, which gave me the spirit and determination to face the persecutions that were becoming more intolerable every day.

To my great surprise and disappointment, a few Jewish families in Florence took actions that I would never have expected and about whose effectiveness I had strong doubts. Some of them tried to prove they did not belong to the so-called "Jewish race." Others made completely false declarations in order to be "discriminated" from the rest of their co-religionists, amounting to one discrimination within another. How could these poor souls hope to survive persecution by grasping at bureaucratic loopholes? Aside from the shame of denying one's own faith, they would in the end follow the destiny of their brothers. In the final accounting, the Fascists would not distinguish between the Jews who remained Jews and those who had tried to prove they were not. We were all in the same boat.

My new work life changed some of my habits. Once I had been very active: I walked and rode my bicycle doing errands for mamma. Now I spent eight hours a day sitting at my little table typing letters. I began to put on weight and felt very heavy. So I got the bright idea of joining the Boating Club of Florence. Every time I crossed the Ponte Vecchio or Ponte Santa Trinita, I saw the tapered shapes of the sculls flying over the water, and I envied those boys who sweated while they made powerful oar strokes, bent over the little sliding seats. It was exercise that I would enjoy both to lose weight and to strengthen my muscles.

One Saturday morning I went to the Boating Club opposite the Uffizi and told the secretary I would like to take up rowing. After giving me the once-over to ascertain if I were physically capable of this sport, he said I could enroll and quoted the annual fee. He also asked if I knew anyone who was already a member of the club who could vouch for me. I told him I knew no one.

"Then you will have to come with your father [I was still a minor], so he can underwrite your request."

"All right," I replied, "that won't be a problem."

"Just fill out this form while you're here."

I filled it out, name, address, and so on. At a certain point my blood froze. On one line I read: "Race." I looked up at my interlocutor and asked: "Excuse me, here where it says 'Race,' do I put 'white' or 'black'?" He started to laugh.

"No, just put Aryan or Jew."

"I'm Jewish; now what happens?"

"Then you can't become a member of the Boating Club."

By the way he spoke to me, I realized he was somewhat embarrassed. Even though I did not show any anger or disappointment, I felt that he was sorry to be the protagonist in this painful scene. In a tone of superior calm I said: "Don't worry. I'll find a way to boat on the Arno," and I shook his hand. The poor secretary of the Boating Club could not manage a reply, and when he gave me his hand his face turned red as a beet.

Outside the door, I took my bicycle and cycled as far as Ponte S. Niccolò. Looking along the left bank of the river, I saw a little man washing rowboats and went down the escarpment to talk to him.

"Do you rent boats?"

"Certainly. Do you want one?"

"Yes. But I would like to reserve it for one hour a day three times a week, from seven thirty to eight thirty. And please give me a good price." The deal was quickly closed. His terms were very favorable, especially considering the fact that I was the only fool who went rowing at seven thirty in the morning. Thank heavens I did not have to fill out any form with my name and race. I had accomplished my goal, in spite of Mussolini and his hierarchy. To be sure, rowing a shabby little boat stripped of paint, with two oars resembling tree trunks, was not exactly the same as sliding on the movable little seat of one of those hulls shining like mirrors and pointed as a needle. Never mind. The important thing was to get some exercise and lose a few pounds.

Three times a week I got up an hour earlier than usual and had a good breakfast because of the physical effort I would make. I pedaled to Ponte S. Niccolò where the little man was usually busy washing his boats.

I rowed energetically, and when I grew warm I would take off my sweater and then my shirt, until I remained in my undershirt. I went toward Rari Nantes, rather far upstream from Ponte S. Niccolò. Along that tract the Arno is very wide and the two banks are green with vegetation. The landscape was very rural and at seven in the morning in the winter months there was usually a light, low-lying fog giving it a surreal appearance. Everything about it suited me: the rhythmic movement, the sound of the oars in the water, the sun rising, the dissolving fog—it all gave me a great sense of peace and well-being. I asked myself: "How is it possible that in such a beautiful country so many contemptible and frightening things can be happening?"

I would continue rowing to the point where I had to turn around, and with the current in my favor, I came back to my point of departure with less effort. I dressed in a hurry, saluted the little boat man, and went quickly to papa's office by bicycle.

More disquieting news came from Germany. Hitler's speeches grew more strident and aggressive before ever larger crowds over which fluttered ill-omened flags with the center swastika. The dictator assailed what he called "the wealthy Judeo-Masonic conspiracy that was the cause of all the evils afflicting the world." He vaunted the claims of the great Reich over the little bordering countries and angrily insisted on the necessity of subjugating all inferior races, which were many according to him, considering the fact that there was only one superior race, the Aryan.

Listening to him on the radio haranguing those fanatic masses made shivers run down my spine at the hate he put into his bellowing, which, though incomprehensible to me, I felt served to instill the same hate in his listeners. What gave me the shivers even more was the huge roar of approval that underscored the *Führer*'s speech. I thought that if a Jew should happen to be in the middle of that crazed mob they would tear him to pieces in seconds. I thanked heaven I did not live in Germany. In comparison, Italy seemed much more tolerable. True enough, the anti-Jewish laws had seriously affected our way of life with all the inconveniences we experienced. After the first shock, however, we gradually found a modus vivendi that allowed us to go on with dignity. Aiding and abetting us was the innate Italian proclivity for disobeying laws, the innate ambivalence of the Italian legislators who make laws and then forget to apply them, and, above all, the character of the Italian people who, thank heaven, could in no way be compared to the Germans.

I considered the German fanatics evil and capable of any cold-blooded wickedness. I am sorry to say that subsequent events proved me right. I considered Mussolini a clown, a ham actor who tried to impersonate some great leader from Roman times, surrounded by a gang of little bosses wanting to cultivate their own little garden plots to ensure their well-being for a lifetime. Still, the danger remained that, because of the agreements between Hitler and Mussolini, one horrible day the Roman clown would have to follow the intemperate and powerful Berliner in his mad endeavors.

In 1938 came the first warnings, the first sinister signs of catastrophe. In February, Hitler assumed the command of the German armed forces that occupied Austria in a move supported by the vast majority of Austrians. On September 30, France, England, Italy, and Germany signed the Munich Pact, allowing Germany to occupy the Sudetenland territory of Czechoslovakia. Then, on November 9–10, came the tragic *Kristallnacht* in Germany, with the destruction of synagogues and arrests of Jewish citizens.

In England, Foreign Secretary Anthony Eden resigned in protest against Prime Minister Neville Chamberlain, the man who instead of facing up to Hitler and putting an end to his arrogance, had followed a policy of appeasement, shuttling between Berlin and London, and in the end signing the Munich Pact that was not worth the paper it was written on.

CHAPTER 6

A New Life Begins

In 1939 my days were measured by some constants, primarily by my work, in which I took an ever-growing interest. I had a friendly and cordial relationship with father's employees and had increased my typing speed, thanks to the Olivetti course. In addition, my English was progressing, with lessons at the Berlitz School.

After a day of work I would usually get together with a friend. I kept more and more to a circle of Jewish friends and acquaintances, and one of the places we most often gathered was at Alberto and Margherita Passigli's home, a splendid two-story house on Via Benedetto Varchi. They lived there with their children Piero and Fioralba, Aunt Gina Procaccia, and her daughter Giuliana. We spent many happy hours in their home talking about everything under the sun, and together went to a concert at the Teatro Comunale or the Pergola, or just strolled around Florence. Often Alberto and Margherita took part in our conversations, and I liked being in their company because they were good and understood young people.

It did not take long for the drums of war to begin to beat. Germany provoked a crisis in Danzig and invaded Poland. Having recently signed a defense treaty with Poland, Chamberlain had no choice: he declared war on Germany. Hitler invaded France. The Maginot Line, which was to be a defensive wall insurmountable to the Germans, proved useless, and the Wehrmacht began its systematic occupation of the northern part of France and the Atlantic coast.

In the beginning Mussolini took a wait-and-see position and abstained from entering the war. As soon as he saw that things were going well for the Germans and that France was rapidly capitulating, he made the "heroic" gesture of sending the glorious Italian troops to occupy the southeastern part of France as far west as Toulon, the nearest objective and easy to reach, a gesture rightly branded as "a stab in the back of a Latin sister."

The Duce's speeches to the enormous crowds were fanatical and also fanciful. According to him the Italian people had overnight become a people of warriors and heroes who, hand in hand with the glorious Third Reich, would destroy the English and French armies. Instead, this race of heroes had to cope with the enormous problems of survival. There was a shortage of everything, even a shortage of metal to produce big guns, rifles, and bullets. To offset this shortage the Duce mandated a collection of iron. Every Italian had to sacrifice whatever metal object he possessed and bring it to the center of piazzas, where the metal was placed in great piles. Beautiful wrought-iron gates and fences were demolished. Balconies were stripped of their iron or cast-iron railings, which were then substituted by bricks. Out of a kind of patriotic impulse, my father decided to give to his "country" an old bronze bust—the figure of a Capuchin brother, if I remember correctly.

Not satisfied with having made a raid on iron, Mussolini cooked up the bright idea of "gold for the country," obliging men and women to turn over their wedding rings. This time my father played it cagey. Because he had never possessed a wedding ring, the only one to give the country was mother's, a shining, massive ring. Father had a jeweler friend make a very thin ring of gold and alloy and took that to the "sacrifice." So mother kept her ring for the rest of her life. She left it to me when she died and I have it to this day.

The government announced a general mobilization in order to put together something that might seem like an army. Mussolini thought the blitzkrieg Hitler had just started would take over the rest of Europe in a few months. He wanted the right to sit at the peace table where the conditions would be imposed on the defeated and the spoils would be divided. As the saying goes, the bearskin was sold before the bear was dead.

Naturally, new laws were decreed to safeguard the integrity of the "sacred" Italian soil from the attacks of the wealthy Judaic-Freemasonry. The only law I regarded as intelligent was the one that prohibited the "Judeans" (we were demoted from

"Jews" to "Judeans") from taking part in the Italian armed forces and therefore of being killed on the front. With all the negative things that had already happened to us, and the things that were on the horizon, I thought this a very generous gesture toward us.

The anti-Jewish propaganda machine proceeded on its inexorable path. It became more aggressive with the articles of a publication with the despicable title of *Defense of Race*. It was founded in 1938 by Telesio Interlandi, and the chief editor was Giorgio Almirante. This publication of Interlandi and Almirante, which never had true exponents of Italian culture among its collaborators, strove to explain "scientifically" how the Jews were an inferior race, illustrating the bizarre theory with photographs of ugly Jewish faces placed beside black faces from Abyssinia or other black African states. After the war, Almirante founded the Movimento Sociale Italiano, a party that had neo-Fascist overtones.

The movies also entered the fray, with dubbed German films shown in our theaters. The most typical of these films was *Jud Süss* (The Jew Süss), based on a novel by Lion Feuchtwanger, which was authorized by Goebbels and which Himmler made obligatory viewing for the Nazi troops and the infamous SS in particular. I remember what revulsion I felt at the part where the Jew is put into a cage and exposed to the mockery of the people. After the war the director Veit Harlan was tried twice (in 1949 and 1950) for crimes against humanity, but was acquitted both times for lack of convincing evidence that he had been responsible for the final version of the film. The actor Ferdinand Marian, who played the unfortunate protagonist Süss Oppenheimer, was banned from the movies and, contrary to rumors of suicide that circulated at the time, he died in an automobile accident in August 1946.

These were dreadful things, but we were strong and tough enough to bear them. What did leave a profound mark on our family was father having to close his office. A telegram from Charles Roditi in Paris gave the order, motivated by a hard reality: no American would buy even a pin from an Italy allied with the monster Hitler. Many Italian firms were feeling resentful when they began to realize the abyss the country was sliding into because of Mussolini. Small consolation for papa who had to face the problem of maintaining a family of four with no income. I realized how wise he had been all these years to make us save everything we could. The "rainy day," to our misfortune, had arrived.

While in the throes of this predicament, we got the news of Grandmother

Evelina's death. All four of us went to her funeral in Bologna. My cousins from Cernobbio were also there with Aunt Lory, and I was happy to see them after such a long time. We exchanged news about the latest events, but in general I saw that they, too, were facing them calmly enough.

Mamma and Liliana, Grandmother Evelina's favorite, were heartbroken. I remember that the funeral took place on a beautiful, warm, sunny day. After the funeral we went to grandmother's house where Aunt Matilde, who had lived with her, read Grandmother Evelina's will. To each of us grandchildren she left 50 lire inside a shiny leather coin purse. We were pleased about that: considering the times, it was not an inconsiderable amount, and frankly we had not expected her to remember any of her grandchildren except for her favorite. When I returned to Florence I could not wait to put my 50 lire in the bank.

Papa was going through a very difficult time, and mother got the brunt of his bad moods. He often unjustly accused the poor woman of spending too much on groceries—she who watched every centesimo. Mussolini came to father's aid in a way by instituting food rationing and the notorious ration cards. Even if you wanted to, you could not spend more than a certain amount for food.

Mother had some good ideas. We had a small garden behind our house and she bought two hens and a rooster. In a short time some chicks were hatched that became hens after a time. Every day mother collected the eggs. Some she used for pasta, and the others she preserved in lime water in a large ceramic vase. This supplied us with eggs even when the hens were laying little or nothing. Mamma then bought several kilograms of sardines, cleaned them well, and put them in salt. In other words, she was putting together a supply of food for every eventuality.

Because I was without work, I tried to make myself useful by helping mother with the housework: polishing the wood floors, making the beds with mother, and going on my bicycle to shop at the central market where things cost less. But this was not enough to soothe the pain of forced inactivity. I decided to look for other work. Having acquired good typewriting and office experience, I believed I had my papers in order to apply for a job. Of course I could not apply at an "Aryan" company, because I would surely be turned down, so I directed my search in a strictly Jewish environment.

In light of these considerations, I turned to one of our distant relatives, Vittorio Bemporad, who had a wholesale textile firm in Prato with offices in Florence. It was a large business in which his older son, Sergio, also worked. To my great joy, Vittorio agreed to hire me to work in his Florence office. I would start my new job the following Monday. I sped home on my bicycle and ran up the stairs two steps at a time in my hurry to tell my parents the good news. Naturally they were happy about it. I was happy to have become so unexpectedly a source of help to my family in that difficult financial time.

I made an agreement with mother that at the end of every month I would give her all my salary, which I did. The coveted pay envelope arrived at the end of the month. Inside, to my great surprise, there was 500 lire, ten times more than what I earned working for papa! I was overjoyed. I went at once to thank Vittorio and to tell him how much I appreciated what he was doing. He was pleased, and slapping me on the shoulder, he said: "You earned it. Keep up the good work."

One of the problems that arose with Italy entering the war was the interruption of communication with Malta, a British possession and an important strategic point for English control of the Mediterranean. We learned from the Swiss consulate in Florence that the only way we could get in touch with Franco was through the International Red Cross, by means of postcards stamped with various messages. We were obliged to put a cross beside the message we wanted Franco to receive. This was not a great way to communicate, but it was better than nothing. We sent the first postcard. Now it was up to Franco to reply using the same system, and we began our patient wait.

The food situation in Italy was rapidly growing worse. Every kind of necessity was scarce. The so-called autarky was not enough to satisfy the smallest need. Mussolini instituted an obligatory plan for farmers to pool the food they produced, and a "Battle of the Grain" was instituted to reward those farmers who distinguished themselves in this production. The results were not remarkable, to judge by the bread that every day grew more inedible. It contained every kind of disgusting thing to make it seem like real bread: flour from sorghum, flour from vetch (seeds normally used for chicken and other bird feed), pieces of potatoes, and anything else that became available from time to time. Everything but authentic wheat flour!

Butter, coffee, sugar, olive oil, meat, and sausages had become practically impossible dreams and could be bought only in the smallest amounts with a ration card. Mamma continually went through contortions to get something together resembling a dinner.

One day mamma heard from a friend of hers that on Via dei Conti in the center of town there was a little *pensione* called Bellettini, where one could get a decent meal at a reasonable cost. The owners had a little land in the country and therefore had many things not found in the stores any more. We tried it out by going to dinner one Sunday. We could not believe our eyes when they brought in four bowls full of homemade tagliatelle with rabbit sauce! In a little basket were four slices (a little thin, to tell the truth) of white (!) country bread that had by now become only a distant memory. For the main course they served us roasted rabbit with potatoes and fruit. We ate ravenously and for the first time in many months got up from the table satisfied.

Papa arranged with the owner for us to go there for dinner every Sunday, and this became the most important event of the week. Every Monday I started counting the days until the next Sunday. Luckily mother still had hens that gave us eggs. The production was a little scanty since the poor hens had their fast also. Do not even mention wringing a hen's neck. For mother they were now an integral part of the family.

Papa tried as well as he could to earn a little money. He had many good friends among the numerous Italian factories that he had given plenty of work to in the past, and he began to give them ideas for things to make and then tried himself to sell them in Florentine shops. Things went well for a few months, but then gradually fizzled out, leaving him depressed and worried, since his only source of income was the small amount of rent he got from three apartments he had bought over the years. It was not much, but with the small contribution of my salary it was enough to survive without having to get into the little capital that father had managed to lay aside with much effort on his and mother's part.

As for summer vacations like those before the war, forget it! In August of 1940, Liliana and I arranged to go with friends by train as far as Trento or Merano and from there trek through the Dolomites and sleep in a different shelter every night. The duration of the vacation was directly linked to the duration of the food we carried with us. Those were wonderful days. In the morning we awoke no later than seven. Our washing up was of short duration because of the icy water, and often before we could pour the water from the pitcher into the bowl, we had to break the thin crust of ice that had formed overnight. We even managed to forget the problems we would have to face when we returned to Florence and talked about whatever came to mind. Every evening we had to put bandages on the blisters our heavy, uncomfortable boots made. We took photographs and returned to our homes reinvigorated by the pure air we had breathed on our beautiful walks.

Returning to Florence was returning to offices that stank of cigarette butts in ashtrays and taking up that sedentary life that little suits a young man of my age. But such as it was, it was better than wandering around the house with nothing to do. As for my health, thank heaven I have always been healthy and robust.

The war continued its implacable course. Every once in a while we learned that one of our non-Jewish acquaintances had been called to the army. I must say that none of them ran to defend his country's sacred borders with enthusiasm, and they used every possible means to get an exemption, something very difficult to obtain. I thanked heaven I had been declared exempt from military service, but I felt sorry for those poor fathers of families who had to enlist, leaving behind work, wives, and children. It was a steep price to pay for being "Aryans."

CHAPTER 7

Forced Labor

When I turned 18 I went to the city hall to apply for an identification card, an indispensable document—particularly when young men were at war while I stayed undisturbed in Florence. Through an office window, a nice young woman gave me a form to fill out, with all the usual rigmarole. I glanced rapidly over the questions, looking for that fatal "race."

In block letters I wrote all the information requested and when I came to "race," out of spite, I wrote in slightly larger letters: JUDEAN. I handed the form back to her, which she quickly scanned. When she came to "race," she said: "You're a Jew, aren't you?"

"Yes."

"Then why did you write 'Judean'?"

"Because that's what you call us and I thought it would be easier for you to understand."

The poor thing did not grasp my polemic spirit and just said: "Oh, all right." And after putting my request in a file she went back to work.

The following week I returned to the city hall to pick up my identity card. In the middle of it was stamped JEWISH RACE. And so I went away with my stamp.

Mussolini continued to keep a close watch on the Jews in Italy. On the war front luck was changing, and the first battle casualties were announced. The fact that the Jews could remain tranquilly at home did not seem fair, so to make them less tranquil a "civilian mobilization" was instituted. Those citizens who for whatever reason had not been called to fight (and I was one of these) would be recruited to do manual labor in the public interest.

On September 28, 1942, I was called up as a ditch digger in the service of the Land Reclamation Syndicate of Sesto Fiorentino. Naturally, many other young and not-so-young Florentine Jews were recruited along with me. They were family men who were forced to leave their legitimate work and come shovel dirt from morning to evening. My work consisted of going every morning to a place in Sesto Fiorentino to dig canals for irrigating the countryside. These canals were 60 centimeters wide and varied in depth from 50 centimeters to 2 meters according to the lay of the land. The first, softer, layer of earth we dug with a spade, and the work was not too difficult. However, as we dug deeper the dirt became harder and drier and we had to work with pick and shovel. We went in twos: one of us would work with the pick and the other would throw out the dirt with the shovel. For this work of high engineering skill they paid us the considerable sum of four lire a meter. Considering it took two men two hours to dig a meter, each of us earned one lira per hour, truly no lordly sum.

Similar action was taken in many other Italian cities, but the hardest work was assigned in Florence. The organizer, if he can be called that, of this (un)civil mobilization was a certain Diego Sanesi, president of the Provincial Council of Corporations. We recruits, naturally, tried every possible expedient to get excused from the summons. Many reported sick, as one might do for military service, pleading physical inability to do such heavy labor. Some, to their good fortune, were successful, but only a limited and fortunate few cases of men of a certain age could show just cause. I, thank goodness, was strong and healthy and had the right physique for digging ditches, so there was no way to get out of it.

I received some small favors thanks to a young woman by the name of Bombassei, who worked for the Chamber of Commerce and was in charge of the recruitment of Jews. She was very attractive, both physically and in her manner, and every once in a while I went to see her in her office, complaining of a backache or whatever my imagination could come up with, and she—who was good-hearted and evidently did not like the work she had to do—would give me two or three days off to get back in shape. But that is all I could ever wrangle.

I started keeping a diary of my adventures and misadventures at this time. It is this diary and other documents from that period that provide the basis of the story of my youthful years.

Obviously, the day I was recruited I had to leave my work with Vittorio Bemporad. Papa and mamma took the news of my ditch digging very badly. They were particularly worried about my health, because I was not accustomed to that kind of work, especially in the cold and damp, not to mention the fact that my contribution to the family expenses, even though minimal, would be missed. There was nothing I could do about it. I assured them that as far as my health was concerned there was nothing to worry about.

A new stage in my life began that was totally different from anything that came before, with unaccustomed rhythms, hard physical labor, and total mental relaxation. In fact, while I was digging, working with the pickax, or shoveling dirt, my mind was free to roam. I thought about past times, about my family and friends. I assessed what was happening to me and to my Jewish brothers in that anxious time, and I tried to imagine what the future had in store for us. But as hard as I tried, I could not construct any logical forecast based on that illogical scenario of wars and persecutions. Being fundamentally optimistic, I looked for the positive side of that particular moment, such as the physical advantages of being outside all day to participate in this "sport" without having to go fight on the front. The fact that so many young men of my age had been sent who-knows-where to make war gave the illusion that the anti-Jewish laws, though subjecting us to severe discriminations, were in a sense saving our lives.

After I had given my imagination an acceptable rationale and resigned myself to the way things were, I faced the new work with good humor, trying to do it prudently and with the greatest moderation, spending as much time as possible talking quietly with my partners in crime. And that is what I did.

I would rise every morning at seven. With the lunch mother fixed for me, I would take a streetcar to the station and from there take another streetcar as far as Sesto Fiorentino. I walked a couple of kilometers to reach the place where I met with my fellow workers and the supervisor named Fantechi who showed us where to dig each day.

In the beginning we were a small group of about ten young and not-so-young men. Among my best friends I remember Umberto Calò, Renzo Sornaga, Gianfranco Sarfatti, Mario Baer, Luciano Servi, Nello Leoni, and Enzo Cortesi. We decided to go to work regularly and not kill ourselves with fatigue. It was enjoyable to be together, and between one shovel of dirt and another, we talked about our common interests and decided what we would do in the evening after work. When we came home we would hurriedly wash, change our clothes, and meet to go to a concert or to one of our homes to spend a pleasant evening together.

Gianfranco and Luciano were learning Morse code. They often had mysterious meetings with someone I never knew, but whom I was certain had something to do with the underground anti-Fascist movement. I did not want to ask because I was not interested in becoming involved in clandestine activities. Although I recognized the importance of their work and admired their dedication, my sole objective was to survive the persecutions and help my parents do the same.

Gianfranco was an unusually intelligent young man with a sharp sense of humor. I liked talking with him and Mario Baer, who was a few years older than we were, and who had a notable fund of knowledge. He was also very pleasant and amusing. He talked to us about sociology and many other interesting things of which I was totally ignorant. I envied his having been able to attend the university.

In the summer months work on the plain of Sesto Fiorentino was depressing. Apart from the suffocating heat (being formerly swampland and in a hollow without the slightest breeze), the mosquitoes were the worst annoyance. Great clouds of them settled over our heads, buzzing continually and attacking every part of our uncovered body. They were much larger and more hardy than those that usually live in the cities, and their bite left a mark. During our breaks, when Fantechi went away on his own business, we would get inside one of the ditches we had dug and cover it with a straw mat. In this way we were sheltered from the sun, the mosquitoes, and the heat for a short time.

We had never-ending discussions about anything that came to mind. Mario and Gianfranco would come up with the most interesting subjects. From time to time we looked to see if Fantechi was in sight. If by chance he was on his way back, the one on guard would advise the others by saying: "*Mamzer*[11] in sight!" and, making the straw mat disappear, we would bend over inside the ditch and start to dig. I also had the time to immortalize some of us by taking photographs while they were busily excavating or while we killed time doing pseudo-gymnastics.

The ditches we made ran along rows of vines. Consequently, as we dug we encountered the roots. According to Fantechi's rigorous instructions these roots must

---

11. A Jewish pejorative, "bastard."

be saved, but every time we found one we chopped it off with a well-aimed blow of the spade. After this was done we would cover the stump of the root with a little dirt so Fantechi would not notice. It was a way of rebelling against our slavery; contravening one of their orders made us feel freer and gave us a little satisfaction.

It was not the only episode of the kind. After some time, with a good part of the excavations finished, some of us were chosen to build the network of pipes to irrigate the Sesto plain. It was a matter of laying the terra-cotta pipes, which had a diameter of about 20 centimeters, along the bottom of the canals we had dug. The pipes were connected by a joint made with cement that was mixed in a little box. Every 100 meters a vertical pipe was attached in the same fashion from which water would flow to irrigate the fields. When this work was finished we had to cover it with the dirt we had dug and smooth out the ground. We carefully carried out the pipe work under the attentive eyes of Fantechi who, however, had no idea what we planned to do when our work was completed. Before covering up the pipes with dirt, one of us had the job of breaking every terra-cotta pipe with a spade or pick. It would not be noticed for a long time, because water was not to be pumped into the irrigation system until the end of the project, that is, after about a year. I am sure that irrigation project never worked.

At home, after the initial shock of my forced labor, things returned nearly to normal. Mamma did everything possible to keep the family going. Some good friends who had small places in the country occasionally gave us foodstuffs we could not find in the stores, and this helped us out. Papa had given up the idea of doing any kind of work. There was nothing he could do, even if he had wanted to. He spent his time sitting in his armchair listening to mother read to him after she finished her chores. It was very touching. Papa often dozed off while mother read, and she would let him sleep, quietly taking up her tasks again so as not to wake him.

One of papa's favorite occupations was to plant himself in front of the radio with an ear stuck to the loudspeaker in order to hear what was said and still keep the volume low enough so the neighbors would not know he was listening to Radio London. Colonel Stevens usually gave the war news and for us this was a vital connection with the free world. Unfortunately, the Fascists began to interfere with the transmission of Radio London and it became much more difficult for papa to understand what they were saying.

Liliana had her own friends and often went to visit Aunt Matilde in Bologna. She continued studying English at the Berlitz School and had become very proficient. We got along and never had any reason to disagree, and each of us had our own lives and friendships. One day we had the joy of receiving a message from Franco on one of those stamped postcards from the Red Cross like the one we had sent him a long time before. He had written: "Everyone in excellent health." We were overjoyed. We spent a good quarter of an hour trying to guess the "real" meaning of that sparse sentence. In the end, we concluded that it had to be taken literally, that Franco and our relatives in Malta were fine.

This news was very comforting because the Italian air force had begun bombing Malta every day, and the triumphant news bulletins from the Italian command spoke of the great destruction visited on the small island. If you believed all the Fascists' lies, Malta would have sunk to the bottom of the sea countless times, but in reality it showed itself for what it was—invincible.

We attended concerts at the Teatro Comunale when we could, and naturally always bought the cheaper seats in the gallery. Giving ourselves over to the music meant forgetting our everyday problems, and that was truly magic.

Thanks to those concerts I became friends with Mimma Castelnuovo Tedesco, daughter of the famous criminal lawyer. She was very nice and had a cheerful disposition. Besides music, she liked sports and took hikes in the hills around Florence. We found we had a lot in common and began to see each other often, along with our other friends. Not much time went by before I had a crush on Mimma, the first crush of my life.

Diary

February 21, 1943: Mimma has been sweet and kind. I'm in love! I would like so much to tell her how I feel. But I hold myself back for fear of upsetting her (perhaps also, and mainly, because I'm a coward and am afraid of being rejected). For now I'll be satisfied with just being her good friend, in hopes that with time things will develop according to my burning desires. Before now I've never been so deeply in love.

March 1, 1943: Went to Cherubini School of Music to hear "Le quattro stagioni" by Vivaldi. Magnificent. Hall full of Jews. Saw Mimma and gave her the photographs. She was happy. Sweeter than ever. She com-

mented on my tan. I saw her father; who knows what he thinks of me.
I want so much to be alone with Mimma.

With this new adventure that gave me such pleasant feelings, I passed the days
working on the Sesto plain, dreaming about when I would see Mimma again. It
was a special time for me. So many things were happening at the same time. Of
course the danger that we Jews were running made true friendships easier to form.
We each felt the need to compare our own reality with that of our friends. We de-
rived strength from being united against the storm that had struck us. But above
all, we felt an indisputable, overpowering sense of optimism that allowed us a life
full of activity and relationships that satisfied our most basic needs as young people
who unfortunately had not yet received much from life.

In retrospect it seems impossible that a minority like ours, so barbarically marginal-
ized from the life of the country where it lived, found so many resources to face
the persecution with spirit and vitality instead of becoming disheartened and depressed. I have to admit that, fortunately for us, the people around us were more
occupied with surviving the enormous difficulties arising from the war, the bombardments, the shortage of necessities, than with paying attention to anti-Jewish laws.
Many of them showed solidarity on our behalf and helped us to the limit of their
possibilities. At worst, they were indifferent. I do not remember anyone displaying
antisemitic sentiments or contempt in my presence. Obviously, in the echelons of
the Italian government there were those whose job was to apply the anti-Jewish
laws, but they did it in the manner typical of state employees who just want to get
through their workday the easiest way they can.

I sought every possible occasion to be with Mimma. As I said, I was rather occupied with the work of a laborer that took most of my time and energy, and I now
began to feel less like devoting my little spare time to my friends and even my parents and sister. I had become selfish and apprehensive about my relationship with
Mimma, which I hoped to deepen. I knew she also liked to go to concerts and I
racked my brain to think of a way for us to go together, but unfortunately my meager finances would not allow me to take her. I also realized that she had a circle of
friends outside my "rounds" that would keep her from accepting my invitations.
Sometimes I phoned her, and if she was not there I left word I had called. She rarely
returned my call, however. I was too much in love to be objective about the situation.

I had just one thought: to stick to my purpose, convinced that one day I would succeed. And so I persisted.

I decided to demonstrate my interest with a concrete gesture.

> Diary
>
> May 24, 1943: I bought a book (50 lire) that I will give Mimma for her
> birthday: frankly, I do not know why I'm giving it to her! But I don't want
> to let this opportunity to strengthen my relationship with her slip by.

After I gave her the book I received a nice phone call from Mimma: she thanked me and said we would see each other the following week. I was hoping for a date with a day, hour, and place, but nothing. I knew it was my fault for letting my imagination run wild; actually Mimma had never been anything more than nice and friendly to me.

I realized my mistake and decided it would be useless and even out of place to persist. It took time to get over my disappointment, but work and friends helped a great deal.

Winter began to make itself felt. Our work was becoming harder, like the ground itself, which seemed like stone. All of us reacted to the intense cold by working as much as we could, warming ourselves through activity and exertion. I wore wool gloves to protect my hands, and protected the rest of my body with a couple of sweaters and an old windbreaker. We went about collecting dry shrubs and vines (if they were not dry, we quickly dried them ourselves!) and built a little fire in one of our ditches. This allowed us to eat our lunch in a relatively bearable temperature.

Understandably, because of the cold the absences began to fall like snowflakes. Some days there were only two of us working. Those who had families to support and those at an age when it was more difficult to bear the discomforts of winter work complained most vociferously about the situation. A young person like me could take it more philosophically.

January and February were killer months. Fortunately March was much milder and we had some beautifully warm days.

> Diary
>
> March 12, 1943: Up at seven. Went to work with Gianfranco, Luciano

and Mario Baer. Dug six meters of ditch. Read *Beethoven*. Enchanting weather. Took photographs. Rode my bicycle during the lunch hour. Began a new ditch . . . Benucci came with two weeks' pay. I collected 35 lire. Mario was demobilized (Benucci told us). I am very glad for him, but at the same time very unhappy about losing his company.

So one of us had reclaimed his freedom.

I continued to see Mario outside work, and this made me want to leave the plain of Sesto Fiorentino as he had done. I asked him how he had managed to get the discharge. He said he owned a textile business in Prato and his presence was indispensable. Otherwise he would have to close it and let the workers go.

He obviously had an excellent argument in his favor. I was not owner of a factory or anything else. Going over and over it in my mind, I came to the conclusion that there was only one way to get out from under the daily slavery: to show I was not physically suited to work as a ditch digger. I talked it over with my parents and naturally they were agreeable. Now it was a matter of finding the way of escape, and I promised myself to talk about it with our family doctor. In the meantime, I went regularly to work with my friends.

For some time I had been using my bicycle to go to Sesto, which was quicker than taking two streetcars whose schedule did not always coincide with mine. It was an old bike that papa had bought secondhand. Mechanically it was in good enough condition. What left much to be desired were the tires and inner tubes. They were in very poor condition and new ones could not be found since rubber products had disappeared from the market, being requisitioned for war purposes.

To reach the workplace I had to go over dirt streets that were full of holes, putting the poor tires and inner tubes to a hard test every day; in fact, they were continually being repaired. Sometimes I had to walk many kilometers pushing my bike with a flat tire. But I relied on this dilapidated means of transportation so much I even used it on rather long trips. One day, March 19, 1943, on a Friday, a group of us cyclist friends pedaled toward Siena to fill our eyes with the splendid paintings of Benozzo Gozzoli and Pinturicchio. Back on the road we stopped at the Hotel Cisterna in San Gimignano to eat and sleep. In that place, and just as we were bent on proving young appetites, something happened to disturb the happiness of that day.

Sitting at a table nearby, some very distinguished men and women were speaking

English. My curiosity aroused, I introduced myself, and speaking in my English, which was certainly not on a level with theirs, I asked how, since they were English, they could stay so calmly in San Gimignano. They explained that actually they would rather not be there as it was a forced visit; that is, they were confined as citizens of an enemy country, England.

We all introduced ourselves and became friendly. We told them that in a certain sense we could consider ourselves in the same situation because, as Jews, we were subject to the famous Fascist persecutions. They fell silent and their faces darkened. Finally one gentleman, the oldest, who must have been the best informed of the group, his face growing even darker, told us in a low voice that he had just heard through unidentified channels that in Germany and Poland the Germans were rounding up the Jews—men, women, children, young people and old—and sending them to concentration camps where they were kept in deplorable conditions. Families were broken up, with husbands on one side and their wives on another, and what was more tragic, the children were separated from their parents. We tried to get more detailed information of the tragic picture that they had just revealed, but that was all they could tell us. They could only advise us to be very careful, since they believed one day or another the same thing was bound to happen in Italy.

This information was deeply disturbing. We lost our interest in sightseeing and decided to go back home. Now we knew. Suddenly the threat of a terrible future ahead of us was very evident. We agreed not to tell our parents in order not to upset them. That night I did not close my eyes, but followed the track of my oppressive thoughts.

We returned to Florence on Sunday evening at seven and told our parents about our wonderful trip, the museums, and the good meals we had eaten—not a word about the English internees. That night, also, I was too agitated to sleep, and the next morning I decided to tell Liliana about it in private. She agreed that we should say nothing to our parents, even though we were sure that sooner or later it would become public knowledge.

Diary

March 25, 1943: Up at seven. Worked with Gianfranco. Dug three or four meters of ditch. Luciano was absent. Weather cloudy and hot. This morning Benucci came to pay us (89.70 lire) for two weeks' work.

Afterward, until almost three o'clock I played cards. Then I worked. Scolding by Fantechi not to gather in groups (he calls them "conspiracies"). Seven workers of the Syndicate (non-Jews) were arrested and handcuffed by twelve carabinieri for striking: they wanted a pay raise. Another three are in hiding.

We all felt solidly behind those poor workers. We Jews were forced to do that work and certainly were not suited for it. They paid us only four lire a meter, much less than what the workers got, but we took it philosophically, as the lesser of two evils, while they did it by choice as a way to support their families.

At any rate, the atmosphere that was gradually being created in that workplace became oppressive and intolerable. It was one more reason to try to get away.

Diary

March 26, 1943: Worked with Gianfranco. Dug a ditch of nineteen meters! . . . There is a good possibility that we will be watched more closely because of the strike yesterday. I think the workers will be tried. Chiti has filed a complaint against them. He won't sleep too well!

After Mario Baer was discharged I teamed up with Gianfranco Sarfatti. He certainly did not have an athletic build, so he would not be much help. I, on the other hand, had a very respectable physique, and our combined strength might bring an acceptable result. I enjoyed Gianfranco's company because he was an extremely intelligent and cultured young man. He had an exceptional sense of humor, and we found ourselves on the same wavelength about many subjects. It was entertaining to make vitriolic remarks about our slave drivers.

One day I asked Gianfranco about the Morse code he was learning with Luciano. He said it was going well. Then I asked him point-blank if by chance it was not all a prelude to his and Luciano's participation in the secret anti-Fascist partisan organizations. He said yes, it was, and made me swear I would not say a word to anyone, a promise I scrupulously kept. I asked him if he had heard anything through his comrades about what was happening to the Jews in Germany and Poland. He said he knew nothing about it. Then I told him about the episode with the English internees and he remained silent for a moment.

Breaking his long silence, he said that the reason he had joined up with the clandestine movements was to avoid just such a fate as those poor Jews in concentration camps. He preferred to fight the Nazi-Fascists with their same weapons instead of ending up like a mouse in a trap. I had to concur with his reasoning. Then he asked: "Why don't you join us?"

"I'm not a fighting man. I consider myself fortunate because I don't have to go fight for Mussolini. I think that if I should ever have to fight for Her Majesty in Britain, I wouldn't refuse, and I'd do my best. But I can't see myself enlisting in a secret organization, even though I appreciate what it's doing."

Gianfranco did not insist. He repeated his admonition to keep my mouth shut, and with that the subject was closed.

March 31 was Liliana's birthday, and mother decided to celebrate it by inviting friends over after supper. We served little homemade cakes and opened a bottle of *spumante* that my mother had procured through the Ruizes, our friends who were still our salvation in emergencies. I gave Liliana two little inexpensive gold-plated hair clips. It was a happy occasion, and along with good wishes for Liliana's 25 years, we wished for a quick end to the war and to the anxieties gripping us.

> Diary
>
> April 1, 1943: Up at seven. Went with Luciano to work. I miss Gianfranco. Dug four meters. Beautiful weather. Met a young peasant girl, very lovely and with an easy manner. My chums judged her too harshly: they are wrong, I think she's nice. . . . I intend to use my health as an excuse for demobilization: I think I have a heart murmur. I'm fed up with the life I'm leading. If I can get out of this work I'll be very glad. I haven't been myself for some time now. I'm more taciturn and serious and seldom laugh. I need someone to love.

The next day I went back to work with Gianfranco. Gina, the daughter of the owner of the farm where we were digging ditches, perhaps realizing that out of all of us I was the one who treated her with greatest regard, came up to where I was digging with Gianfranco and began asking questions about why we were working there, and so forth. I explained in simple terms the situation, and as I expected, she was dumbfounded. Evidently the racial laws were known and understood only by the Italian intelligentsia. A simple soul like Gina could not understand the "profound" significance of all that which you must allow me to call "crap." We chatted away until lunchtime and Gina invited me to her house to meet her father and mother. I accepted gladly, while my faithful co-workers tried to see who could cough the loudest. I could not care less.

I went to eat my frugal lunch in Gina's kitchen. She offered me wine and fruit from the farm. I met her father and mother, who were very pleasant, and I would say better educated than almost any other farmer. I again summed up the reason why my friends and I were working on their farm, and then I left, thanking them for their hospitality. From that day on, my talks with Gina grew longer and the subjects became more personal. She asked if I was engaged. I said no, but that I liked a Jewish girl who up to that time had not shown much interest in me. She said she was engaged and her boyfriend was in the army, on one of the war fronts. That was welcome news. Now our friendship could remain one of mutual regard. The fact is I still loved Mimma, even though I was trying to forget her.

Gina was very beautiful—slender, tall, with long black hair and large green eyes. She did not have the aspect of someone subjected to hard physical labor. Her skin was velvety and lightly tanned by the early spring sun. We were working near her house and often, when she came out to do some daily chore, she would come by and exchange a few words with me.

During the lunch hour we would meet under the shade of a large tree a bit away from where I worked. I had my lunch box with my snack and Gina would bring something to eat. We sat with our backs against the large tree trunk on the fresh new grass. While we ate our snacks we talked of nothing in particular. She laughed easily and this gave me a pleasant, relaxed feeling. One day, after she finished eating, Gina stretched out on the grass with her head resting on my legs and then the conversation took a sudden turn. She looked at me with her eyes emanating a great sweetness and said she loved me and had never felt this way about anyone before. While she talked I tenderly caressed her hair, which almost completely covered my legs. With my eyes I caressed every little detail of her body, which was barely hidden by her skirt and light cotton shirt. I yearned to kiss her and hold her in my arms, but realized that if I did that we would not stop there and things would become seriously complicated.

I worked some monosyllables into her sweet monologue and felt very tender toward that girl who with such warmth, honesty, and abandon was confessing her love for me. She said she had stopped writing to her fiancé; she did not feel like writing him words of love when she realized they were untrue. I was sorry to hear that. I put myself in the shoes of her fiancé, who, unaware of anything, was risking his life on the front. I knew, sorrowfully, what it meant to love a girl without being loved in return and felt guilty for the turmoil I had caused. I told Gina I was very fond of her, but I did not think it was right for her to treat her fiancé like that. I was sure that her infatuation for me would soon pass and she would love him again as before. Shaking her head slowly she said, "Never, never."

Our meetings always ended with a hasty good-bye. I had to return to my work and she to her domestic chores before her parents became aware of her long absence.

That was a very pleasant time for me. I would have liked for it to go on forever. I felt grateful for so much love and this helped me get over my crush for Mimma. "One pain drives out another," I thought. And so it did.

I went to the syndicate to ask to be excused for a while in order to do what was necessary to get my discharge. They gave me leave until April 7, so I went to the Provincial Council of the Corporations where I made an appointment with Dr. Fabiani who was the official doctor. On April 6 I went to my doctor to get a certificate to show Dr. Fabiani. After a very thorough examination, he said I was hypersensitive and indeed verified a slight heart murmur. He filled out a very detailed form which I took to Dr. Fabiani. He also gave me a thorough checkup, and after reading Prof. Pisani's report he nodded and said: "I agree with what Prof. Pisani has written. I think that you can undoubtedly get an exemption from the work you are doing. Good luck," and he shook my hand.

I could not believe my ears. I asked how long it would be before I received confirmation of the exemption. "Three or four days at the most," he told me. I went out happy, my heart pounding with excitement. The following morning I got up at the usual hour and went to the place where the ditch diggers were working. I told my friends I would be discharged and they kindly expressed their happiness for me, but I did not feel comfortable, as though I had betrayed my partners in misfortune.

I started working with Gianfranco, reciting the details of the procedure I had to go through to get the exemption. I advised him to do the same thing. He did not seem too anxious to change his situation. Probably his involvement in that forced work camouflaged him and allowed him to devote himself undisturbed to his anti-Fascist activities.

At the lunch hour, my regular meeting with Gina, I had to tell her about my discharge. She broke into tears, made me promise to come see her in the future, and asked me to give her a kiss. It was long and sweet. While I kissed her I thought about what I was giving up. For the first time I felt her whole body pressing against mine. I realized how attracted I was to all those wonders of nature and how easy it would have been to make love to her, if I had wanted to. I made an enormous effort to restrain myself during those two or three minutes of an embrace and kiss; they seemed quick as a flash and eternal as a benediction.

The voices of my co-workers laughing and joking came to my rescue. The enchantment broken, I returned to reality and gently loosened our embrace. I was sure I would regret that moment. At the distance of an abyss of time, I can say that regret remained with me for a long time.

I continued to work every day, but feeling my freedom close at hand, I took it easy. Instead of digging ditches, I preferred to give Gina a hand cutting the clover. I enjoyed the work, but most of all I could be with her and make the inevitable break less painful.

It did not seem real that after almost seven months of hard work I would go back to a normal life, because for that period of time I had been detached from my family, living in a world they knew nothing about. Now I yearned to assume once more a dutiful role toward my parents. The first thing would be to start earning something to add to my father's ever smaller income. And I had to make them feel all my affection. I knew how much they suffered because Franco was so far away from us on an island now being bombed daily by Italian planes. The triumphant bulletins of the Fascist command spoke of devastating damage to the Maltese military structure and this caused my parents anxiety because they had not heard anything from my brother for months.

For all military, food, and health supplies, Malta depended on the English naval convoys that plowed the Mediterranean waters, stopping at Malta before heading toward North African ports with supplies for the Allied forces. These convoys were also persistently targeted by the Italian air force and German naval vessels, and many of the ships were sunk before they reached their destination. Malta was under continuous siege and we feared for Franco's safety.

I was pleased to continue seeing my former work partners with whom I had formed close ties. This was a great comfort because I needed to feel surrounded by affectionate friends. I was especially tied to Gianfranco Sarfatti, to Mario Baer and his wife, to Luciano Servi, to Giulano Treves and his wife, to all the "gang" of the Passigli, Procaccia, Servi, Benadì, Levi d'Ancona, Orvieto, Belgrado, Donati, Cassin, and others with whom I had daily contact, either directly or by telephone.

Giuliano Treves was a young professor of art history and English who taught at the Jewish school of Florence and also gave private lessons to young Florentine Jews. He was a cultured man, gracious and accessible. I liked his company because he always had something interesting and intelligent to say. I got the impression that he, too, had connections with the Italian partisan movements or directly with the Allied forces, but I never wanted to pry any deeper so as not to cause Giuliano embarrassment.

The news of my work exemption was received with much relief by my parents, and by Liliana in particular. In fact, my sister was going through a difficult time and my renewed presence in the family circle gave her the possibility of an exchange of confidences and advice.

Through mutual friends Liliana had met a young lawyer named Lattes—from Turin, I believe—who was looking for a young Jewish girl from a good family to marry. Their first formal meeting was at our house for tea. *Avvocato* Lattes came alone, as the parents had already spoken with each other. He was honest, cultured, and distinguished. Liliana liked him instantly and after the first formal meeting he returned to Florence almost every week to take her out to dinner or the theater.

I do not know if my sister was ready for a sentimental attachment with anyone at such a precarious time in our lives. Of one thing I was certain, however. My father, though not daring to set himself against his daughter's hopes of finding a good match that might lead to marriage, was opposed to the idea that anyone should carry off his firstborn. This rebellion was manifested in great scenes with my mother and Liliana herself. Those were traumatic experiences for me. On one side papa shouted angrily. On the other my mother and Liliana cried. And I was in the middle, not knowing which way to turn in that hullabaloo! Then, after my father was through venting his feelings, he calmed down and things returned to their peaceful state, until *Avvocato* Lattes's next visit to Florence.

In the end Liliana finally could not take it any more and put an end to the lawyer's visits. From that moment peace returned to reign in the Tayar household. My sister went back to her usual friends and was able to take up her social life again, going to concerts or spending pleasant evenings in good company.

CHAPTER 8

Year of Great Events

Diary

Sunday, April 11, 1943: Up at nine (it was Sunday). Shaved. Papa, mamma, and Aunt Matilde went out at ten. I received a letter from the CPC [Consiglio Provinciale delle Corporazioni (Provincial Council of Corporations)]: I AM DEMOBILIZED!!! Joy, exultation, etc. etc. Luciano came over and I told him the good news.

I was a free man again! I wanted to celebrate the event by going to eat with Liliana at the Pensione Bellettini and, later in the afternoon, I went to play tennis at the Giglio Rosso Tennis Club with Luciano and Elsa Treves. We enjoyed ourselves, and that day I promised myself to learn to play a decent game of tennis. I arranged to play several times a week with some friends on the Giglio Rosso courts. It would serve to keep me in shape, after all the "sport" I had as a ditch digger!

The vicissitudes of the war on the different fronts began to turn more favorably toward the Allies. Air-raid alarms began to sound in Florence on April 12. Most of the time they were pre-alarms, set off after sightings of Allied planes that were headed for Florence but that turned back because they were only reconnaissance planes, or that dumped their arsenal of bombs on Livorno, Grossetto, or Bologna. If the alarms went off at night I often did not even wake up. When they went off in the daytime it was a nuisance because we were obliged to go huddle in an anti-aircraft shelter that had been built under Dante high school and which, according to the Unione Nazionale Protezione Antiaerea, was completely secure! For me the siren wails were like listening to a Beethoven symphony. Finally the war front was drawing near Florence and the frequency of the air strikes revealed that the Allies were beginning a big military campaign that pointed to the liberation of Italy.

I hoped that Florence would be spared the massive bombings that had destroyed a good part of Livorno. Because the city was so full of artistic treasures and, besides, much loved by the English who had visited it for so many years, I hoped it might be considered a kind of "open city" like Rome.

As far as I was directly concerned, I observed that the exemption from forced labor had one disadvantage. In fact, with unbelievable rapidity considering Italian disorganization, my ration of so-called bread was reduced from the 400 daily grams that I received as a ditch digger to the miserable 150 daily grams of a simple citizen.

During my stay at the Sesto plain I had made friends with the shopkeepers, where I often bought something to supplement my snack. These contacts were useful even later for buying food for the whole family. Being a small country community, Sesto had the possibility of buying directly from the farmers.

On April 15 I went by bicycle to Peretola and Sesto to buy some things, and as long as I was there I went to say hello to my former work partners. I also saw Gina, of course, and though I was happy to see her, I tried to behave in a more detached manner. I suggested she start writing her fiancé again and be a good girl!

On the following days I played much tennis with Gianfranco, Luciano, and Elsa Treves. I knew that once I began to work again I would have much less time at my disposal. I even played the morning of April 20, the first day of Passover. At ten I went to temple, where mamma and papa had gone ahead of me, and I saw almost all my friends, which made me happy. After the *bracha,* at noon, we went home, and for dinner we ate the matzos that the Jewish community had managed to procure with great difficulty.

At seven in the evening I went back to temple alone, and after the service I participated in the seder that had been set up in the community. All my friends were there, and Fernando Belgrado officiated. I envied his splendid baritone voice. While he recited the Haggadah, he made the windows of the room shake. Aside from the religious aspect, the supper was excellent and my friends and I hung around to talk afterward.

The free time I had after office hours and other business I dedicated to the problems of the Jewish community. Every Thursday evening there was a meeting in which anyone who wished could participate. It was presided over by a new young rabbi, Nathan Cassuto. A very cultured person and endowed with a great fund of generosity and good will, he attracted the sympathy of everyone. That day, April 29, Rabbi Cassuto announced that he had made an arrangement with Maestro Veneziani, director of the Teatro alla Scala chorus (who overnight found himself bumped from his prestigious position), to come to Florence as often as possible, depending on his availability and financial possibilities, to organize a choir for mixed voices and teach them Jewish religious songs.

I agreed enthusiastically to take part in the choir. It would give my musical and vocal interests an outlet. I liked it also because concerts were planned in the temple with organ accompaniment, with the proceeds going to Delasem,[12] an organization to help Jews who had escaped from German concentration camps. I was anxious to take a more active part in the problems involving European Judaism. After our encounter with the English political internees at San Gimignano, I had not been able to get any more information on what was happening in Germany and Poland, and I was counting on Delasem to get a better idea of the situation.

The first choir practice was set for the next Sunday, May 2. I talked this venture over with my papa and mamma, who approved of my joining the undertaking; mamma even said she would like to participate. I was pleased by the idea of being able to sing with my mother. Besides the fact that she had acquired a good musical sense through her piano study, she also had a very beautiful contralto voice. With his beautiful tenor voice I thought papa might like to take part in the choir. When I asked him he said he would think about it and I suspected he would like to, but might be uncomfortable around a group of young people.

Finally, Sunday afternoon at three I went to the community center for the audition. A piano had been placed in the corner of a big room. With the rabbi was Maestro Veneziani, a middle-aged man with glasses, thick hair, and a musician's face with lively, penetrating eyes. The others trying out arrived a few at a time, and with great surprise and pleasure, I counted 22 women and 19 men. Veneziani sat at the piano and had each one of us sing something. There were beautiful voices and also bad ones. Some were off-key and some not.

---

12. Delasem stands for Delegazione Assistenza Emigranti Ebrei (Delegation for Assistance to Jewish Emigrants).

Veneziani divided the group according to singing voice: soprano, contralto, tenor, baritone, bass. I was the only bass. Veneziani said I had an excellent voice and chose me for the choir. Unfortunately, not everyone made it. When the audition was over I offered to accompany Maestro Veneziani and his wife on foot as far as their hotel downtown. I hoped to become friends with such an important personality in the musical field: it was the first time something like this had happened to me. While we walked I asked him many questions about famous singers that he had known during his career at La Scala, and I did not neglect to let him know that papa had studied voice and mother would like to be in the choir. He said that obviously I had inherited my parents' singing voices and musical ability and that I should study voice. In any case, he would be able to evaluate my possibilities during the lessons in the coming weeks.

I had not expected such compliments and encouragement. I said good-bye to the couple at the door of their hotel and returned home on my bicycle, happily singing "La calunnia è un venticello" with what by now I was convinced was an excellent bass voice.

After the musical euphoria had passed, I plunged back into my office work. I was still a little in the air as far as my precise duties were concerned. Besides that, I did not feel very well. I tired too easily, and felt weak and empty-headed. Perhaps I did not get enough to eat, just as my parents and Liliana did not get enough. I decided that every day I would go by bicycle to Sesto to buy food from my shop-keeper friends, where I could find a bit of everything at reasonable prices. This trip would also give me the opportunity to see my friends who were still digging ditches. I saw how few remained. Some were on sick leave; others had managed to get exemptions. There was an air of winding up. Everyone talked about how the war was going badly for Italy and Germany and something important was about to happen.

Diary

May 4, 1943: Went to Brozzi to get the photos I had taken of Gina; she was very beautiful this evening. She told me her fiancé had left her, and her sister-in-law confirmed it, but when I seemed upset, she said it was a joke. I would like to know the truth. I'm very fond of her.

That was the last time. From then on Italian political events, and in particular those affecting me, kept me occupied with other things, and because of circumstances beyond my control I never had the opportunity to see Gina again. What a shame.

Diary

May 8, 1943: A decree for Jews appeared in the newspaper: they may not belong to a union. I don't know yet what will be the consequences of it. Actually it had no personal consequence for me or for my friends. Apparently more than anything else the Fascist party meant it to show that the Jews were being watched and that the bite of persecution was still strong. Its relevance primarily concerned the real boss, Adolf Hitler.

The same day mamma decided to go to Maestro Veneziani's first lesson, something that thrilled me much more than Mussolini's decrees. On May 9, Veneziani returned to Florence, and May 10, at nine in the evening, we gathered at Via Farini for the first lesson. We were all there, including mother.

Diary

May 9, 1943: . . . I can say it wasn't bad. Veneziani is a very strict teacher, but a good one.

Actually it was not easy for him to get so many different voices to harmonize, especially when they were so out of practice. Choirs are ordinarily made up of people who have a basic knowledge of singing. We were a ramshackle gang and so Veneziani had to be tough. Otherwise he would get nowhere.

The following evening, another lesson.

Diary

May 11, 1943: After supper I went to choir practice with Luciano: 16 men. Too few. The choir is beautiful and has made some progress. Veneziani gets very annoyed when he teaches. This evening I'm a little hoarse; I'll take something for it.

One of my difficulties with learning the songs was that I did not know how to read Hebrew very well, so I had to transcribe the Hebrew into the Latin alphabet. Most of my singing colleagues knew how to read the Hebrew correctly.

In spite of his just severity and demands, Maestro Veneziani was very humane with us. He realized that we were trying to help our less fortunate brothers, and he urged us not to become discouraged if we could not get the right note the first time.

The following day, May 12, in spite of the long, stressful work day I went to the community center in the evening after supper for choir practice.

> Diary
>
> May 12, 1943: It went rather well: I really thought choir work was eas-ier. I was mistaken. Everything you want to do well requires study and effort. Rommel sneaked out of Tunisia, and Messe had to remain. Stupid alliance! I hope it's all over soon.

Needless to say, this news that the Fascist propagandists unwillingly revealed filled me with happiness and the hope that before long the war would end with the complete defeat of the Nazi-Fascists.

I often asked myself: "How can a maniac like Hitler devote himself so tena-ciously to the persecution of my people when, thank heavens, he has so many mili-tary irons in the fire?" Evidently he used the anti-Jewish persecutions to distract his people's attention from the real problems gripping Germany: not only to distract attention from the difficulties in perpetuating an insane war, but also to make people forget the serious damage they were suffering from the Allied bombing, the enormous loss of human life—military and civilian—and the scarcity of every kind of basic necessity. The Germans, whom History describes over the centuries as a people capable of the cruelest and most shameful acts, felt victorious just at the thought of being able to hunt down the poor, defenseless, old, young, men, women, sick or well Jews. In this war they knew how to distinguish themselves, and, unfortunately for us, they were having their greatest triumphs.

> Diary
>
> May 13, 1943: Went to choir practice at nine: a lot of people didn't show up. I sang some wrong notes: my voice is weak. Veneziani gave

me a hard look. Today the war is over in Africa, that is, it was announced today in a rather dramatic news bulletin. I don't believe that any Axis soldier can return to Italy from Tunisia, except Rommel and Messe, of course. Now I'm waiting, or rather, everyone is waiting, for a campaign to begin in grand style by the Allied air power and for Italy to be attacked. I think the Allies are thinking of first occupying the important Aegean and Ionian Islands (Crete, Rhodes, Lampedusa, Dodecanese) and then attacking Bulgaria and Greece by way of Turkey. Churchill is in Washington talking with Roosevelt about the war. It will be a wonderful day when I can go boating at the Florence Boating Club!

The news was too exciting, and I absolutely had to enjoy it with my old work buddies. So the next morning I quickly did everything I had to do and went to the outskirts of Sesto Fiorentino.

Diary

May 14, 1943: After lunch at three I went to see my friends at Peretola; poor guys, I felt so sorry for them, knowing how much better it is to be demobilized! I took Gianfranco back on my bicycle, while Luciano towed Gianfranco's (which had a flat tire) as he rode his own bicycle. We spent many happy hours together celebrating the military failures of the Axis. When I went to choir practice at six thirty, the women were leaving their rehearsal, but Veneziani was in a good mood and didn't get mad.

On Sunday morning, May 16, there was a long choir rehearsal: we began at nine and were not finished until eleven thirty. The number of choir members had increased, which pleased Veneziani. Actually, the more participants there are, the better the choir. One of the things I especially liked from all the things Veneziani taught us was countermelody, something I had already learned from the Alpine choirs. Finding it again in the Jewish choirs was ever so gratifying, and I must say I managed it well. While we sang I never took my eyes off the Maestro's face. From his expression I understood how we should change the inflection of our voices. His hands moved constantly, signaling the various sections to increase or reduce the strength of our voices. We obeyed his smallest request instantly and the result was fantastic.

I appreciated this man's great stature, for years accustomed to directing choirs made up of hundreds of mature and perfectly trained voices. I asked myself how he could put such concentration and energy into teaching a small group of beginners. I imagined him during performances at La Scala, bowing while he received ovations that filled the theater. How could the poor man be reduced to what he was doing because of the infamous racial laws?

Yet, while he directed our little choir, I felt the same strength, devotion, and great skill as must have emanated from him at La Scala. I admired and respected him for this and was infinitely grateful. Only a person of his distinction could have such modesty and dignity.

Diary

May 17, 1943: Went to choir practice at 6:45. It went well. I heard Veneziani praise mamma, who is the only good contralto. She knows the music well, sings in tune, and has a beautiful voice. I'm happy for her. After the rehearsal, at eight, I went to Mario Baer's house to take the sheet music for his wife Eva, who will join the choir. She was in bed, not feeling well. I explained the pieces to her and afterward we talked with Mario. From there I went to Matilde Cassin's to take her some sheet music. A long chat with her and her mother. We talked about how the choir will turn out, etc. etc. Let's hope that no bombs fall on Florence before the day we are to sing: no one would come to hear us.

I was anxious for the choir to do well and above all for us to make some money. I saw with what dedication Veneziani was teaching us, and I hoped that the work of such a worthy teacher would not go to waste. He did everything without compensation, assuming the expense of the trips and the time he gave us. I did not want to disappoint him. The days went by calmly. My only interest was the choir.

Diary

May 20, 1943: The practice went well: we three basses were highly praised by Maestro Veneziani, who said the basses and the contraltos were the best. But, alas! The prefect has denied authorization for us to have a choir; Rabbi Cassuto will speak to him. Let's hope he convinces him, otherwise it will be too sad for us.

To say that this news left us thunderstruck is to say too little. What could be the reason for prohibiting this choir? What was so dangerous about our singing religious songs in our temple? I was very angry with that idiot prefect who played the super-zealot to satisfy his Duce, naturally in the hope of receiving who knows what high recognition. I could do nothing less than launch a curse in the prefect's direction.

What made me most angry was the abuse of power freely exercised by those incompetent little bosses who had free rein, thanks to the immunity granted them by the regime. They tried their best to see who could dream up the most sensational thing to make news and increase their own worth on the stock market of the idiotic administration. I felt an emptiness in the pit of my stomach every time I saw those bosses walking through the streets, strutting around in their ridiculous uniforms and shiny boots, with the bird sewn on the front of their caps, their wide belts of black leather, the long gloves also of black leather, and every kind of fake decoration sewn on the front of their uniforms, testifying to heroic deeds certainly never performed.

On the other hand, what could we expect from these second-raters when their Duce, the supreme commander, behaved exactly as they did? When He (the capital letter is obligatory) stands on the balcony of Piazza Venezia, in front of the tempestuous sea of black shirts, I am astonished by his histrionic performance. The grimaces he makes with his mouth, his eyes bulging as though he would like to gobble you down in one bite, his chin jutting skyward, his fists planted on his hips, the silences regularly following his words that provoke the inevitable roars of approval by the masses huddled like sheep at his feet, his expression of satisfaction as the ovations go on infinitely.

This spectacle masterfully directed by the Duce almost makes the content of his speeches of secondary importance. I often compare him with his companion in crime, Adolf. I will always be grateful to the Lord for having given us the Duce instead of the Other. Mussolini recited a part assigned him by circumstances. His speeches were primarily of the boasting variety worthy of Don Quixote. His behavior clearly alluded to the pomp of the Roman emperors, who in truth were men of steel.

Mussolini sang a song he considered right for his people's ears, and with his bluster he seemed a twin to Nero of Petrolini. The Other, instead, was simply a deranged criminal worthy of any insane asylum. He had the evil and sadistic genes characteristic of a large part of his people. His every word was an incitement to hate and to execute the most abject crimes invented by man. When he spoke there was nothing histrionic in his gestures, only fanaticism and sheer madness. He was truly frightening, as were his people, who obeyed him and followed him in his blind furor against the Jewish race.

And while all this was going on, I was worrying about what would become of our little choir!

> Diary
>
> May 23, 1943: At five o'clock we were at the temple. All the choristers were there, women and men. Alas, the rabbi gave us the official word that the chief of police had prohibited the choir to continue at the temple. We will try to get permission to meet in a private home, but I'm afraid they'll refuse; they don't want so many Jews meeting together. Just the thought of having to give up the choir makes me very unhappy. It's amazing: when they find a way to get at you they do it with all their might! I'm certain we'll get our revenge and that the day will come when we can have our choir where, how, and when we want. In the Community [center] I met a man of German origin by the name of Grosser who said I had been assigned a special mission within Delasem. I hope to do a good job. I would like to work for a good cause. Afterward I accompanied Veneziani to his *pensione*.

We walked in silence for a few minutes. Both of us were overcome by the great disappointment. It was late in the evening and the streets were deserted. We heard only the rhythmic sound of our footsteps. I broke the silence first. "What a shame we can't sing with you anymore. You don't know how much I appreciate all you've done for us. It's like we've been awakened from a dream, with anger in our hearts."

The elderly Maestro nodded while I spoke, then he said: "Look, Tayar, you are still young and fortunately have not had many opportunities to see the world collapse around you, except for what we are all experiencing now. In my long life I've had plenty of disappointments. Do you think I got where I am now without having to fight? Not at all. But I've become calloused about these things. Even though I'm sorry that the choir can't be, I'm glad I've had the opportunity to teach all of you to love music and singing in the few meetings we've had. Don't give up singing. You have talent. In fact, let another maestro hear you sing to give you a second opinion."

With a hand resting affectionately on my shoulder, he continued: "Let's try to forget this unfortunate little incident. Let's look ahead and hope the future is generous and gives us the opportunity to meet again. Good luck, my young friend."

"Good luck to you, too," I said with a knot in my throat. "And God bless you."

We left each other like two old friends who were starting off on a long journey in different directions.

While I bicycled home that evening I remembered the evening after my first meeting with Veneziani when, in the thrall of euphoria, I sang "La calunnia è un venticello," already considering myself a Fyodor Shalyapin. "How quickly our beautiful dreams can end," I thought bitterly.

Diary

May 24, 1943: Today, May 24, is the anniversary of Italy's entering into war against Germany in the first world war of 1915–18. I saw a flag waving from a balcony today. A mistake, provocation, or old style patriotism? Whatever the reason for that banner, I think whoever hung it out must have spent a bad 15 minutes. At 6:45 I was at the choir practice where, alas, they confirmed the prohibition. Immense sorrow for everyone. We have begun to collect money to pay Veneziani. He did not want to accept anything. I gave 100 lire. Now we'll organize something to meet together other times. It was really a nasty trick, one of many. But we know how to remember until time is ripe.

This had been the beginning of something so important to us, something that would have been good for us and for those poor fellow Jews escaped from concentration camps. All of us felt sad. Veneziani said good-bye, thanking us for our good effort to learn how to sing, and for the little economic contribution we finally convinced him to accept. His eyes were glistening as he shook our hands.

We promised each other that once our human freedom and dignity were restored, we would meet to take up the work where we left off. Rabbi Cassuto was also sad to see the unhappy ending of the project that he had thought up and that he had hoped to bring into port, but with firm words and looking us straight in the eyes he said we certainly would find another way to help our brothers. He added: "I count on those of you who have always shown pride in being Jewish to help the less fortunate who are suffering. Let us not kid ourselves about the future which awaits us even in Italy. The worst is yet to come." It was not only a horrifying prophecy, but also a warning not to let down our guard.

I went home with my mind in turmoil. As I feared, I saw my mother grow sad at the events of that evening, the confirmation of the prohibition and Veneziani's departure. To lighten the atmosphere I announced that the rabbi supported Delasem and that I would be part of the organization. My parents were pleased and encouraged me to devote as much time as possible to this necessary work.

When the first meeting of the finance board of Delasem met in the community center, we set up a plan for collecting money from the Florentine Jews and, going over the list of the community members, we selected the names of those we thought could make a substantial contribution to our campaign. Then we formed little groups to contact a certain number of people from the names chosen. I worked with a friend and went with her from house to house to ask for contributions. We worked consistently, and the results were immediately encouraging: we got offers of a thousand lire at a time—really important and generous amounts, given the unprosperous economic conditions of most of us. But even those who could only give smaller amounts received the same warm thanks.

Every week we took a report to the community center and turned over the money we had collected. Through Delasem I was able to get an account of the atrocious pogroms carried out against the Jews in Czechoslovakia and brought it home to read to papa. This was the first truly upsetting news that gave details of the atrocities. I thought it only right for my parents to know about it even if it disturbed them.

The only comment papa made when I had finished reading was: "Let's hope to God that nothing like that happens to us in Italy." I replied with the words Rabbi Cassuto had spoken in the community center the evening of our farewell to Veneziani, words that had frozen my blood. But papa did not give in to his usual pessimism and replied that Rabbi Cassuto exaggerated. I think he was trying to hide the cruel reality from himself with fake optimism.

Recently papa's spirit had had its ups and downs. Most certainly his being forced into inactivity at the time the war broke out and his office was closed had a negative impact on his morale. He felt useless and in spite of the efforts he made, he could not get any kind of job. He had nothing to distract him, neither reading nor going to the movies.

He and mamma often visited with the Lattes, who were about their same age. Signor Lattes also was practically without work and therefore he and papa were in the same psychological condition. Together, at least twice a week they took the streetcar to Vingone and walked a good way after the last stop to reach the villa called La Ragnaia, where mother's relatives, the Archivolti, lived. Aunt Gina was Grandmother Evelina's sister, and her husband, Carlo, was a retired army general.

As is suitable for an ex-general, Carlo had a military character, and when he spoke he seemed to be haranguing his troops. Gina was a tiny woman, exactly the opposite of her sister Evelina, may she rest in peace. In fact, whereas Evelina had a very strong and authoritarian character, Gina was perpetually whiny. Her brother Guido always said that Gina was a "pain."

Papa listened to the war bulletins on Radio London. Then he would relate the news to us and we would discuss it together, each of us with a different opinion. But this was a normal thing in a family like ours! Every once in a while papa came home with a new book for mother to read to him. They were usually dull books, such as the history of the Medici or the life of Michelangelo. He wanted to improve his knowledge of Renaissance Florence, and mamma, who had the onerous job of reading them out loud, was bored to death, even though she hid it behind her usual calm exterior. I watched this with a feeling of real tenderness for them both.

Another one of papa's occupations was to keep weekly tabs on the finances. Even here mother's assistance was indispensable because papa could not read the numbers on the receipts. Sparks often flew between them at the end of the week when papa thought we had spent more than we should. Mamma then had to give him all the particulars about what she had spent and on what and to this end had to save all the store receipts. It was a thankless as well as a useless task. But that was the way papa wanted it, and in order not to irritate him any further she did it as he wished.

Playing the piano was a great comfort for mamma. After finishing her housework she would sit at the piano and play for an hour or two instead of resting, as she would be justified in doing. She wanted me to take it up again; I had taken piano lessons from the age of ten until these lessons began to interfere with my school work. I played well enough and it had become a great pastime. Because of mamma's insistence I started playing again to make her happy, going over the exercises I had done hundreds of times. They were a little monotonous, but in the end I had the satisfaction of making progress, and I quickly climbed up the slope to which I had descended after quitting the lessons.

Sometimes mamma would sit beside me while I practiced and correct my mistakes as I made them. I loved her attitude toward life and her deep serenity. She was rarely in a bad mood and if it happened it was certainly someone else's fault. To be precise, in the order of responsibility, I would say the variations of maternal mood were caused first of all by papa, then Liliana, and finally me.

To me she was the most solid pillar upon which our family rested, and I also appreciated her being a woman of few words, since those few words she spoke were always full of goodness and wisdom. Like every good mother, she worried about Liliana and me, along with Franco, of course, but avoided excessive indulgence and had a very strong will when reminding us of our obligations. However, it was not difficult to obey these reminders that were delivered with a firm and ever-peaceful voice, never altered by harsh tones.

Mamma was endowed with an enviable dexterity and sometimes fixed things around the house that normally would have required the services of an expert. For example, if the upholstery was worn, mother would buy a piece of fabric and casually replace the old material, using nails, hammer, and pliers.

She was a very skillful draftsman. When I was small I loved to look at the folder where mother had saved many pencil drawings she made as a girl in high school in Bologna. They were mostly drawings of architectural details, such as decorated capitals or colonnades with arches. She also knew how to do needlepoint embroidery, and once she undertook a truly complicated piece, nothing less than a portrait of Pope Pius IX, standing beside a throne. It was about 1.2 meters high and took many months for her to finish. Technically it was very well done, in beautiful, bright colors and it looked just like the pope, but I never understood why mother chose to embroider his portrait. Our house was certainly not the most appropriate place to hang such an image!

Besides handiwork and embroidery, mother knew how to sew very well and made all the necessary clothing alterations for the entire family. Sadly, it was usually a matter of taking something in, because we kept getting thinner from the scarcity of food.

For many years we did not buy new clothes, but if the occasion called for it, mamma could be creative. Once Liliana had been invited to go to a party at a friend's house and did not have anything new to wear to make a good appearance. Out of a chest mother fished one of her old long scarves of light wool, with many colored stripes, like an Indian dancing girl's scarf; took Liliana's measurements; and made a simple, straight, sleeveless (because there was not enough material) dress that turned out "new" and beautiful. Liliana was able to attend the party, as elegant as if she had just come from a dressmaker's.

There were not many such social opportunities for my sister, but she had both male and female friends (with whom I had little in common, considering our age difference) that she went out with often, to concerts or meetings. Or she went out with mother to visit her friends. The days were sometimes long for Liliana, and I knew there were boring moments. She tried to escape the monotony by going to see Aunt Matilde, who would invite her to stay a few days with her in either Bologna or one of the places where she went on vacation.

As I said, Liliana rarely bought new clothes because of our lack of money. It was mother who made her simple skirts and blouses. But Liliana was a beautiful girl and therefore even when she was simply dressed she made a good impression. I remember when she was 18 papa had some photographs made by a professional photographer, and I will never forget how shocked I was when I saw them, because in addition to her face, Liliana showed a bare shoulder. Of course the photographer had resorted to this stratagem to make the photograph more artistic, but I could not rest until Liliana assured me that nothing more than her left shoulder was exposed.

Papa liked to be properly dressed. He was especially fond of a heavy wool suit that kept him warm, but the jacket was worn in many places. Mamma noticed it and decided that he needed to take the jacket to a tailor to be turned. The work was well done, with the single drawback that the handkerchief pocket that is normally on the left side was now on the right. Everyone would know he was wearing a jacket that had been turned. I must say that when the tailor pointed out this problem to my father, he answered him very wittily: "If anyone asks why, I'll say I'm left-handed and it's easier to keep my glasses in my right pocket!" And he wore with pride his jacket with the pocket on the right side!

The war continued relentlessly. The Allied air bombardments became more frequent and many Italian cities were badly hit. The Florentines did not pay much attention to the air-raid alarms because they were too frequent and regularly turned out to be nothing. If we had had to run and hide in the anti-aircraft shelters at every siren our lives would have been paralyzed. So we ignored them all.

Returning home on the evening of June 4, 1943, I found my parents talking with a Belgian woman by the name of Adler who had just come to Florence after escaping from a German concentration camp in Poland. The poor woman was in terrible condition. She was extremely thin and her face showed signs of the physical and moral suffering she had undergone. She was speaking French with my parents. I had trouble understanding what she was saying. Mother translated what was most important. Signora Adler was the only one of her entire family who was lucky enough to escape the camp. She had decided to try to go to Palestine where she had relatives and where she thought she would be safe. I could not understand how that poor woman could leave her husband and children behind and go away alone in search of salvation. I realize now that after one has suffered so terribly the will to survive becomes strong enough to make one forget everything but one's own safety.

My parents comforted the poor woman with a supper that mother prepared just for her. Afterward we sat in the living room and listened to this woman's sad story, which was the story of millions of our brothers and sisters. She told us about the Germans bursting into her house in the middle of the night and taking away her, her husband, and their children. There were horrible scenes of beatings and inhuman screams. They were loaded onto a truck, were taken first to one concentration camp, and then each was taken to a different camp. From the moment of that terrible separation she knew nothing of her husband and children.

I said that I could not understand very well what the woman was saying because she was speaking French, but one thing was very very clear and easy to understand. It was at a certain point in her story when she rolled back her sleeve to show a number tattooed on her arm. This was our first introduction to this cruel, monstrous practice, and we were horrified by it.

Shivers ran down my back as I looked at that number stamped on an arm become skin and bones. Mamma, papa, and I were struck dumb, and within the walls of the living room the monotonous voice seemed unnatural and unfeeling as it recounted a story whose words were lost on me, but not their meaning. The sound of the foreign language and the silence that surrounded her seemed like something from a different world, inconceivable for the mind of someone who, like me and my parents, had up to that time lived a normal, if troubled, existence.

That poor woman, branded like a beast for the butcher, kept on talking and who knows how many times she had had to tell of her misfortune. For her, only one thing was certain: she was alive; she had escaped from an inferno inhabited by monsters. In her heart she nourished a single hope: to reach Palestine.

She slept in our house and in the morning I took her to the community center. When I left her I gave her my heartfelt wishes that she reach the Promised Land and one day embrace her dear ones. Heaven knows how this story ended. From then on in my money-collecting campaign I had a true story to tell about Signora Adler, which, I hoped, or rather I was sure, would touch the feelings of my fellow Jews in Florence.

The days were longer now and summer was definitely in the air. I began to feel the urge to take a summer vacation and to do some physical activity, which had been practically reduced to zero after I quit digging.

I decided to go to the section of the Alpine Club of Italy in Florence and ask if I could join and participate in some of the excursions they organized every summer in the Dolomites. I was greeted kindly enough by a secretary who had the appearance of someone who had made mountains a way of life. I asked if I could become a member, and to avoid any ugly surprises popping up later, I told him right off the bat that I was a Jew. He replied that he did not give a damn about that ("Excellent beginning," I thought), but I would have to wait a few weeks for the club to consider it. The visit was not a success, but it was not a total loss, either. In the course of our talk I had seen that a camping trip was planned in Val d'Aosta, at the foot of Mont Blanc, that I knew I would like very much. I went away with the hope of being able to go there.

On the evening of June 7, there was another meeting of Delasem. I was pleased with what I had collected, and in fact, that morning I had received another donation of 1,000 lire from my mother's cousin, Lello Archivolti. The other community members collecting money were doing a great job, even if we all understood perfectly well that it would take millions and millions more to help so many poor refugees, and we were not able to get more than 1,000 lire at a time. However, we could not lose heart; we had to be patient and steadfast in our work.

Mario Baer was doing a great deal for the Jewish refugees coming from Poland, Austria, and Germany. They had fled from their cities to take refuge in France, but now, after the Germans had made their life impossible in France, some of them were crossing into Italy through the Alpine passes. Through Delasem, Mario contacted these refugees and had them come to Florence, where he settled them with various Catholic families. He ended up resettling more than 120 of these poor people, and the most amazing thing was that those who took them in most easily and with the greatest enthusiasm, hiding them and risking their own lives, were those most humble souls in the poorest sections of Florence, such as San Frediano and Santa Croce.

The rumor was spreading that the Germans were amassing large numbers of troops and war materials in Florence with the help of the Fascists, who tried to keep it secret. This news was disturbing. It was one thing to know that the Germans were fighting with the Italians in some other part of the planet, and another to have them in your own backyard without even knowing or imagining the reasons for this undesirable presence. As long as this was limited to the Wehrmacht troops, the harm was in proportion. My worry was that the SS might come to take care of matters in quite a different manner than the strictly military ones. It had not happened yet, at least apparently, so we were getting by.

On June 12 Pantelleria, an island between Sicily and Africa, fell, which was a sign that the Allies were not slowing down their offensive.

> Diary
> June 14, 1943: At 5:45 I went to a meeting of Delasem. Several people were missing. A reliable source said that some Jews are spies in OVRA. This is very bad news.

I never would have thought that a Jew could denounce his own brothers, taking part in one of the most odious organizations created by Fascism. Everyone knew that the OVRA agents tried to infiltrate the possible anti-Fascist organizations to uncover plots and denounce the guilty. This danger made us very cautious around strangers who asked leading questions or claimed to be philo-Semites and anti-Fascists to earn our confidence. That there might be even one Jew among us who could belong to the OVRA amazed me. Even if someone were capable of denouncing a fellow Jew, he could still get kicked out of the OVRA himself one day and then be treated like all the other Jews.

Personally I was not worried. It was obvious that to be a Jew was synonymous with anti-Fascism. How could it be otherwise? Therefore, if one of those spies denounced me I would never deny a fact so obvious as being anti-Fascist, that is, hostile to someone who was oppressing us in every way. Instead, I was worried about my friends Gianfranco and Luciano because of their contacts with the anti-Fascist opposition that worked against the regime and did not limit itself to talk. I phoned both of them to put them on alert. They had already been warned and were able to discover the traitors who, eventually, would be adequately punished.

On June 16, I went to the community center for a Delasem meeting. We counted our donations and planned the next visits. At the end of the meeting it was announced that it was Delasem's last session, but the collection of money would continue anyway. Rabbi Cassuto would be responsible for delivering it. I was a bit surprised but asked for no explanation. Obviously whoever made the decision had a good reason.

The evening of June 17 was the community's usual Thursday meeting. The rabbi and I talked about OVRA and about our prospects for the future. I expressed my opinion about the OVRA. Concerning the future I told him of my fears about such a massive presence of German troops in Florence. The rabbi reaffirmed his pessimistic view of the future. In the paper a notice appeared that all Jews born between 1907 and 1926 would be "rigidly organized" into work programs. This did not worry me overmuch. Even if they should call me, unlikely after the exoneration I had obtained, they certainly could not make me do any harder work than I had already experienced.

As for the general situation of the Jews, this new restrictive intervention was a sign that Mussolini had not forgotten us and that he wanted to keep us under pressure to show his colleague Hitler that he was serious about the Jewish question. I began to believe that Rabbi Cassuto was right to be pessimistic.

Over the last few weeks in almost daily encounters with my friends, I got better acquainted with Gianna Orvieto, a lawyer's daughter. She was a few years younger than I, rather pretty and slender, very intelligent and sensitive. She spoke slowly as though weighing every word. I liked her a lot and wanted us to become closer friends. From what I could see, Federico also liked Gianna, but I did not think they were romantically involved yet. There was just a feeling of mutual affinity between them, I told myself, and therefore there would be nothing wrong with my trying to get closer to Gianna. We will see what happens, I thought. The worst that could happen would be to be left stranded, as with Mimma.

On June 25 Liliana and I were invited to Gianna's house after supper. It turned out to be her birthday. I was unshaven and wore the same suit I had worn to the office that day. All the other guests were elegantly dressed. I felt so out of place that I tried to stay apart from the others. The refreshments were excellent but I did not enjoy myself because I felt so shabby. The next day I called Gianna to apologize. I had gone to her house without shaving, without changing my suit, and above all without the ghost of a present. I had not known it was her birthday.

She had noticed that I kept to myself and had not understood why. She tried to console me by saying that she really gave no importance to a person's exterior. "What counts is what one has inside," she said. I felt encouraged and asked Gianna to meet me in town at five. To my joy she agreed. This time I shaved carefully and put on a decent suit. We met at Piazza Vittorio Emanuele and from there went directly to Seeber bookstore on Via Tornabuoni where I asked Gianna to pick out a book as my birthday gift to her. She chose *Tutti i romanzi di Pirandello* (The Novels of Pirandello), and I spent 70 lire.

Afterward we went to sit at a bar on the Lungarno. We talked and then walked along the river until suppertime. We walked slowly, stopping once in a while to admire the sun that was setting behind the Cascine and coloring the muddy water red.

We had a quiet conversation that jumped from one subject to another. I liked Gianna's openness and the fact that she knew how to listen as well as to talk. As we walked side by side, my arm would involuntarily brush against hers. She did not try to avoid these occasional contacts, which made me happy.

I walked her home and she thanked me for the gift and for the nice afternoon we had spent together. Before I left I had a great desire to kiss her on the cheek, but I did not for fear that she would not like it. I limited myself to a light caress on her face. She blushed and we parted with the promise to see each other again soon.

> Diary
>
>   July 1, 1943: At Castello a train coming from the Brenner Pass collided with seven freight cars that unfortunately (?) were uncoupled by another train blocking the tracks. A slaughter. Sergio went to see. The passenger train had become a heap of two engines and eight cars. People said they were German VIPs. I don't know if it's true.

Immediately we began speculating about this very mysterious accident. If, as they said, there were Germans on the train, this could only be an act of sabotage, which pleased me very much, naturally. I wanted to ask Gianfranco if he knew anything about it, but I did not because I was sure his answer would be negative.

July 2, Mimma phoned to say that her father had been arrested by the carabinieri for "precautionary reasons" (political). I told her I was very sorry and that if they needed anything whatever, they could count on me. She thanked me and we said good-bye like old friends. It occurred to me that this arrest could be connected with yesterday's train accident.

In the morning I went to the Provincial Council of Corporations (the CPC, by its Italian initials) to find out about the announced mobilization. They will notify us individually by postcard. I continued to be unconcerned. I had been vaccinated! I got telephone calls from alarmed friends who had received the postcard from the CPC to go to work. They had gone as far as the letter *C*. Federico Benadì, Sergio Bemporad, and Marcello Campagnano had been called. I tried to explain to each one of them that this new summons had nothing to do with the ditch-digging work I had done. It was probably some kind of light work that would allow the police to keep an eye on the potentially dangerous young Jews.

On July 4, there was more trouble with the trains: electric lines were cut at Porretta. They do not know if by Allied parachutists or someone else. The Castello accident was confirmed as intentional. Ion Antonescu, the military dictator of Romania then on the Nazi-Fascist side, went to Rome to meet either with the king or with Mussolini. They talked of eventual negotiations for an armistice between Italy and the Allies. These could be fantasies, but too many strange things were happening that had never happened before. I was beginning to hope it could be true. I hoped to heaven the war was really about to end. How many things in our lives would change.

On July 5, I received a phone call from the head of Delasem of Genoa. After the customary compliments and thanks for the work I had done in Florence, he asked me to transfer to Genoa and work for them full-time. They needed young recruits with innovative methods to help collect money for the Jewish refugees whose situation was a growing tragedy. I thanked him for the honor, but had to decline. I could not think of leaving my family and work and everything that tied me to Florence, especially at such a critical time. He was a little unhappy with my refusal, but thanked me and said he understood my reasons. We hung up cordially.

That phone call plunged me back into a world from which I had been slowly retreating: what I had learned from the head at Genoa did not allow much optimism and it reminded me of Rabbi Cassuto's prophecies that things would get worse. I began to reflect on the Jewish situation as a whole. What was happening in Italy was only a small part of the whole Jewish problem: the largest problem was taking place in Germany and in all the countries Hitler had occupied, particularly in those places where the persecution was more virulent and more ferociously organized. Furthermore, it seemed evident that with every military defeat the Nazis countered with a worsening of their anti-Jewish fury. What would happen if, as was rumored, Italy, with an army reduced to practically nothing after the beating it got in Africa and other parts of the Mediterranean, signed an armistice with the Allies? What would be the reaction of Germany and its still powerful war machine toward an ally that betrayed it?

My mind was whirling with questions, but I did not feel like talking about it with my parents in order not to upset them. So I kept it all inside, which made it even worse. For a distraction I went to the Alpine Club to find out if they had received a reply in regard to my application. To my great surprise, the gentleman I had spoken with the first time, that mountaineer type, told me that the reply had been received and that Jew or not I could join.

I was happy: it did not seem real. It was a concrete sign that things were changing in Italy. This did a lot for my peace of mind. I joined at once, paid the initial fee, and went away with my fine Alpine Club of Italy membership card in my pocket.

Practically speaking, the possession of this membership card was not of great importance, but I considered it a kind of revenge.

That evening Liliana and I decided to hike around Lago Santo, in the Modenese Apennines, together with some other friends. We got our knapsacks ready with what little food we could wrangle and went to sleep with the prospect of a nice weekend. It was a good five-day trip, which I really needed, and it helped us come out from under the leaden cloud created by the news of the German atrocities against the Jews and by fear of repeating their sad destiny. We restored our energy by walking many hours every day and breathing the fresh mountain air.

I would have liked for Gianna to be with us. She could not come because she had to stay to help her father. I phoned her from one of the mountain refuges where we stopped for the night and I told her how much I liked her and of my desire to be near her. If it was not a proper declaration of love, it was close. Gianna said she was happy about my feelings for her, and this was enough to put me in a good mood for the rest of the trip.

We returned to Florence the next day, happy about how our trip had gone, and our parents greeted us with glowing faces. While we were in the Apennines a message had arrived from Franco. The usual few words—"Everything fine"—an example of concision, but still good news. Although we did not know exactly where he was, the easing up of the bombardments on Malta after the war front in North Africa had been closed had already mitigated our worry, and now came the confirmation that he was safe and sound. Perhaps in the wake of his euphoria caused by the message, papa wanted to give Liliana and me 250 lire each as a contribution toward our expenses at Lago Santo. We appreciated the gesture, knowing the situation of the family coffers.

On July 17 Churchill and Roosevelt sent a message to the Italian people, inviting them to capitulate and free themselves from Fascism. This invitation was difficult to accept for a people accustomed to obeying the Duce's orders and seldom using their own heads. Things had been going along like this for 20 years. How could they overnight find the courage to do something that in all this time they had not been capable of? Undoubtedly Churchill and Roosevelt thought they were sending their message to a democratic and politically mature, free people like the English and Americans. I doubted the Italians would do as they were requested without strong support from the Allied armies.

CHAPTER 9

July 25, 1943: Mussolini Falls

Diary

July 25, 1943: . . . Got up and went to the shelter as usual from 8:45
to 9:15. No air raid. Did nothing in the morning. In the afternoon went
to see Gianna and took a walk with her around downtown Florence,
talking about the events of the last few days, of what we will do after the
war is over, and many other things. Came home and went to bed.

I went to bed too early. That night was not meant for sleeping. At eleven o'clock
a friend of mamma's, Signora Bruno, telephoned. She was excited to tell us
that, according to a communiqué from Rome she had just heard on the radio,
MUSSOLINI HAD RESIGNED and had been arrested by order of the king!

It was the end of Fascism. The king had taken command with Badoglio as prime
minister. The war was continuing.

This was the greatest thing that had happened to me in my whole life. It would
bring incalculable change. It ended, thank God, a dictatorship that had lasted more
than 20 years.

I was so dazed by the incredible news that I could not sort out all the many ideas
and questions crowding my mind. Would Mussolini be tried and condemned for
the misery he caused? Would the Fascist party members endure the same fate?
Now that the regime had fallen, would the Allies be willing to sign a peace treaty
with Italy? And what would Germany do?

I was in no position to answer these and the many other questions I put to my-self. I also asked myself if there would be an anti-Fascist movement in Italy and if there would be a settling of accounts between opposing factions that led to bloodshed. I was curious to go out on the street to see how many were still wearing the Fascist emblem, the so-called *brigidino*. This last question was quickly answered: not a single person went around with the *brigidino* in his buttonhole.

Each of us began to plan for the future. Mamma hoped that Franco would come back soon; papa thought about reopening his office; Liliana thought about going to some other country, even the United States. I thought about the possibility of resuming my interrupted studies, even of getting a degree in medicine, my original aspiration. And not the least, with my freedom restored I would be able to join the Boating Club!

I got on the phone and in spite of the late hour called all my friends to tell them the great news. Most of them had not heard anything and were already in bed. Only a few knew about it and, like us, were still up talking about this astonishing turn of events.

After I finished making my calls (past midnight), I continued my line of reasoning. If Churchill and Roosevelt had sent that message to the Italians just eight days ago and today Mussolini had fallen, it meant the Allies had been alerted by someone who knew what was happening to Fascism. It meant that at a certain higher level people were working to overturn the situation in Italy and help the Allies eliminate Italy as a hostile force. This thought gave me hope for further improvement of the situation. I seemed to be living a dream and I was afraid of waking up.

The calmest one of us all was mamma. Her sole concern was to have her family reunited. This was of utmost importance to her. We went to bed after one. I tossed and turned for a long time without getting sleepy. It is strange, but when we are in the dark with our thoughts, things assume a very different aspect from when we get up with the others in the light of day or in the lamplight. In the solitude of night, doubts and fears come alive. Those maddening phantoms of the mind kept me from sleeping until nearly dawn.

I got up earlier than usual, at six thirty, dressed quickly, told everyone good-bye, and dashed to the office. I was anxious to find out what would happen around me after the unexpected reversal.

Diary

July 26, 1943: Went to the office. Watched a demonstration from the office balcony that I'll never forget. Went down to take part. Took ten photos. Met friends on the street. Great jubilation and happy crowds reign in Florence. Afterward I went to Gianna's house. Fioralba, Giuliana, and others were there and I went out to celebrate with them. Very moving scene. Returned home at eight. A unique day in my life.

To find myself amid such irrepressible joy made me forget my doubts and fears of the night before when I could not sleep. Of course, among all those people who had come out to express their joy many were really happy anti-Fascists. However, the suspicion lingered that among them were also some who until two days ago raised their arms in the Fascist salute and were ready to make the supreme sacrifice in the name of the Duce. Besides, who filled the piazzas and cheered Fascism during those 20 years? People either with short memories or champions at speedily switching allegiances.

Strangely enough, we Jews were not filled with a spirit of revenge, even though we had plenty of reason to be. All the suffering we had experienced in five years of privations, humiliations, renunciations of the most basic things, all seemed to melt like snow in the sun. We had only the desire to get back all that had been taken from us, even the banal things that had a great significance for us. One thing important to me and my friends was to take a vacation by the sea, on those beaches where for five long years we had been forbidden to go. It was on our last vacation at Lido di Camaiore that we learned of the promulgation of racial laws.

Some of us voted for the sea and others for the mountains. So no one would be unhappy on this auspicious occasion, we decided that the mountaineers (including me) would take a tour of the Apennines and the Apuan Alps and end up in Versilia to join the "mariners."

As for the crimes committed by Fascism in general and by single Fascists in particular, we thought it right to leave to the Allied military tribunals the pleasure of imposing just prison sentences.

Another thing that pleased me and that reflected well on the non-Jews of our acquaintance was that none of them came to "relieve" themselves, but continued to offer us friendship as they always had during the years of persecution. And they cheered the fall of Mussolini's regime as much as we.

With the fall of the regime and the uncertainty of the new situation, I wanted to talk to Gianfranco and ask him what he intended to do or what he knew about the status of things. I met him the next morning, July 27, in downtown Florence. We walked slowly along the Arno toward the Indiano, one of the places I liked to go as often as possible to relax with a book or talk with a friend.

I immediately broached the subject and Gianfranco answered my inquiries plainly. He was not reassuring. In his opinion, the disappearance of Mussolini from the scene did not mean peace. We had to deal with the Germans, who, according to the information gathered by his organization, were amassing great numbers of men and equipment for occupying the regions in Italy not yet in Allied hands. There was no sign that the anti-Fascists were relaxing their efforts. In fact, they were preparing for the worst.

Gianfranco's words gave substance to those fears and doubts that had kept me from sleeping the night of July 25. He and Luciano were ready to take up arms in the event that the Germans should attempt a military action in the Italian territory that the king had placed under Badoglio's administration. This prospect was distressing. I felt very close to Gianfranco and it worried me a lot to know that he was engaged in risky actions. I prayed that nothing bad would happen to him or Luciano.

I also asked Gianfranco if his parents were fully aware of what he was doing. Yes, they knew about it and had always encouraged and supported him. Gianfranco said all this in his typically dry, calm manner, without the slightest emotion. I admired him, but I admired his parents even more, because they made no objections even knowing the risks he was exposing himself to.

I changed the subject and spoke to him about the idea of all of us meeting in Versilia for a brief respite from worry and politics. He was enthusiastic and on this positive note we separated at 9:30, the hour I went to the office.

I worked until 12:30 and then I met Federico and Piera Campagnano, who took me to a bicycle shop because I had learned that bicycle tires and tubes had suddenly sprouted forth. Evidently they had been hidden, waiting for the prices to go sky high before they were put on the market. This seemed like a rotten thing to do. However, I had no choice. The tires on my bike were shot, and because they were my only means of transport, I had to buy tires if I could afford the price.

I showed the shopkeeper the condition of my tires and tubes. He opened his eyes wide and said: "How in the world did you get around in this condition?" I explained that I had not been able to find replacements and had had to get along the best I could. He motioned for me to go to the back of the shop with him where he uncovered some brand-new tires and inner tubes hidden under dirty old tarps. Anxiously, I went directly to the question of price. He asked what I wanted to spend. "As little as possible," I replied, "because my father hasn't been able to work for five years. I had to do forced labor and so there really wasn't much money in our house. As you probably guessed, we are Jews."

His face was illuminated by a big smile. He gave me a slap on the back that left me breathless for a moment and then said: "I hear you. I'm poor, too. What you see here is all I own. But I've been poor all my life, so it won't surprise me if that's the way I'll always be. Know what I'll do? I'll give you the tires and tubes for what I paid for them three years ago. I'll pretend the Germans stole them. How about 200 lire for both?"

Anything but rotten behavior! I had been too hasty in my judgment. I was about to hug him. If he had been a woman I even would have kissed him. But he was not. I could only say: "You're a good man and heaven will reward you."

"Let's not go overboard," he replied. "I don't believe in those things. Your thanks will be enough."

He took my bike into his shop, threw away my worthless tires, and put on the new ones. Then he put a brush in a jar full of a concoction that was anything but inviting and spread it on the two tires. "What are you doing?"

"I'm camouflaging them a little. If someone sees they're new they might snitch them."

I was infinitely grateful to the mechanic for this crumb of wisdom that was certainly acquired through experience. I paid him and we shook hands while he winked in complicity. This was the first occasion in a long time that being a Jew turned into something positive for me! I returned home a happy man. It did not seem real to be able to calmly pedal along without fear of getting a flat at any moment. I told my parents the story, thinking they would be pleased. Mother was. But my father was angry about my public enthusiasm over Mussolini's fall. . . . I was irresponsible, I did not understand anything, and he added that I was seen in Piazza Vittorio Emanuele cheering the downfall of Fascism, shouting, and getting worked up with the others. He ended his tirade with a slap on my face.

I was so shocked by his unusual behavior that I did not have the strength to react. I looked at my mother who had tears in her eyes but dared not say anything. I left the living room and locked myself in my bedroom after slamming the door. I cried because of the rage I felt and did not join my parents and Liliana for dinner. I could not have eaten sitting next to my father. What had gotten into him to treat me that way?

My mother explained it to me later. After she ate and cleaned up the kitchen, she knocked on my door: "Enzo, open the door. You have to eat something." I opened the door and mamma handed me a plate with my share of zucchini omelette and a piece of bread. I thanked her and forced it down, although I had a knot in my throat that made even swallowing water difficult.

Then mother began speaking in her soft, calm voice, quietly so that papa, who had gone to rest on his bed next to my bedroom, would not overhear.

"Listen," she said. "Papa is going through a difficult time. It seems like a paradox, but he slapped you to show how much he loves you and how afraid he is that one day, if things should take an ugly turn, someone might remember you, and make you pay for your display of happiness. I'm sorry he had to take it out on you. Try to understand. At that moment it was the only way he could express his feelings."

I understood and gave her a big kiss and jokingly said: "The next time papa wants to talk to me, I'll keep my distance."

Thinking the incident over quietly, I realized how dramatic the precarious situation of the country must appear to a man as fragile as my father. One also had to keep in mind all the years of tension, undernourishment, deprivations, frustrations, and the forced inactivity caused by the anti-Jewish laws. I felt bad and wanted to make up with him, but my pride would not let me. Instead, I took my bicycle and went to see Mimma who had phoned that her father was now home after being let out of prison.

I congratulated Signor Castelnuovo and told him I hoped he would never find himself in such a dangerous spot again. Staying to talk with Mimma gave me the clear idea that for her I was only a good friend and would never be anything more. I went away torturing myself with the thoughts of a broken dream, the one of being able to share with Mimma the days of our youthful existence. I was always in search of a close tie of affection with someone. I felt it as an absolute necessity and the doubt flashed through my mind that it was my fault that I still had not managed to acquire one. I lacked sufficient faith in myself to move with decision and reveal my real feelings, because of my fear of being rejected.

> Diary
>
> July 28, 1943: Great demonstrations of joy this morning: they said the armistice had been signed. Unfortunately it was not true. The crowd was crazy with happiness. This morning they confiscated the newspaper *La Nazione*. Very stormy morning . . . I think it is just a question of days before peace is signed. Everyone is weary by now.

The country had fallen into a state of confusion. Any sensational story that came out would be believed and spread like wildfire. In plain words, people believed what they wanted to believe and what they passionately wished for. A general fatigue was joined to a vague sense of disillusionment. After enduring 20 years of Fascism they wanted everything to change for the better overnight, with the past dead and buried, the war over, and with it the dangers and suffering they had to submit to in silence without the possibility of rebellion.

The days followed in absolute, total calm, with no more demonstrations. Everyone refrained from making predictions or comments. It seemed as if everyone was waiting for something to happen, but no one was able to imagine what this "something" was.

The important thing was for it to happen. But nothing happened, and so life flowed along smoothly. I saw Federico, Gianna, Fioralba, Lamberto and the others. Fioralba's parents and Piero invited us twice to Montorsoli to spend some pleasant hours: we talked about music, listened to records, and played silly parlor games, just for distraction. We felt the need to be carefree and not to think about anything important.

On Monday, August 2, I had a long discussion with papa and mamma about leaving Florence for fear of Allied or German air raids. Papa had spoken with our Archivolti relatives who remained in their Villa La Ragnaia, outside Florence. They would be more than willing for us to stay until the fear of bombardments was over.

So it was decided we would move bag and baggage to La Ragnaia. I was not very happy about it. It meant being far from my friends, and I would not be able to use the telephone when I pleased, but I did not say anything. That afternoon mother gave me a mattress to take to La Ragnaia. I rolled it up tight like a salami, loaded it on my bicycle, and peddling with my knees apart and panting up the hills, I reached La Ragnaia and unloaded it.

When I got back to Florence I took care of some personal things. I went to the Alpine Club to finalize my membership, and because I was in the "normalizing" vein, I went directly to the Boating Club to do the same. Mentally I had prepared a fine little speech to give to the head of memberships—in revenge for the bitter defeat of the past when my request was denied and I had to satisfy myself by renting an old boat.

I went in. It could not have been planned better: before me was the same man I had dealt with before. I greeted him courteously.

"You certainly don't remember me," I said. "I came to you about four years ago, but because I was Jewish (and still am, naturally), you told me that the racial laws forbid my becoming a member."

"I seem to remember something of the sort," he replied.

"Now, as you know, Mussolini is in prison, while I am still here, determined more than ever to become a member of the Boating Club. Also, now that I am of age, my father's permission isn't necessary. I would appreciate it if this time you would accept my request. As I told you the first time, I don't know any member of the club who could sponsor me. Therefore you have to decide."

He stood thinking for a few seconds while slowly extracting membership forms from a drawer. He finally said: "I understand what you're saying, and I'm glad your personal situation has changed. However, there are rules governing the memberships that have to be observed. I can accept your request but I can't guarantee that it might not be refused for other reasons."

I could not argue with that, and I said: "That's fine. I'll fill out all the forms you want and please speak with the club board and tell those men that here is a young man who has waited for more than four years to be accepted, and who only wants to come here to use one of your boats to go peacefully boating on the Arno, paying the same fee as everyone else. I don't think it would be so nice if I had to return to the boatman at Ponte S. Niccolò a second time, do you?"

He gave me two forms that I filled out. I crossed out the space where it asked for race. I gave them back to him without a word. He seemed to have grasped the idea that to refuse me would be asking for trouble.

I asked him to phone me at home about the decision as soon as possible, after which I would come by to complete my application and pay the membership fee. I said good-bye with a wave of the hand and went away satisfied for at least having got the pebble out of my shoe, as the saying goes. I was feeling rather confident that they would accept me and told mother to take a message if anyone should call while I was out.

The next day I went back to work in the office. An atmosphere of expectation was there also. None of us could keep our minds on our work, and we accomplished very little. Even Vittorio left for many hours without giving us a number where he could be reached in case we needed him. I realized the office was in a very precarious state, which was not a comfortable feeling, but there was nothing I could do about it. We had to wait until "something" happened.

I met with Federico, who said his parents had also decided to leave their house because of the air raids. They would stay for a while with friends in a villa not far from La Ragnaia. The prospect of being near Federico at least was heartening.

At home I found the atmosphere a little stormy. Liliana had been invited to spend a month at Rimini with friends, but papa said she could not go. Liliana and mother were very unhappy because it would have been a good opportunity for Liliana to get away from the family and have a peaceful time on her own. I, on the other hand, thought papa was being fair in light of his refusal to let me go to Val d'Aosta. I decided to stay out of it. Things would settle down on their own.

When I returned home in the evening mother said a gentleman from the Boating Club had called, leaving word that everything was in order and I could go by to complete my enrollment whenever I wished. Wonderful! It had finally come through and represented a victory. Now that I knew I could join the Boating Club I said I would do it in good time and complete my registration after returning from the vacation planned with family and friends at the sea and mountains.

Our departure was set for Sunday, August 8. I made a series of phone calls to coordinate plans with the various participants. There were nine of us now. The prospect of this vacation by the sea cheered Liliana and mother, who hoped to convince papa to go also. It would be good for him. Poor man, for years he had not budged from Florence. Undoubtedly it would do him much more good to breathe a little salty air than to stay in Florence in the August heat.

I packed the necessities for a few days in the mountains and by the sea. My backpack was stuffed to overflowing. Thank goodness I did not have to worry about carrying food also; I would not have known where to put it. I took a little bit of the money that I had put aside and figured how much I would need for the whole vacation.

Sunday morning we left Florence by train for Maresca, and from there we walked straight to Lago Scaffaiolo without stopping, reaching it late in the afternoon. We spent a week hiking around and sleeping in shelters at Abetone, Lago Santo, and Foce al Giovo. Crossing Garfagnana we climbed to the Apuan Alps: Pania della Croce, Pania Forata as far as Matanna where, on August 16, we reached Viareggio. Our friends were waiting to give us a festive welcome. The next day everyone got on paddle boats to go out for a swim.

I was not a swimmer. When I was a child and could have easily learned to float and swim, no one took the trouble to teach me. Like all self-respecting children, I had been afraid to jump into deep water. Instead of giving me a push and making me tread water to stay afloat, mother said that no one should force me to do what I did not want to do.

I had grown up without learning how to swim, but that day I made a big decision and announced to everyone that finally I, too, would jump into the water when we reached the open sea. No one believed me. When I jumped in and, to my great surprise, stayed afloat, I started doing a kind of frog kick, and everyone broke out in applause. It was an important event for me and from then on, though no champion, I could swim like the others.

Those carefree days spent at the sea with my best friends were a real cure-all for me and the others. We felt liberated. Finally, after so many years of abstinence we could enjoy the beautiful beaches of Versilia like everyone else, lying on the boiling sand and roasting ourselves in the sun. When we got hot we jumped back into the sea and wallowed around like children indulging in previously forbidden pleasures. We were all happy, but no one more than I, because I could be with Gianna and enjoy her many good qualities.

Wednesday, August 18, with the arrival of mamma and papa, the old vacation times seemed to have returned, with long walks along the shore toward Forte dei Marmi. Both were in the best of humor and felt restored by the salty breeze blowing off the sea.

I had to interrupt my vacation because my work called me back to Florence. On

Tuesday, a holiday, I decided to make my entrance at the Boating Club. I saw the same man who had given me the membership forms and I completed all the formalities for joining, including paying the annual fee. All the local spots were practically deserted, because in August almost all Florentines go to the seaside, and only those who cannot afford a vacation or have work responsibilities remain in the city.

I wandered around in the boat storeroom where sculls of every kind and size were resting on special trestles. They were all very shiny and seemed to have just come from the shipyard. I ran my fingers over them lightly and it was like caressing velvet. I was overcome by the desire to row one of those sculls, which were so tapered and lightweight. I asked the guard if it would be possible to put a one-man scull into the water. Unhappily I could not because the Arno was low and could not be navigated. We had to wait until it rained for several days.

Because I was there and did not feel like going back home, I put on bathing trunks and went to sunbathe on a barge moored in front of the club. From there I watched the tourists enjoying the panorama from the Ponte Vecchio. I gazed at the buildings on the Arno, which seemed much more beautiful and inviting when seen from that perspective. After lolling there for a couple of hours, I decided I had had enough sun, got dressed, and went away satisfied.

I yearned to spend the weekend at Viareggio with my friends and Gianna. I felt abandoned, roasting in hot Florence, and imagined them lounging half-naked on the beach. But there was nothing to do but have patience and keep faith with the motto that duty comes before pleasure. My only consolation was to go to the Boating Club and put on my bathing suit.

One day I invited Massimo Meyer to go with me, and because the Arno was still low, we lay on the old barge in the sun on our backs, our eyes closed to avoid the reflected light, daydreaming about what we could do and wanted to do from that day on.

I still had my heart set on becoming a doctor. Massimo advised against it because of all the years I would have to recoup. I admitted that if I had actually been able to attend high school and university without losing even one year, I would have graduated when I was 30 years old, totally dependent for 9 years on my father, and his finances would not have supported such a burden. Otherwise I would have had to do it myself by earning some money with a part-time job, which would mean leading a dog's life before starting a career in some hospital.

Massimo was right. I gave up my dream of becoming a doctor and thought about a future in the export business with papa, capitalizing on the work experience I already had. I spoke to papa about my decision and could tell he was pleased. It would be a great relief for him to be able to reopen his office with me as his main associate. "It remains to be seen if conditions are right for reopening the office. Let's not put the cart before the horse." It was one of his favorite maxims, and in this case it was very apropos.

After work I would phone my few friends who had stayed in Florence and go around the city with them. I spent an afternoon with Wanda Lattes, whose exceptional intelligence I admired, to shop and walk around and talk politics. According to her, the moment had come for us Jews to make some choices in a way that enforced our ideas with the party that was most similar to our way of thinking. According to Wanda, I should give some thought to joining one of the many political parties that were already in existence.

Frankly, I did not feel ready for anything like that. The only thing I was sure of was my total and visceral aversion to Fascism and to any kind of dictatorship. I did not even feel attracted to Communism which, though the antithesis of Fascism, was still a dictatorial regime. If I ever had to make a choice, I think I would turn toward a liberal movement. "Therefore," I said to Wanda, "I don't think I am suited for just any kind of political activity. Not only because of my total lack of preparation, but also because, after all, being a subject of Her Britannic Majesty, I have little to do with Italian politics." And that ended the subject once and for all.

The first of September my parents decided the moment had come to move from Via della Cernaia to our Archivolti relatives at La Ragnaia. I was as mad as a wet hen. I saw no reason for moving those few kilometers. If the English bombed Florence they could hit La Ragnaia just as easily as Via della Cernaia. I let papa, mamma, and Liliana go in the morning, telling them I would join them after supper.

In the afternoon I invited Federico to have a snack at my house and I bought some things from Calderai in town. We spent several hours listening to records. We talked about the evacuation and he said that his parents would be leaving their house in Florence in a few days, too. He did not understand the reason for that disruption either. We also decided that he would make an appointment with Maestro Guetta, who would give me his competent opinion about my singing abilities.

I gathered up the few things I would need for my removal to La Ragnaia and, saying good-bye to Federico, got on my bicycle and reluctantly pedaled toward Vingone. That night the air-raid alarm woke me and it was a long time before I could get back to sleep in the unfamiliar bed. The next morning I had to get up earlier than usual in order to get to the office on time. What a pain, I thought. Especially since even my family went to stay in Florence during the day and returned to La Ragnaia only to sleep.

Diary

September 3, 1943: After work I went with Federico to see Maestro Guetta. He listened to me, said I have a beautiful voice, and that it would be a shame not to study singing. Federico is excited about having the idea of taking me to Guetta. Now I'll see what I should do. I'll have another maestro listen to me, and if his judgment is also favorable, I'll take up the study. It would be wonderful to have a singing career. I went home. Papa and mamma agree that I can study singing.

After supper I talked with my parents for a long time about the possibility of studying voice seriously. Father, who had taken voice lessons, spoke in detail about the difficulty of finding the right pitch, of learning to breathe properly, of singing "from your head" and not "from your throat," of pronouncing each syllable perfectly, and so on. "However," he said, "if you feel deeply committed I'll be happy to help you. But, remember, the operatic world isn't all roses. You'll have to work hard to reach a respectable level and you'll have to fight hard to get ahead in your career."

At that moment a world was opening up before me that I had never before considered. It is true that Maestro Veneziani had been complimentary when I sang in his choir. Now, however, after my audition with Maestro Guetta, I understood that I had some positive reasons for learning to sing—something to do besides medicine or office work. If I made it, I would be able to go around the world singing in the famous theaters and earning stacks of money. I could see my name on the playbills of the New York Metropolitan Opera or La Scala. I would sign autographs and receive deafening applause. Not bad as a career. Not to mention success with the women!

My imagination was galloping faster than a cowboy. I loved to dream with my eyes wide open. And anyway, what is wrong with that?

Diary

September 4, 1943: The Allies have landed in Calabria and are making good progress. They have enormous power at their disposal and no one can stop them. The situation in general seems to be coming to a head: the Italian troops in Calabria put up no resistance. That means something is behind it. Could it be a secret agreement between Italy and the Allies? Not at all unlikely. I think we'll know something definite soon.

I was excited by the fast-moving events. It seemed as if a great puzzle were coming into place piece by piece, in a predetermined arrangement. Was it possible that my fate and that of all Jews was about to take a decisive turn and a happier time was about to begin?

I prayed that the Allies continued their advance in Italy and on the other fronts. I prayed for the total defeat of Germany and for the disappearance of the Nazi curse from the face of the earth. I prayed for those poor Jews who for years had languished in German concentration camps, for their survival of such suffering and illness, and for their liberation from that inhuman martyrdom. For all this I prayed to our Lord, hoping He heard me.

The following day I made up my mind to try again to go rowing on the Arno. It had rained for two days and I thought the river should be navigable. I arrived at the Boating Club at seven sharp in the morning, but no one was there. The sign read: Open at 8:30. I wandered aimlessly around town. The morning air was nice and fresh. The street sweepers were at work, one sweeping the right sidewalk and one the left. They kept even with each other, and while they swept they talked, recounting the events of the previous evening. They never looked up as they swept and talked, and it was amusing to stand there and watch them.

Finally, at half past eight I was able to enter the Boating Club. The same custodian let me in and I asked him if it was possible to put a boat into the water. He gave one look at the water level and said, "It's deep enough. But be careful not to go near the shore where it could be more shallow. Stay in the center of the Arno."

I thanked him. He put a one-man scull on his shoulders and I took two oars. As he gently slipped the scull into the water I handed him the two oars, and he put them into the oarlocks. With one hand he held the boat firm, alongside the landing wharf, while with the other he helped me get settled in the movable seat and put my feet where they belonged.

Never before had I sat in such a thin, lightweight boat. At the slightest bodily movement it swayed frighteningly to the right or left. I had to find a position of perfect equilibrium and maintain it constantly or be sorry!

The custodian noticed my lack of expertise at once. "Are you sure you can manage it?"

"I think so. But if you'll hold it still to give me time to get used to the back and forth movement of the seat, I'll be grateful."

He kindly held the scull still with one of the oarlocks and let me practice moving backwards and forwards on the movable seat, bending and extending my legs. At the same time I moved the other oar with both hands, as though rowing.

The trial lasted a couple of minutes. I felt more secure and told the custodian to let go. I moved carefully away from the wharf and finally gripped the oars and began to row. The scull responded instantly to the push of the oars. It was as light as if made of paper. What a difference from the battered old boat at Ponte San Niccolò!

I remembered the custodian's advice and steered toward the center of the river. After a few strokes I was already passing under the central arcade of Ponte Vecchio. There were two tourists leaning on the bridge's parapet watching me, perhaps envying me. I tried to row in a flawless manner, coordinating the movements of my legs, the seat, and the oars. It was work keeping them all under control, but I gradually gained confidence and relaxed, giving a slow, regular rhythm to my rowing.

I took as my objective the central arcade of Ponte Santa Trinita. I passed under it and made a maneuver to turn about. One single stroke with the left oar was enough to turn completely in the opposite direction. Such sensitivity in a boat surprised me. This time I was rowing against the current and instantly felt the greater effort required to make it go upriver.

I passed again under Ponte Vecchio and reached the club wharf. The custodian had stayed there to see how things went. One never knows. There is a lot to fear with a greenhorn. I gave him a timid wave. He gestured as if giving me a spanking. I interpreted that as encouragement to go ahead and so I came about again and made the trip to Ponte Santa Trinita a second time. It all went well. The next time I would not have any problem.

When I got out of the scull it was 9:45. I helped the custodian put the boat and oars in storage with all the other marvelous long and shiny boats. I was truly pleased.

Diary

September 5: Sunday. At ten o'clock I went with Liliana to Montorsoli where we stayed all day visiting the Passiglis. Excellent lunch. Excellent company. Federico and Maurizio were also there, with whom I discussed the war events. We agreed that a radical decision would have to be made within the week. I think it might be a secret armistice unknown to the Germans. Allied planes tossed out a kind of booklet over Florence. It was a not very interesting speech given long ago by Wallace. No bombs. So be it.

The next day, September 6, was papa's birthday. As already planned, I gave him the records I had bought in the last few days. He was very happy with them. At lunch mother brought to the table a cake she had baked herself, and we sang "Happy Birthday." We toasted with a *vin santo* that papa poured into four small-stemmed glasses with gold trim, used for special occasions. These glasses and others like them were kept in a wooden case inlaid with mother-of-pearl and tortoiseshell, along with four little bottles with glass stoppers. Besides papa's toast, we raised our glasses with good wishes for Franco, who was still far from us.

I returned to the office until five in the afternoon, the hour I went directly to the Boating Club to do some rowing. The same custodian. The same ceremony. This time, however, without the shivers. I rowed for nearly two hours. The rhythm of the oars was faster than the first time. I perspired profusely, but I was glad to be finally participating in a sport I had always liked but had never been able to do. This time I pushed upstream from the club as far as Ponte alle Grazie. It was pleasant to glide between those austere and elegant old buildings flanking both sides of the Arno. Now that I had more confidence in my boat, I could afford to look up every once in a while and admire the panorama.

Diary

September 8, 1943: I left the office at six thirty after a full day's work. Federico was outside waiting. We went to Gianna's where we learned the wonderful news: Italy had asked to surrender! Things were developing from July 25. General rejoicing. We can finally listen to Radio London without interference. Tomorrow we'll find out the details. These are thrilling days. I can't wait to hug Franco again. Returned to Gianna's house after supper to celebrate. Tomorrow I'll take the day off.

I thanked the Lord for hearing my prayers. It was a moment of great excitement. Because we were all talking at once, we could not understand what the others were saying. Everyone made his own strategic predictions about what turn the war would take. In our euphoria we now considered Germany defeated. It was only a question of a few months before the Germans would ask to surrender!

CHAPTER 10

September 9, 1943: The Party's Over

Diary

September 9, 1943: From my office window overlooking Piazza Vittorio Emanuele I saw an officer shoot a civilian during a protest. The crowd attacked the officer, turning him into a colander (dripping blood instead of water). He deserved it. A day full of emotional and sensational rumors of every kind. The truth: the Germans occupy Bologna, Modena, and Reggio. Because of terrifying rumors stayed home in afternoon until five o'clock. Went out with Federico, Giuliana, Fioralba, and others to see what was happening downtown. Nothing in particular. Long telephone conversations with many people. Listened to radio from many countries.

The news on Radio London did not give much hope for Italy's future. Incensed by Italy's surrender, Germany had gone on the counterattack, beginning to occupy the country from north to south. They advanced without firing a shot. The Italian army was in chaos. After the surrender the soldiers had taken off on their own. Sporadic news began to filter in about single actions of small groups of partisans who fruitlessly tried to stem the German advance. The joyful intoxication of yesterday's news was rapidly wearing off, replaced by a deep sense of apprehension.

Diary

September 10, 1943: Went to work as usual. Getting a fine cold. News coming fast and furious. Seems the Germans are headed for Florence. Still nothing certain. Fear everywhere. Stayed home in afternoon with cold. Piero came to see me. The Passigli family has come back to Florence from Montorsoli. This afternoon the Germans are at Vaglia. Expected in Florence tomorrow. Anxiety in the air. For the time being we are calm. Seems the Italian troops in Florence will surrender without resistance.

The horizon was covered with big black clouds. As though under a spell, I was plummeted into the same state of mind as in the early months of the war. This time, however, things were much more serious. We had the Germans in our backyard. I cursed myself for being an idiot. How could I have thought Hitler would not react to what he saw as the betrayal of his Italian ally?

The difference in strength between Germany and Italy was enormous. Hitler would have a free hand over all Italy. The situation was getting bad for us Jews. I mean very bad.

Diary

September 11, 1943: The Germans arrived around nine thirty this morning. Orders: don't leave home. Things have gone "normally": no combat. The Florentine troops surrendered in mass without making the slightest resistance. We didn't go out all day. Only at seven did I go to the station with Liliana. Just in time to witness a shoot out. General pandemonium. The Germans took every bicycle they found, in addition to valuable objects from people. Great terror everywhere. Not many Germans: about 1,000 to 1,500. But they've occupied all Florence.

The time was fast approaching when our very existence would be at risk. We had passed from Fascism to Nazism, with all its horrendous implications. My mind ran automatically to the concentration camps where Jews were amassed in inhuman conditions. What difference could there be between a German Jew and an Italian one for the SS? The only difference, luckily for us, was in the fact that Italians were very different from Germans. In Germany no Jew had been able to escape the systematic manhunt made by the whole population. I did not think anything like that could happen in Italy. At least I hoped it could not.

Diary

September 12, 1943: Spent the morning going around to help some Jewish refugees liberated from concentration camps. I was able to do some good. After lunch I went to the Passiglis. It was Fioralba's birthday. We had a pleasant afternoon together. I made a visit to the Terni. A large contingent of Germans left this morning. A great feeling of relief all around. I think tomorrow we'll transfer to La Ragnaia to have more peace of mind. Mamma went to visit La Ragnaia. A lot of hate for the Germans everywhere. They say Mussolini has been liberated.

Unfortunately it was true. German parachutists were dropped over the Gran Sasso where Mussolini was held prisoner, and with one blow they liberated him, taking him to northern Italy. The same day Mussolini founded the Republic of Salò, with the support of the most diehard and fanatic Fascists.

In other words, we had gone from the frying pan into the fire. Everything would not be just as before, but worse than before. Humiliated by the events of July 25, the Fascists would undoubtedly want to take revenge on their enemies. And first in line, we Jews.

We could expect anything. In order to pay their debt to the Germans for liberating their Duce and for permitting the founding of the Republic of Salò, the "new" Fascists would go to any length to do whatever might be required, and most important, to establish "order" and hunt down the Jews. This consideration was made more shocking, on the same day, by the revelation of some Jews who had escaped from German concentration camps. The general opinion was that the Nazis shut Jews up in concentration camps in order to keep an eye on them and to prevent them from interfering in their cause. After the war was over, we had no doubt that they would be given their freedom.

The reality was something else, and more atrocious. What those poor refugees revealed went beyond the worst thing imaginable. The Nazis subjected the Jews—men, women, old people, children—to the most abject and indescribable torture. They did experiments of every kind on them that usually ended with their death. The women were tortured and abused sexually by their guards, the able-bodied men were used for backbreaking work. The children, torn from their parents, were destined to die of hunger because they were useless.

We learned the heartbreaking truth of Hitler's "Final Solution" for the Jewish people, ordering their total extinction. Those infamous places for collecting Jews were monstrous extermination camps, where crematoriums daily burned the bodies of the Jews killed in gas chambers. It was a macabre "cycle of production" that harvested thousands of victims a day and that the Nazis had organized to perfection, thereby distinguishing themselves for their abject, inhuman, bestial, sadistic brutality.

I was profoundly distressed by the discovery of this horrible reality and decided I absolutely must bring it to the attention of my family, friends, and coreligionists, so they could quickly make the necessary plans for their own safety. Otherwise, it was a matter of certain death, after indescribable suffering.

I asked myself how the Eternal could allow His People to be decimated by a madman like Hitler. By what enormous guilt were we stained to deserve such tragic punishment? Through the ages my people were always protected by the Lord who helped defeat His enemies, and He did it in such a way that the Jews emerged from every war stronger and more numerous.

What was happening now could not be compared with what had happened over the past millennia. I was firmly convinced that all this was part of a Superior Will of which I was unable to grasp the importance or the ultimate goal. I had absolute faith in the God of Israel, and in His justice and goodness toward His people. Very likely this monstrous catastrophe that had befallen us would bring some benefit in the end.

If my mind and spirit found comfort in these certainties, my physical being was falling into a deep depression. If at first I had seen only black clouds on the horizon, now I felt I was in the middle of a devastating cyclone. My family had been living in a kind of limbo where life seemed to flow by in relative tranquillity, and whose most serious worry was the danger Franco was exposed to on an island under bombardment. Now we risked extermination without the possibility of defending ourselves, whereas Franco's days of fear were over with the cessation of aerial bombardments. At least one member of our family could be considered safe.

We desperately needed to find a safe haven. I did not want to end up like a rat in a trap. My first thought was that I should separate from my parents and Liliana.

To stay together, given my youth and greater visibility, could constitute a danger for them. The three of them could escape Florence to live with farmers in the Casentino area who Mirella Levi d'Ancona knew and who would undoubtedly take them in.

I told Federico about my intentions, and he was of the same mind. He said he would talk to his parents about it and let me know their decision. For the first time in my life I had to make my own decisions and face dangerous situations alone. Although my life was clearly in danger, I remained lucid and did not let sentiment sway my reason. I realized how sad it would be for my parents and Liliana to be separated from me, but I knew how to convince them. By splitting up we increased our individual chances for salvation, and this was the most important thing. Deep in my heart I hoped this separation would last only a few weeks, or a few months at most.

> Diary
>
> September 13, 1943: Got up at seven thirty and spent all morning shopping. Now they're selling potatoes without a ration card to keep the Germans from stealing them. They've taken all the food. In a few days we'll be starving. After lunch I said good-bye to Gianna in person, and by telephone to all the Passigli, and to my other friends, advising everyone to get out because I knew that the Germans were "interested" in us Jews. We moved to La Ragnaia. I took my mountain gear in case I had to take to the bush. Walking along I met Federico; he also left for Soffiano. He talked with his parents and shares my ideas. We'll go together to Chianti, near Radda, where the Benadìs have a little farm. We'll be farmers until the storm passes.

I remember we had just finished eating, and I was in the kitchen helping mother. She washed the dishes and pans while I dried them and put them back in the cupboard. We talked about the plans we had just made when the phone rang. I ran to answer it with a certain trepidation. In those days every phone call could be critical. He did not say his name, but I recognized his voice. He only said: "This morning the Germans took the list of names. They've started taking people from their homes. Get out immediately." And he hung up.

I ran back to the kitchen. "Mamma, leave everything, and let's get out of here.

Someone from the community center phoned to say that the Germans are taking Jews out of their homes. Let's hurry before it's our turn."

Mother stood there open-mouthed with a plate in her hand, and with typical feminine reasoning, said: "Let's finish the dishes, at least."

"What for?" I said firmly. "Who cares if the Germans find dirty dishes. Let's go, mamma. Pay attention to your son this once!" Convinced, she left everything just as it was and went to her room to dress. Papa and Liliana did the same and in a flash we were out of the house.

Papa, mamma, and Liliana took the streetcar to La Ragnaia. I wanted to stay in Florence to warn my friends of the danger and tell them good-bye. I raced on my bicycle directly to the area of Via Benedetto Varchi where many of them lived, trying to make the visits short. It would be too much if the Germans nabbed me in one of my friend's homes, but I also wanted to warn as many people as possible.

Farewell to work, to the Boating Club that until a few days before had represented an enormous achievement, to the Alpine Club of Italy and mountain trips, to the classical music records that had kept me company, to the piano and the concerts at the Teatro Comunale. All this now belonged to the past. The present and the future were devoted to our survival—no small matter. And what can be said of my parents' sorrow at having to leave their house to the mercy of the tempest, with all the things that they had managed to collect over many years of sacrifice? With a smile and loving memories of my parents I think today of the "treasure" that papa, in those dramatic days, had put in a bank security box: the albums of stamps that mamma had patiently collected day after day from the time she married. It was her passionate hobby and that collection really represented a small treasure to her.

> Diary
>
> September 14, 1943: Got up at seven thirty. Toward eight thirty I met with Federico. Ate very well at Scandicci. At six Federico returned. We'll leave tomorrow morning by bicycle with our backpacks. This evening I got everything in order for the trip. May God help us.

It was truly an extraordinary day at La Ragnaia. As the hour of my departure drew near, I became more aware how difficult the break would be, especially for mamma and papa. I tried to appear as composed as possible to instill a little calm.

A pious hope. Mother's eyes were red, which meant that she cried copiously when no one could see her, as only a mother can cry at the pain of separating from her child. In planning for my departure, we tried to imagine all the situations I might have to face during my flight. My primary concern was how to support myself in the future. Papa gave me a few thousand lire from his depleted reserve. I promised him I would try to save by working as a farm laborer. Luckily I had acquired some good experience with the pick and shovel.

I remembered that I had always worn my mother's *Shadai* on a chain around my neck, and that it had become almost an integral part of myself. I did not want to give it up. At the same time, if someone—Fascist or Nazi—stopped me and saw the Hebrew writing on the gold medal, he would know I was a Jew. I decided then to keep the *Shadai* out of sight. I had mother sew it into the lining of my trousers, waist high.

Another thing my mother thought to sew in the lining was a small diamond she had had for many years. She said: "Enzo, if, God forbid, you should be captured by a Fascist or Nazi, try to bribe him with this diamond in exchange for your freedom." I promised mother that on the blessed day when we are reunited after the exodus, I would give her back her little diamond intact. Actually it was more a hope than a promise.

I watched my mother sew the *Shadai* and diamond into my trousers (the only pair I would take with me). Her hands were trembling and her eyes glistening. I know she was silently praying to the Lord that I return home safe and sound. Papa did not express his feelings. He kept everything inside and by doing so increased his suffering.

The Germans published a proclamation in which they "invited" all Jewish citizens to register at a city office. It was, according to them, only a simple census without any ulterior motives. The aim of this "census" was obvious. Even so, when father heard about the proclamation he told mother that perhaps they should register to avoid complications. To this she replied tartly: "You can be sure to avoid all complications by registering. Most of all, having to breathe!" And with this the subject was closed forever.

Liliana shuttled between Via della Cernaia and La Ragnaia, taking from home everything the three of them would need during the exodus, things which they had forgotten in their hurry to get out of the house. She was taking a big risk because with the arrival of the Wehrmacht vanguard in Florence an SS patrol had also gone directly to the community center to get a list of all the Florentine Jews with their addresses and telephone numbers. Therefore, there was the danger that while Liliana was in our house to get the necessary things, a Fascist or Nazi might come to get her. Luckily she managed to get everything they needed in two or three trips.

Diary

September 15, 1943: Woke up this morning at six fifteen. Ate, said good-bye to everyone: General emotional turmoil. Not I. (!!) I was very calm, as was Liliana, who accompanied me for a time. She is an angel of a sister; may the Lord bless her. Because Federico was late we left at seven thirty instead of seven. Met some Germans, but nothing happened. Excellent trip. Arrived at Radda at twelve fifteen. We are staying with farmers. Ate. Went to sleep. Took a walk through the fields. Had supper and went to bed. It's a beautiful place and nice to be here. At last I can lead the farmer's life I like so well.

The separation from papa and mamma was very painful. I tried to appear calm and serene in their eyes, but inside I was dying. Mamma cried without any attempt to restrain herself. She held me tightly and kissed my face; sobbing, she advised me to be careful, not to take unnecessary risks, and to be sure to send news of myself, writing down the address of some farmers in the Casentino where they would be going.

Papa gave me a big hug also and the same advice as mamma and, placing his hands on my head, gave me his blessing. His hands and his voice trembled as he did so, and I could not keep back the tears. I thought about that very sad moment when papa slapped me for celebrating the end of Fascism in the piazza on July 25. How right he had been! Promising to take good care of myself, I kissed his damp cheeks.

I left the house with my bicycle and my backpack on my shoulders, blessing the day I had bought new tires and inner tubes. Now more than ever I did not need a flat.

Liliana walked with me and Federico for a few meters. The customary words, the customary replies. We stopped in front of a little house at the beginning of the main road that led to Siena. I hugged Liliana and thanked her for all she had done to help me. I asked her to take good care of papa and mamma and with our good-byes we added, "See you soon!" We tried not to let our emotions get the best of us. Then Federico and I got on our bicycles and began to pedal toward our goal.

CHAPTER 11

The Flight with Federico

The partially cloudy sky and cool September air helped us to brave the hills without too much discomfort. The dirt road occasionally wrapped us in a cloud of dust when a truck or automobile passed. We stayed one behind the other, keeping to the far side of the road. Every once in a while we traded who had to "pull," as they say in cyclist jargon. We were about halfway there when we noticed what seemed to be a column of military trucks coming toward us in the distance. We stopped to make out more clearly what it was and saw the German insignia with the black swastika painted on the side of the trucks.

We rapidly reviewed our options: it was useless to try to avoid them because there was no side road between us and the column of trucks; to avoid them, we would have to fling ourselves and our bicycles across the fields, which would look very suspicious. We had no choice. Getting back on our bicycles we pedaled calmly as though it were nothing, but instead of riding one behind the other, we rode side by side, the better to talk with each other and give the impression of people who had nothing to worry about.

When the first truck was a few meters from us, we raised our hands in a friendly greeting. To our enormous relief, the German driver did the same. After that we were literally engulfed by big clouds of dust stirred up by the column, and I think the Germans that followed were unaware of our existence.

It was a long column and we did not mind eating the dust that was our salvation. After the danger passed, Federico and I had to stop and catch our breath and especially to release the tension that had gripped us for those short, but seemingly very long, moments.

We sipped water from our canteens and walked for a while since the road was quite steep. We continued to talk about the fright we had both had.

It was about eleven o'clock and I was getting hungry. Federico said we should not stop there, and it was better to avoid crowded places, because you never know who you might meet. I said he was right and we continued pedaling until we were in sight of Radda in Chianti, a pretty little town on top of a small hill covered with vines of red grapes.

"Look," Federico said. "My farmer's house—Duro—is down there, right at the foot of Radda." It was a small, white construction, immersed in a sea of vines. And isolated. The nearest house was almost a kilometer away and the main road was at least three kilometers.

I liked the fact that we would be far from the rest of the world. The fewer people who saw us the better. I was enchanted by that panorama, a succession of gently rolling hills where the flourishing grapes announced the harvest season. Here and there on the slopes of the hills the sea of vines was interrupted by rows of cypresses or other trees close to ancient cottages. The enchanting scene reminded me of the background of certain Renaissance paintings. I felt the magic of being part of it, as though my bicycle had taken me on a voyage back in time and perhaps to more tranquil times. Even the silence was magic, and enriching this silence more than interrupting it was the distant sound of a barking dog or the proud crowing of a rooster. I was happy about the decision I had made that was about to make me the inhabitant of a place so romantically captivating.

It was nearly noon and beginning to get hot. Finally we reached our destination at precisely twelve fifteen (time to eat, my appetite kept telling me). We rapidly calculated the kilometers we had traveled and thought we had made good time, considering that neither of us were great cyclists.

We came into the farmyard paved with large, irregular stones worn completely smooth from countless years of use. Chickens scratched around for food and a small dog, tied by a chain, began to get restless at our approach.

It was the dinner hour and a man with a youthful air looked out the window: *"Buon giorno, sor padrone!"*

"Buon giorno, Santi," Federico replied to the man in charge of the farm, as he

came out to meet us in the yard. In the meanwhile we leaned our bicycles against a mulberry tree and put our backpacks on the ground.

Energetic handshake with Santi Gatti. He was married to Giulia and had three children: Iolanda, 18; Sergio, 14; and Marina, 10. Then there was "Uncle Vico," a good man, up in years, who was dislodged from his bedroom to make room for Federico and me. The poor man was packed off without pity to sleep in the barn along with the mice, grain, and useless contraptions.

After a rapid exchange of news and greetings we went up the stairs to eat. My eyes popped out of my head: tagliatelle with rabbit sauce, stewed rabbit and potatoes, and country bread. All to be washed down with a nice ruby-colored wine. I could not have asked for a better beginning.

We washed in what was to be our bedroom. A flowered majolica pitcher and matching basin sat on an enameled iron stand. I poured the water from the pitcher into the basin and soaped my hands. The hard water did not rinse the soap off easily; a strange effect, but it did not bother me.

I asked Federico: "Now what do I do with this wash water?" He did not waste time with explanations, but opened the window and said: "Just give it a toss!" I did not have to be told twice. I looked out to see if anyone was crossing the yard: only the chickens. I took the basin and heaved the contents out the window. A couple of duly dampened chickens squawked loudly and ran off.

As I dried my hands I looked around the room. It was clean and smelled of bleach; they must have recently washed the brick floors. There was a small iron bedstead painted black. In the center of the headboard was a small oval, also in black iron, with a colored decal of a young girl wreathed in flowers. At the foot of the bed was a chest of drawers in dark walnut, with the top of white marble and an oval mirror framed in the same wood, supported by two columns. Stuck between the mirror and frame was an old photograph of Santi with his wife in a bridal gown. On top of the chest of drawers stood a figure (in papier-mâché, I remember) of the Madonna dressed in a brightly painted dress, studded with false jewels, all covered with a glass bell that failed to keep the dust off this sacred image. Two towels were placed on the two chairs. On a wall hung two prints of women in long dresses, kneeling in an attitude of prayer.

No light. Electricity did not come this far. They used acetylene lamps to light a large area such as the kitchen, while we had two little oil lamps for the bedroom:

two *bugie,* as the Tuscans call them. Each little lamp had a small wick that swam in olive oil and, slowly burning, gave off a very dim light, but sufficient to keep one from running into things. A small wire hook could attach the lamp to the head of the bed. It looked like Aladdin's magic lamp. From a small window (the one used to dump the wash water) we enjoyed a splendid panorama of the surrounding countryside.

Ablutions finished, we joined Santi and his family and sat down at the table where we made everything disappear in a flash. I enjoyed every mouthful of that fresh and genuine food, the likes of which I had not tasted for a long time.

During dinner I told our hosts about myself and saw that they were surprised by the fact that I had dug ditches for many months. They looked at me with a certain admiration. I was one of them, after all!

They were very simple people, of course, but with an innate intelligence. They quickly grasped everything I told them. They were friendly and pleasant, and I felt perfectly at ease. The kitchen, large and spacious, was dominated, like many country kitchens, by an enormous fireplace that practically covered one wall. The mantle extended from the ceiling to about two meters from the floor. Inside the fireplace sat two large andirons on which two great oak logs were burning. On either side of the andirons nestled two small wooden benches resting on stone posts, called *canto del foco* in Tuscany.

In the middle of the kitchen a large oak table, probably more than a hundred years old, showed the signs of many meals and libations. Against one wall stood a piece of furniture called the *madia,* used for making the dough and letting it rise before baking. It also held the bread after it was baked in the farmer's own oven. On the opposite wall stood a sideboard with two lower doors and two upper doors with rough, opaque glass. Stuck between the glass and wooden frame of the top two doors were a series of family photographs and postcards with views of country towns. Inside was the good china service, decorated with little flower decals, and small green glasses from Empoli. The whole room was typically rustic, and very clean and orderly.

When we had finished the sumptuous dinner, Santi, his wife and children had to go back to work in the fields. Federico and I, tired from our bike ride, went to sleep for a few hours. It was a restorative sleep, both physically and spiritually. When I woke up I did not know where I was. It seemed as if a century had passed since I had left my parents that morning. Nothing of the emotional parting had stayed with me. I was perfectly at ease and looked on the future without foreboding. If the Germans went into our house, they would be left empty-handed, thank goodness.

Federico woke up and we talked about what we would do in the coming days. For one thing, we decided it would be opportune to camouflage ourselves a little. We would let our beards and mustaches grow; that would change our appearance and at the same time save us the bother of shaving, a rather arduous undertaking with the limited bathing facilities in that house.

I said that I would like to do some work in the fields—physical exercise, such as my ditch-digging experience at Sesto. With that work I would also be useful to Santi and pay him back in part for his hospitality. And finally, the days would go by more quickly, because I was afraid we would be spending quite a number of them there.

We got up and took a walk around the fields. Santi and his wife were cutting grass for the oxen. The farm was not large, but it was well tended. The rows of vines were far enough apart so that wheat or other kinds of grain could be cultivated. The vines were heavy with red grapes. I tasted one. It was small and had a slightly sour taste. The eating grapes that came from the Mediterranean islands were completely different, but also their use was different.

We walked all over the farm. Federico pointed out different houses in the distance, inhabited by Santi's farmer friends who would be safe for us to meet, because their political views certainly did not favor the Fascist regime.

The day was drawing to a close; the sun was low over the crown of hills against the horizon. The sky, after turning yellow, soon changed to orange and from orange to fiery red: a beautiful spectacle. We watched motionless. Such sunsets are not unusual in September, but at that moment it seemed like an exceptional event and I took it as a good omen for us refugees.

We walked slowly toward the house with Santi whose wife had gone ahead to fix supper. When we entered the house, wood was already burning in the fireplace, spreading the delicious odor that has always appealed to me. We washed our hands and face and went down to the kitchen to watch Giulia prepare the meal. She moved about unhurriedly and with absolute assurance; obviously she had repeated those motions hundreds of times a year. The pot of water was sputtering over the wood in the fireplace. It was time to toss in the pasta.

Santi cut slices off a loaf of crusty bread, holding the bread with his left hand against his chest and pulling the knife toward him with the right, in the country manner. We all sat down at the table. The glasses were instantly filled with wine. "Buon appetito!" In unison we bent over our plates and quickly did justice to their contents.

We each got up slowly, almost unwillingly, from the table. Santi, Federico, and I took places in the *canto del foco* and stayed to *veglia.* There is an unwritten law among the country folk that when they go to *veglia,* that is, to spend a few leisure moments at someone's house, they may discuss any subject freely, but lies are not permitted. Perhaps it's a bit like Christians going to confession. I found it very pleasant to sit in the fireplace and watch the oak logs burn, talking of whatever came to mind.

I took the poker and poked at the logs to keep them burning. Every time I did it little exploding sparks went up the flue, making me feel happy.

Santi's wife joined us after she had cleared the table and put the kitchen in order. I told Santi I would like to help him in the fields and was delighted when he accepted so enthusiastically. Santi was a tall, handsome man, with a well-trimmed mustache. He expressed himself in correct Italian and to the native intelligence typical of all Tuscan peasants was added an experience of life greater than what I would expect from such a relatively young man. It was pleasant to sit there talking to him and his wife until Federico and I began to feel our eyelids grow heavy after our busy day and the copious libations that I certainly was not accustomed to.

We excused ourselves and went to our room. Each of us had our own oil lamp that we attached to the head of the bed. Yes: the bed! We looked at it and mentally tried to compute its proportions in relation to our size. Federico and I looked at each other: "Frankly, it's a just a wee bit narrow," I said. In order to be the least bother to each other, we decided to try to sleep one at the head and the other at the foot. It was not an ideal solution, but it would give us more room (so to speak) to sleep. We slept fairly well.

When I woke up in the morning, all drowsy, I could not understand what was going on. I had forgotten our arrangement of the night before. The effect of the wine, I think!

The days flowed by very peacefully. We had brought some books with us and took them to read in the pile of straw where it was cool, soft, and quiet, without having to be seen by strangers who might come to visit Santi. We alternated reading with long hours of working in the fields. The first day we knocked walnuts from the tree with long bamboo canes and gathered them in a sack. We helped Santi make a deep, wide trench to plant new vines. It was quite fatiguing because we had to dig the large hole with pick and shovel in the rocky ground. Then we filled the hole with stones and dirt to make a drain, indispensable for the vines to grow. It was a hot day and we were as sweaty and dusty as horses. When the work was finished we went to the wash house over a spring near the house to bathe in the cold water. It was such a nice relief that from that day on the wash house became our bathtub for a more thorough cleansing than was possible in the house. The only drawbacks were that we did not have the privacy necessary for an all-over sponging and the water was icy. Aside from that, to bathe under the sun's rays was truly a pleasant extravagance.

Another daily job that Federico and I took over was grinding the wheat to make bread flour. It was an illegal operation because by law every farmer's wheat had to be stockpiled. In exchange, the farmer received a part of the wheat ground by a mill controlled by the authorities. This amount was expected to be sufficient for making enough bread for the whole family, which was completely unrealistic. Consequently, at harvest time every self-respecting farmer would hide enough wheat to feed his family, but he could not have it ground at the mill or he would be found out; therefore, he had to resort to a machine something like a coffee grinder, which took hours to produce enough flour for a couple of loaves. But all of us took this philosophically and were excited by the risk we were taking by cheating the Fascist state.

At eight o'clock on the morning of September 18, Federico's father arrived. He had left Florence by bus at dawn to avoid meeting German soldiers. In a letter he brought me from mother she wrote that all three of them had decided to go stay in the Casentino as we had discussed. I quickly scribbled her a note for Signor Benadì to take back with him when he left for Florence at ten.

The three of us, Federico, his father, and I, took a walk around the farm and talked about what was happening in Florence. After the first great fright, the Jews had scattered in all directions, and luckily no one had yet been taken by the Fascists. It was necessary for us to take the greatest precautions not to be seen by any stranger, because the Fascists were also hiding among the simple country people, and it would be easy for anyone to recognize that Federico and I were not part of the local scene.

We said good-bye to Signor Benadì and of course I asked him to give my family my good news.

> Diary
>
> September 20, 1943: I spent the morning cracking up with laughter. I did an awful job cutting Federico's hair: he looked like a priest. We shaved a seven days' growth of beard, leaving the mustaches and goatees which we'll let grow. We always keep within the farm's boundaries. It's funny how a road of a little more than one kilometer that separates us from Radda, the only town around, is enough to keep us completely divided from the rest of the world. We don't know anything about the war. Occasionally we hear a bit of unlikely news from a farmer, which generally turns out not to be true.

Because there was no electricity in the farmers' houses there were no radios, and therefore we were totally isolated from the rest of the world. Not that I was so unhappy about it, because when all was said and done, it was another way to keep calm. But I was nervous about the idea that if something really important happened, whether positive or negative, we would not know and would not be able to take the proper precautions.

One day Santi came in all breathless to tell us that the English had landed at Grosseto. I did not get too excited about the news because it seemed too preposterous to be true. I asked Santi to find out more about it that evening by going to Radda and listening to the radio in a bar, which he did. And, in fact, it was not true.

One morning I asked Santi to call the barber at Radda because my hair was too long. I would have preferred not to have him come because everyone knows how barbers love to talk while they cut hair or shave their customers. He would most likely let it slip that he had cut the hair of a young man with such a mustache and beard who could not be bothered to come to his shop at Radda. And the logical deduction would be that the young man was in hiding.

I had to risk it, hoping that the barber would be discreet. He came and I introduced myself as Enrico instead of Enzo, even if it was not a great disguise. While he was cutting what had become a forest, he asked some questions that I answered evasively and in monosyllables. He got the idea I did not want to talk and quit quizzing me. I told him to cut my hair almost to the bone. Then I would not have to get it cut for a long time. He took me at my word, and as they say, he scalped me!

As long as he was there I asked him to trim Federico's hair, which had been the victim of my pitiless ax job a few days before. When the barber saw him, he asked: "Oh, my, who did this to you?" We did not have the courage to explain. He took up his scissors, and even more effectively, his clippers, and gave Federico a shearing similar to mine. We were both satisfied. We paid him and said good-bye. I am sure he thought he was dealing with two less than normal individuals.

That evening Santi invited some of his friends from the neighboring farm, called La Spugna. He assured us they were absolutely trustworthy, being anti-Fascist anarchists. They all arrived at the same time: a band of merry, noisy people who filled the house with their laughter and cigar smoke. We played a card game until late and were grateful to Santi for this pleasant diversion. Federico was an excellent card player; I was just so-so and always lost.

On the morning of September 25 we were awakened by the arrival of Federico's parents. They brought a letter from my parents and Liliana giving me the details of how they were comfortably established with a farmer's family in the Casentino area. I had feared that living in that environment might be difficult for papa, both because of the unaccustomed diet and because of being confined to a small house without light, radio, or the slightest diversion. However, from what I could judge from the letter, he was fairly well settled and the days went by pleasantly.

I read the long letter twice and set about to write a reply. I wrote 16 pages while Federico visited with his parents. It took almost four hours. I turned the precious missal over to the Benadìs who promised to deliver it. They left for Florence at four thirty in the afternoon. That evening the news came that Florence had been shelled by Allied bombers, but it seemed the damage was light. That evening we went to La Spugna to visit the family who had come the night before, and another interminable card game ending with my defeat, naturally.

By September 26 we had been Santi's guests for 12 days. I thought it only fair to pay him something for our expenses, because I did not want him to think I expected a free ride. He had diligently recorded everything his wife had bought for Federico and me at Radda. To this we added what he produced himself and used for our meals, and Federico and I divided the total of 1,000 lire between us.

Diary

September 26, 1943: Paid Santi. Rather steep amount, but I have to remember what things cost.

I wrote a letter to my parents and gave papa the total of what I had spent up to that day. I knew it was important for him to know I had enough money to last the rest of my exile.

The weather began to change. We had rainy days and the temperature was more like autumn. Federico and I immersed ourselves in reading books of all kinds, which Federico's parents brought us. We really glutted ourselves, and besides, what else could we do? Following my example, Federico began to keep a kind of diary.

Diary

September 27, 1943: Got up at eight thirty. Ate breakfast. Went to read in the straw stack until eleven o'clock, covering myself completely with straw to stay warm. Returned to the house to attend to the little girl's infected heel: it went well. Ate. Prepared the ingredients for a grape flatbread. Prepared the oven for baking bread. Rained all afternoon. Learned from a newspaper details of the Florence bombing: luckily Via della Cernaia wasn't hit. A bomb fell on Via Puccinotti. Damage along tracks to Rome. News came of a second raid on Florence with much damage: very discouraging. I'm worried about my house. Rained all night.

The bad weather kept Santi in the house, where he caught up with various little jobs in the house he normally did not have time for. He started making a pair of work shoes from scratch. As a young man he had learned to make shoes, and we watched him in admiration as he worked with skiver, awl, and other tools, fashioning what I considered a splendid pair.

While he worked he patiently explained what he was doing. While he was at it, I had him sew the soles of my boots that were beginning to show their age.

We were invited to supper at the Brogis (the family who lived at La Spugna). As always, it was an excellent supper of hare, the usual conversation by the fireplace, and finally the habitual card game with Federico's victory and my defeat.

The following evening after supper some other neighbors came over. Apparently the news had spread that Federico and I were Santi's guests, and all their friends wanted to meet us. However, it was getting out of control. On the one hand, we liked spending time with the good people, but on the other we were afraid so much exposure might backfire. But it was not up to us to limit the freedom of our hosts, so we adapted to the situation.

Federico's parents came to stay at Radda in a small *pensione* for one or two weeks, to get away from Florence where the atmosphere was no longer good for their health. This afforded us the opportunity to get the latest news about the war; there was electricity at Radda and the radio, in addition to the newspapers they brought us every day.

On October 4 we began the grape harvest, and the bad weather we had had for so many days cleared up, so we could cut the grapes in the sun and get a tan at the same time. We stuffed ourselves with grapes while we cut great bunches and continually talked and joked with the other men. Federico's father also joined us.

We carried the grapes in an ox cart to the cantina where we put them into tubs, and before pouring them into oak barrels, we crushed them with large wooden clubs. The sweetest grapes were put aside for a different process to make *vin santo*.

When the vats were full, we jumped inside and stomped the grapes with our bare feet. While we performed this operation the odor of the must made us slightly intoxicated.

We stopped working on the grape harvest because October 8 was the eve of Yom Kippur. Federico and I had decided to observe the fast and that day we ate supper at four thirty, so we could begin the fast at five thirty. We spent the day reading and resting. I thought of all the past Yom Kippurs with my parents. This was the first one I had celebrated without them. I asked the Lord to pardon me for all the sins I had committed during the year and to protect me and my family, keeping us all far from harm and sickness. I prayed for Gianna and her family and for my fellow Jews who, like me, were trying to survive the Nazi persecutions.

Normally, during the Jewish celebrations in the temple, it was very easy to concentrate on praying. The atmosphere was concentrated and the hazan's voice and the choir harmonized well with my thoughts. Here, in the middle of the country, lying on the straw under the blue sky, the situation was quite different; but once I achieved a certain level of concentration, I noticed that the intensity of my prayer was just as strong as it had been inside the temple. I thought about how difficult it would be for the Jews in Florence to gather at the temple to celebrate that Yom Kippur. It would be an open invitation to the Fascists and Germans to rake them all up in one fell swoop.

In the afternoon a sudden downpour lasted nearly an hour. Then, as though by magic, the sky cleared and the clouds moved toward the horizon. At that moment a great rainbow shone in all its multicolored beauty against the background of clouds still lingering in the distance. I stood looking at that spectacle for a while. I have always been charmed by rainbows, but on this particular Yom Kippur, I interpreted it as a sign of peace and pardon and a good omen for the year that was just beginning.

We ended our fast at 6:30 the next day, and at 6:40 we sat down at the table: chicken broth, tagliatelle with sauce, boiled turkey, steamed rabbit, roast rabbit with roast potatoes, and grapes. Not a bad way to end a fast. Of course we explained to the family in simple terms the significance of Yom Kippur and our fast. They listened in respectful silence without making any comment.

In the meantime the war news in the newspaper was encouraging. The Allies had landed at Termoli. Sardinia and Corsica had been evacuated. The Russians had developed a great offensive on the Eastern front.

After the grape harvest was finished we began to prune the vines under the direction of Federico's father and Santi. We used pruning shears and the *gattuccio,* which is a small saw for cutting the larger vines. I learned to distinguish between the vine shoots that should be pruned and those that should not. The longest shoots had to be bent in a certain way and tied to the wire that ran along the vines. It was interesting work, but not easy.

When the pruning was finished, Santi asked if I felt like trying to work with the oxen. I agreed and grasped the plow after hitching the two oxen to the yoke. I learned how to make the oxen move ahead and stop, gradually managing to plow the first furrow along the row of vines. The successive furrows were easier to do. It was a tiring but satisfying job. The two animals, so powerful and yet so patient, docilely followed my commands, snorting and slavering. Periodically they would stop to take a mouthful of grape leaves.

The next morning we felt somewhat groggy, but the stinging air and work we had to do woke us up and brought us back to reality in a few minutes. We had to kill a 20-pound suckling pig that Santi had bought at a good price. It would help us save on meat expenses.

Certainly for two Jews in hiding to help kill a little pig a few days after fasting for Yom Kippur was not very kosher. Very likely our Lord wrote this down as a sin to ask forgiveness for at the next Yom Kippur!

With our religious qualms under control, we set to work. Santi went to get the animal from the enclosure where he had put it the day before. Because the room was so small it was easy to grab and tie the piglet quickly by the legs.

After preparing a basin to collect the blood, Santi stretched the animal on the ground. It was my job to hold it by the back legs and Federico's to hold the forelegs. Santi took a long, thin kitchen knife suitable for the occasion, and with a gesture that spoke of familiarity with the procedure, inserted the knife into the animal's neck, going straight to its heart. While all this was going on the pig was squealing nonstop, making the scene so much more bloody. It was like a massacre of the innocents.

It was not easy for Federico and me to hold the furiously thrashing animal. Thankfully, after the coup de grâce the pig stopped squealing and thrashing. It was struck dead. Santi carefully let the blood drip into a basin he had ready for that purpose. Then, he began to strip the bristle covering the animal. Finally, Santi hung the pig from the ceiling of the cellar by its hind legs and slit it open completely, removing the intestines. Every day we cut off a small portion that Santi's wife baked or fried.

I continued to help Santi with all sorts of jobs. Autumn was approaching so we had to chop firewood for the fireplace and oven. I went to the woods to cut small oaks that I then carried to the yard to split with an ax and stack in a pile. I pruned the vines and plowed the fields for planting wheat. These were all things I liked to do and in time the work got easier, an indication I was in good physical condition.

Federico's parents came to spend some time with us every day. I liked talking with them, but I noticed that Federico became different—quieter and more serious. He may have felt intimidated and not as free as when we two were alone.

Federico's mother left for Florence October 15. Her husband accompanied her, but promised to return in a few days. I wrote a long letter to my parents to bring them up to date about the latest events and gave it to Signor Benadì to deliver. In that letter I answered my father's concerns about the expenses for my upkeep. Because his last letter expressed a growing reluctance to contribute to my expenses, I wanted him to understand that I could get by with what I had. Understanding his anxiety, I tried to justify how much I spent, though I realized the amount was high.

In addition, I knew that papa was afraid he would never work again because of the condition of his health. So in my letter I tried to reassure him of my intentions for the future. I knew he counted on the fact of my taking up his work, and thus giving him the possibility of making a contribution. I knew that talk was futile as I had nothing concrete. However, knowing papa's apprehensive character, I could at least make his vision of the future more agreeable and instill some tranquillity as the times required.

Knowing that Liliana was taking care of mamma and papa was also reassuring. Her presence was decisive in giving them comfort in places where there was little comfort to be had. Besides, if necessary, she went to Florence to get the things they left behind in their hurry to escape. It was a great risk to return to the city, but she was the only one who could do it.

Along with the farm work, I found time to provide occasional first aid at the request of some of Santi's family friends. One of my most important "cases" was a 13-year-old boy's abscessed foot. He had run into the metal point of a harrow three days earlier, his foot and lower leg were already swollen, and he was in pain.

I do not know where I found the courage, but after disinfecting the skin and instruments, I took a razor blade and made an incision in the center of the infection. A large quantity of purulent matter came out, giving off a terrible odor. I could not understand the reason for all that putrefaction until the boy's mother finally confessed that she had tried to cure the boy on her own with a poultice of sage, boiled oil, cobwebs, and other disgusting things. I scolded her and had her buy some Antipiol and tincture of iodine. I then carefully disinfected the wound, covered it with an antiseptic salve, and bandaged the foot.

The boy was in so much pain during the treatment that at one point he threw up. The entire family looked on in fear and trepidation. Federico, who pretended to be my assistant, looked away whenever he could so that he would not vomit as well.

I ordered the boy to stay off his foot. When I came back the next day, his foot and leg were still in bad shape. When I cleaned the wound again with Antipiol, I discovered another small infection. I made a series of little punctures and more pus came out. I medicated the wound, rebandaged the foot, and left.

The third day his foot was less swollen, and from then on it began to heal. I medicated it once a day, and after five days it was completely healed. The family could not thank me enough and they gave me food that I passed on to Santi's family.

This incident gave me an aura of respect in the eyes of the families who knew Federico and me. They often came to ask me medical questions. I explained that I was not a doctor and that curing an abscess did not mean that I could cure every illness.

Our visits to the neighboring houses had by now assumed a frantic pace. An evening did not go by when we were not invited to go somewhere. We were two young men who aroused curiosity, especially with the young girls our age. Not that we were anything special, just different from the young men they ordinarily talked to. They were very curious to know how we spent our evenings in Florence. More or less like the way we spend them here, we replied. But this did not seem to satisfy them. They obviously imagined brilliant evenings, luxurious houses, elegant women, and who knows what else.

The next morning Signora Benadì returned from Florence. Happily, she brought us a chess set. We needed distraction from the various shepherdesses in the neighborhood. Chess would be an excellent diversion. We inaugurated it at once and just as quickly I had my first defeat. Federico was much better than I. It was obvious he had played often and had acquired a good strategy. In comparison I was an amateur. However we enjoyed ourselves just the same.

I watched Federico and his father play a game and learned that certain moves should be made at the start. I realized that one must plan a series of moves in order to capture pieces. I had just made one move after the other, following the procedure of my adversary. And by doing that I merely put myself in his hands.

Federico's parents returned to Radda for another long stay, because the atmosphere in Florence had become unbearable. The various country tasks continued their inexorable march. We finished the vine pruning. I plowed, and with the oxen had passed the "40 teeth" over most of the land that had been previously fertilized and now waited to be sowed. Sowing is work that requires skill, as the seeds have to be scattered in a homogeneous manner. Santi did this going behind me as I passed the 40 teeth over the ground with the oxen. With a wide swing of his arm he tossed the seeds, incredibly covering every part of the field.

The little pig we sacrificed was quickly eaten. We had Santi buy another that met the same fate. This time, as is often the case, it made less of an impression: the procedure had become routine. Every day we cut off a small piece of meat and Giulia baked it in the bread oven.

We had the barber return to cut our hair and shape our goatees, which now had a mature and professional aspect. While he was there the barber also gave Federico's father a trim.

The work in the fields had practically reached the point where it was up to Mother Nature to do her part. This left me some free time. There was a limit to how much I could read or to how many card and chess games I could play every day, so I decided to devote some time to teaching the most elementary things to Marina, Santi's youngest daughter, and to one of her little friends who, by coincidence, was called Gina. Marina, poor child, was obtuse and had little desire to study, whereas Gina was vivacious with a quick intelligence and enjoyed doing the exercises I gave her. They came to me every day for a lesson. I taught them the multiplication tables, which Gina learned almost immediately, while Marina had to spend quite a few days on it. It just did not want to get into her head, but finally I succeeded.

After a week of pedagogical activity, one of Santi's friends begged me to take his little girl under my wing also. She was about the same age as the other two. It was no problem to take her on, so I had a class of three little girls. It was entertaining and helped the days go by quickly. Federico also devoted himself to teaching and took on another little girl.

One day Marina came to class and I noticed that her homework was done much better than usual. I was very surprised how she had made such extraordinary progress from one day to the next. I asked her if she had done the homework by herself or if someone had helped her. She lowered her head, blushed, and burst into tears. She confessed that her older sister had done it all. I was more angry with Iolanda than with her. I sent her away and told her that if she did that another time I would not teach her any more. She took it rather badly, but by the time we went to the table for supper we had made up.

The chess games continued, and with the help of Signor Benadì I began to understand chess much better and become more confident in planning the game strategy, imitating what Federico and his father did. I reached the point where I also began to win some games. It was now more entertaining—also for my adversaries who were battling on a more even field.

When Santi's older daughter became ill with a cold and a toothache, they asked me what they should do. I told them to buy some aspirin and after two days it was all gone. Then I caught her cold and cured myself with aspirin and *vin brulé*.

The season became more autumnal. The days grew shorter and the temperature gradually cooler. Not having brought any warm clothes with me, I asked Concetta, a local girl who had befriended me, if she could find a kilo of sheep's wool to buy, spin by hand, and then knit me a heavy sweater and two pairs of long socks.

Concetta happily accepted the assignment. She found a kilo of raw wool for 100 lire, washed it with sulfur to make it whiter, dried it, and spun it into a very fine and twisted thread. She put the wool fleece on a stick and from that fiber gradually pulled out a little into a thread. She then twisted it around the wooden spindle that she turned constantly with two fingers of her right hand. I was fascinated by her skill and dexterity. She then wrapped the thread into a large skein from which she made balls for knitting my sweater and socks. I paid Concetta 50 lire for her handiwork.

I began taking walks with Federico in the area around Radda. We went randomly from hill to hill, avoiding the busy roads and only taking paths through the woods. We ranged far and wide, discovering the most beautiful places. I had my little camera with me that I had asked Signor Benadì to bring and made some beautiful photos of the most outstanding panoramas.

On November 2, Federico's parents came from Florence. They had met with Liliana and gave me her news. They also brought letters from her and from my parents and a gift for my birthday that was coming up, a nice book. They said Liliana would have tried to come visit me much sooner but was waiting to see how safe it would be.

I learned that other Jews were hiding out in Radda and arranged to meet with them. They were not Florentines, so we did not know them. It was a short meeting in which we told each other of our experiences as exiles and wished each other well.

The next day we took a walk to Badiaccia, a small place where Santi's daughter Iolanda lived with her aunt and uncle. It was an enchanting walk. We arrived at ten and were given a hearty welcome by Iolanda and her aunt and uncle. We spent all morning with them and in the afternoon we met with some Florentine Jews who were hiding there, among whom were Virginio Vita, Leone Passigli, the son of Goffredo, Cesare Levi, and a certain Belgrado, all related to each other. We had the usual discussions of how we were getting along, but nothing more.

Strangely enough, encounters with these fellow sufferers always left me dissatisfied. One would think that when two people running the same risks got together after a long time it would be an emotional meeting. But that was not the case. One asks the other how it is going and the other gives a very bare-bones response, asking the other in turn how it is going. There is a cool reserve, as if each one were afraid of giving himself away. Perhaps each thinks he is privileged in comparison to the others and feels guarded about letting it be known. Or who knows why.

On November 5, we got up and noticed it had really turned cold. I put on my woolen sweater to avoid further colds and that day the lesson with my three little students was held around the fire burning merrily in the fireplace. I read a little of my book *(L'innocente)* and told Federico good-bye, because I was going to see Concetta and preferred he not come with me, for obvious reasons.

The next day I got up early and went to buy more wool for Concetta since according to her the first amount would not be enough. When I returned to Duro I had the surprise of my life: Liliana was there. Extreme happiness for both of us. I was crazy with joy. I had not seen her since that fateful day I left Florence to come to Radda—almost two months. She was very well; she had not expected to see me with the beard and mustache, which had "a strange effect" on her. Anyway, she thought I looked fine and in good shape, though a little heavier (with all the food I had eaten).

Liliana brought letters from papa, mamma, Gianna, and greetings from different friends. She recounted the vicissitudes and fears she had to go through before coming to visit me. One day, returning to Via della Cernaia to get some warm clothes for our parents, just as she was about to enter the house, she saw two Germans coming out of it. Undoubtedly they had come to get us and, not finding anyone, were going away to return another time. Liliana waited until they had left in their automobile and then entered the house furtively. In the greatest hurry, confusion, and fear, she grabbed up everything she could, put it in a suitcase, and took off as fast as her legs would carry her.

Such was her emotional state when she got off the streetcar stop closest to where our parents were hiding that she suddenly lost her way. By then it was dark, without even the light of the moon to help her. Unable to see three meters in front of her, she could not find the narrow, twisting little path leading to La Ragnaia. She stopped to collect her thoughts, desperate because of the surrounding darkness and no houses nearby. Suddenly, when her thoughts were the blackest, an enormous brightness lit up the sky, followed by an explosion. With that light that lasted several seconds, she was able to find the little path and finally reach La Ragnaia. At that moment Providence wanted a German gasoline tank to blow up.

The next morning, carrying the suitcase with my clothes, she took the bus to Radda, sitting in one of the back seats to be as hidden as possible. As usual, the bus was overcrowded. Arriving at a military checkpoint, the bus was stopped by a squad of German soldiers. In order to check the documents of all the passengers, they ordered everyone to get off with identity papers in hand. Liliana had no document and she felt like dying. It was not possible to hide under the seat because there was absolutely no space. Trembling, she remained seated and waited, while the other passengers began to complain loudly about that unscheduled stop. They were in a hurry to reach their destination and refused to get out to show their documents. If the Germans wanted to see them, they would have to come on the bus.

Calculating the astonishing number of people in the vehicle, the Germans, with gestures and swear words (understood by their tone), gave up, sending the bus and its human cargo to the devil. When the bus started up again Liliana felt reborn and thanked the Lord for saving her.

I spent all morning listening to every detail of how papa and mamma were, what they did every day, where they lived, the people who gave them hospitality, and everything that was happening in Florence that by now had become a distant memory. I did not feel homesick for any of the things I left behind. I was concerned only for my physical salvation and that of my family and friends.

We ate lunch, talking without taking a breath, and afterward Liliana went to bed to rest. I played a game of chess with Federico and later read some pages in my book. After supper I walked Liliana to Radda where she would spend the night. Federico and I went to visit some neighbors until eleven thirty, playing cards and telling slightly off-color jokes, in the country fashion.

ABOVE: We three children *(left to right)*: Enzo, born in 1922; Liliana, born in 1918; and Franco, born in 1920.

RIGHT: Enzo's maternal grandmother, Signora Evelina Markbreiter, with his father, Ugo Salomone Tayar.

LEFT: Papa and Mamma, Dora Markbreiter Tayar, on vacation in Lido di Camaiore.

ABOVE: Mamma (*right*) and Aunt Matilde, her sister.

RIGHT: Enzo and Liliana, Florence, 1938.

LEFT: Enzo and Grandmother Evelina on one of her visits from Bologna, the day of Enzo's bar mitzvah, Florence, 1935.

RIGHT: Gianfranco Sarfatti as a forced laborer, digging canals for irrigating the countryside.

BELOW: Enzo (*standing second from the right*) and his labor crew, drawn together in devising ways to undercut their Fascist oppressors.

ABOVE: The farmyard at Radda, operated by Santi Gatti and the first hiding place for Enzo and his friend Federico Benadì.

ABOVE: Three of Enzo's fellow workers resting after working in Sesto Fiorentino.

RIGHT: Gianna in
San Gimignano, 1943.

BELOW: In Enzoli, Enzo hid out at a farm with *(left to right)* Antinesca, Settimia,
Beppe, Venusta, and Gosto.

ABOVE: La Consuma, where Enzo took refuge.

RIGHT: Stella, the welcoming owner of La Consuma, Enzo's fourth hiding place, and Jim.

CHAPTER 12

My Refuge at Poggiarso

The following morning, November 7, the scene changed suddenly and completely. We got up at seven thirty. Liliana was already in the kitchen with Giulia, waiting for us to wake up. She looked very serious. "Bad news," she said. And she told us how Federico's parents had arrived from Florence the previous evening, very frightened. They had gone to Florence, as Liliana had done, to get some warmer clothes for themselves and Federico. As they were about to enter the front door of their apartment building, a neighbor saw them and told them to run away because the Germans had broken down the door of their apartment and were inside. The Benadìs escaped by a miracle. They ran off without a backward glance and did not stop until they were on the bus about to leave for Radda.

Shortly afterward the protagonists of the misadventure arrived. We discussed the situation around the kitchen table. We were very worried. Not finding anyone at the Benadìs house in Florence, the Germans could continue their search by going to their farm in Chianti, their most logical hiding place. Therefore it was urgent that we all leave Duro immediately, each going a different way.

These were moments full of emotion and sorrow. I was sorry to have to quit my life at Duro with Federico. I felt very affectionate toward him and his company was very congenial. I was sorry also to leave Santi, Giulia, Berto, and Marina and all the young women we had become friends with. It was upsetting to have to change my life so suddenly. I had established a certain precise rhythm in the work in the fields and in moments of relaxation and I was comfortable in that house and in those habits, just as one becomes accustomed to an old pair of shoes. I would miss someone like Federico to talk to every day, play cards and chess with, and tell all my amorous adventures to.

I now felt secure in that house. I knew they were all good and trustworthy people and I loved having their friendship and had nothing to fear. I did not have the slightest idea where to go. Certainly not to one of those farmer's houses near Duro. Too dangerous.

After long discussions about where the Benadìs would stay and where I would go, we agreed that none of us would sleep at Duro that night, and we would take everything away that belonged to us. We would not leave a trace to incriminate the family.

As a first hypothesis for the immediate move, we thought of going to the monastery of some brothers in the neighborhood. Liliana and I went there and were shown into a kind of parlor. A brother came to meet us whose rank in the hierarchy of the monastery I do not know. He was rather young with a full beard. We described our situation in a few words and asked for his hospitality, assuring him that we would leave as soon as we found an alternative.

I certainly had not expected him to throw his arms around me and greet me like a brother. However, his reaction was far from the vaunted "Christian charity." He mumbled something about the danger that the monastery ran every day because of the Germans who went around plundering food everywhere. He said there was not even one free bed and that, reluctantly (!!!!), he had to say no. I told him that luckily up to that day I had found some farmers who had showed much more sympathy and understanding than he, and that I hoped to find others.

We turned on our heels. I was feeling very angry with that brother and his cohorts. They risk nothing in their life, I thought. They have food and lodging guaranteed until they die. They are isolated from everything that happens outside the circle of the monastery. No political or military event ever comes to disturb their tranquillity. They do not know what it means to struggle for survival and they are not ashamed to show themselves enclosed in an infinite selfishness that keeps them from putting up for a single night a Jew hunted by the Germans.

We returned to Duro and decided to sleep that night at La Spugna with Santi's friends, who were quick to offer us hospitality. To have cured their son's foot, thank heavens, was paying off. Federico and his parents moved that afternoon to a little house that had been empty for some time, since the family had moved to another farm. Carraino, as it was called, was a very small house at the end of a narrow little valley that the sun had trouble reaching. It was completely hidden from sight by thick oak woods and shrubs. It took about an hour of walking to reach the new destination, accompanied by Santi who was well acquainted with the family who had lived there.

Separating from Federico and his parents was not easy. We tried to make foolish jokes as was our wont, but they were not funny. Sadly, we said good-bye with big hugs, wishing one another good luck. It was the end of a particularly important period in my life. I would never forget it.

I watched them go away with their bundles and felt a great pain in my heart, after which Liliana and I moved bag and baggage to La Spugna and settled in a small bedroom. We ate with the family and after supper, while we were around the fireplace talking with our hosts, Santi came to warn us that he heard the Germans had come to Greve and it would be dangerous to go over the main roads or on any road that military vehicles could travel on. This news did not simplify things, but it was not the end of the world. We would take more winding but more secure ways through the woods.

Antinesca, a girl who lived with her parents at La Spugna, said the next day we could go stay with a farmer's family she knew who would be able to keep me for a while. Their house was not more than an hour away, and she would take us there. I did not have the slightest idea where I would end up. It was enough just to get out of that area that had become too "hot" for me.

After supper we went to bed early. I tossed and turned for quite a while without being able to sleep; I had too many thoughts swirling in my brain. I thought of the Benadìs who had gone so far away, alone, far from everything and everyone. Federico's parents were elderly and unquestionably their discomfort was great. The only good thing was that all three of them could be together and be company for each other. I was very tempted to tell Liliana that the next day I would go with her to Casentino to be with papa and mamma. It would be very nice to be able to join them, as Federico had done. Then I changed my mind because my presence would have put their security at risk, and I absolutely could not do that. Finally I went to sleep, but I did not sleep well, and every so often nightmares woke me up.

At five o'clock in the morning we were up, washed quickly, and ate a frugal breakfast. Antinesca was also ready and all three of us left with our things to go to my new refuge. We went down a path through a thick woods while it was still dark. I had my backpack, which weighed a ton, on my shoulders and carried a bundle in my hand. Liliana had her heavy backpack but she did not complain. The air was very cold and we walked briskly to warm ourselves. Reaching the top of a hill just as the sun rose we observed a very beautiful panorama. We were heading toward Valdarno and in the distance we could see the Pratomagno. Descending the hill we went along a little valley for some kilometers, avoiding any busy road. No one was in sight, but it was also very early.

At a certain point Antinesca stopped and pointed out a house perched on the summit of another, higher hill. "That's the house," she said. "We'll be there in half an hour." Seen from a distance the building appeared rather large; totally isolated, it had a 360-degree view of the plain and was an ideal position for my peace of mind, far from the prying eyes.

I decided that in order to avoid unnecessary dangers I would alter my life completely from that day forward. Instead of going to visit every Tom, Dick, and Harry as I had done up to that time, I would stay hidden in the house or in the immediate vicinity. Certainly I would not be as entertained as I had become accustomed to, but my personal health and safety were of utmost importance now. I would read the books I still had and would ask Liliana to send others.

We climbed to the top of the hill by way of a steep, narrow path. Finally we reached a nice clearing with the house where I would hide in the center. It was much larger than the one at Duro, even though not as esthetically pleasing. A strong wind was blowing that whistled through the oak branches surrounding the clearing. We put our baggage on the ground. No sound came from the house. It was a quarter past six. Evidently everyone was sleeping, so we agreed to wait until they got up.

At a quarter past seven a window opened and a woman looked out and motioned for us to come in. We did so and Erminia met us with a cordial smile. She was around 40, short, neither fat nor slender, gray-haired, with a calm, sweet face, even though I seemed to see in her eyes signs of ancient tribulations. She had us sit down and offered us a cup of boiling hot barley coffee. I drank it because it was hot and I was numb from the cold air, but certainly not for its burnt taste.

While we were sipping the so-called coffee, the head of the household came in, Gino. He was about 45 years old, long and thin, and his face was marked by hard daily work. He greeted us pleasantly enough, but I realized at once that he had a rather closed and sullen character. Much different from Santi, unfortunately. I would act accordingly and avoid getting too chummy with him. We explained why I was there, and I realized from their first words that I had nothing to worry about as far as political ideas were concerned. They were fanatic Communists. That was not my ideal either, but given the circumstances, a Communist's house was better than a Fascist's.

One by one their five children at home made their appearance. The sixth was in the army. The first to appear was Leonetta, about 20 years old, of medium height and a shapely figure but with ordinary features—her nose proudly in the air. She seemed to have a strong authoritarian character, but pleasant. The second to arrive was Leonora, about 15. She was tall like her sister, with yellow hair, a moon-shaped face, and sweet features like her character. Leonora was plump, but she had nice legs. Then the youngest came in, Maria, 5 or 6 years old, a sweet little girl. Silvano arrived, around 17 years old. He was a big boy, long and skinny like his father, with a merry, boisterous character and typical peasant features. The last to arrive was Mario, around 12, blondish, with beautiful blue eyes and a handsome face with a sweet expression. He had inherited everything from his mother.

One after the other they sat down at a large table that dominated the kitchen and drank their barley coffee, dunking pieces of bread in it. We continued talking while everyone had their noisy breakfast and as rapidly as they appeared the four older children and their father Gino went out to do their daily chores. Only the smallest child and Erminia remained. She showed me the room where I would sleep, sharing a double bed with the two males.

The house was furnished in a manner almost identical to Santi's: the standard wrought-iron bedstead, the standard ceramic basin and pitcher on an iron stand. I would be the only one to use it because no one washed in the morning and when they did wash, they preferred the stone sink in the kitchen. I had exclusive use of a locker in the bedroom that was more than ample for my necessities.

The kitchen was also typical: the *madia* for the bread, the cupboard with glass doors, two long benches on either side of the table, and a large fireplace with benches and andirons. The ceilings were higher than those at Duro; the thought immediately occurred to me that as a consequence the rooms would also be colder. And in fact they were.

After the exchange of salutations, Antinesca took to the road to go home and Liliana went to rest for a bit on what would be my bed. I stayed in the kitchen to write letters to my parents and Gianna. I sent mamma good wishes for her upcoming birthday. I reassured her about my health and told her I was with people who would treat me like a son.

I had barely finished this letter when Giangio arrived, a friend of Santi's who had come to Poggiarso (the name of the house where I now lived) to advise me that the situation had improved and it was safe for Liliana to go back to Casentino. Now that she was there she wanted to stay with me for a while and decided to leave the next day.

We ate with Gino's whole tribe. Erminia had prepared the kind of sumptuous meal that the country folk put on for special occasions. We stayed with the merry company until the last crumb on the table was gone.

After supper I took Liliana by the arm and led her outside to take a constitutional. A full moon shone as bright as a 100,000-watt spotlight. We sat on a large rock and began to plan our immediate and distant future. We both had firm intentions of getting through the present situation with the least damage possible, and then to take full control of our lives and recoup the time we had lost in the past five years.

I recapped the past days with Federico and my almost-gallant adventures with the country girls, and we had a good laugh at my expense. It was a very peaceful evening for which both Liliana and I felt a great need. Later, after lingering to talk with the family a little, we went to bed.

I had never slept in the same bed with two other people and stayed curled up on my side so as not to bother the two boys. In spite of that, we engaged in a kind of contest for possession of the blanket. The room was cold and the blanket was not sufficiently wide to cover three people. The one in the middle had no problem; only those on either side. I waited until the two boys were asleep and then retrieved my part of the blanket. We slept, but not too comfortably.

The next morning wake-up call came at seven thirty. The boys got up, dressed quickly without going near the sink, and off they went to work in the fields. The same routine with their father and sisters. The only ones who remained at home were little Maria and Erminia. I washed up as well as I could and had what euphemistically can be called "breakfast." While Liliana was mending some of my sweaters, Antinesca arrived with a suitcase of my things I had left behind. She confirmed the more positive news we had already heard the day before. Liliana left at four in the afternoon. I gave her a list of books I wanted her to get me. I made her promise to come back as soon as possible, and I promised her I would send news of myself regularly.

"Come back soon!" "Don't worry!" were our parting words. I watched her go away smiling with Antinesca. I was once again alone. This time more alone than ever. And without Federico.

It took some time for the pain to ease. I began to read *L'Americana*—an anthology of various American writers edited by Elio Vittorini. I sat on one of the benches inside the fireplace, next to the burning log. It was cold and that was the only warm place in the house. Every so often I stirred the flame and added another log. I did not move from that position until the gang of children with Gino in the lead came in, numb with cold in spite of working in the fields.

I forgot to mention another important member of the family: Tito, a very nice black dog, a mysterious crossbreed. He resembled a Scotch terrier and had short, rough fur, a square muzzle, short legs, and a long and squat body. We made friends instantly. It is amazing how dogs can sense right off if someone likes them or not. The first time I saw him he came up wagging his tail as he would have done with an old friend. I bent over and petted him, speaking softly and fussing over him a little. From then on he did not leave my side. He stayed with me all afternoon while I read near the fire. Doubtless he enjoyed the warmth, too. He kept his eyes closed and his muzzle extended on the floor. He seemed to be sleeping, but he was awake and enjoying the heat and my company. Every so often, without moving a millimeter, he would open one eye to assure himself I was still there reading and then close it at once.

As soon as Tito heard the voices of his masters he would abruptly get up and go to the door wagging his tail. Then he would flop down exactly where he had been until one of the children made him move to put a chair where he was lying. Tito complained weakly and took up his original position, but this time under the chair.

Gino began to talk with Erminia about the work they still had to do. There was not much work left in the fields, but there were still the animals to care for. Every day they had to make chaff, a mixture of fresh grass and hay chopped up by a machine with a large wheel and four very sharp, swiftly turning blades. This wheel was turned by hand and I offered to do it every day. My offer was taken up and I began that same day. When the chaff was ready I carried it to the trough in the stall where the two oxen were kept. The meal would be tranquilly munched all night long.

We ate a normal dinner that night. Nothing extravagant like the first evening. After dinner Gino, the two boys, and I played a card game. I was partners with the youngest, who seemed more alert. We won and Gino let loose a couple of curses that were habitual with him. I do not think he even noticed how often he used them. After a while no one paid any attention; indeed, it was a marvel if he ever finished an entire sentence without cursing once.

While we were sitting at the table playing, I saw a bright flash outside the dark window. I looked out and saw in the distance some Bengal lights slowly descending from the sky, illuminating the whole area like daylight. I also heard the light roar of an airplane motor in the distance. It was probably an English reconnaissance aircraft photographing some bombing objectives for the next day. It was a comforting sight and meant the Allies were continuing their war and coming closer to where I was.

Tito woke me up the next morning at eight thirty. Standing on his back legs, he leaned his front paws on the mattress near my face, whimpering to get my attention. I was very touched and lifted him up beside me. The two boys were still sleeping heavily. The night before, their father had said that this morning they did not need to go out to the fields early because it was beginning to get too cold.

Tito settled down next to me and let me pet and fuss over him a little. He had become my best friend and made a great companion, filling the emptiness I had felt since departing from Federico. After five minutes of cuddling I got up. While I washed he stayed on the bed, following me with his eyes.

I was about to go have breakfast when I heard voices coming from the kitchen. One of them was unfamiliar and I knew it must be an outsider. I eavesdropped at the door: it was an assistant to the foreman who had come to discuss money matters with Gino. I could not let him see me. Erminia, very judiciously, brought me breakfast in my room. I gulped it down and got back into bed with the blanket over my head. It was cold and I was shivering. I stayed there trying to warm up and I also tried to go on with my reading, until I heard Gino tell the man good-bye. The way was clear. I jumped out of bed and ran to the kitchen, where a nice fire was burning. Taking my place on the bench I continued reading, warming myself by the blessed heat of the flame until lunchtime.

After lunch I went looking for mushrooms with Erminia. We found many groups of "honey" mushrooms. These edible mushrooms are tasty enough, if a little watery—not nearly as good as porcini.

While we walked in the woods I told Ermina about the last few years of my life, about our fears and the good fortune I had had in finding families courageous enough to take me in. She did not seem to think there was anything extraordinary about my being their guest but thought it good for me to stay hidden, without being seen by outsiders, and even by the assistant foreman, because he might not have approved their giving hospitality to a fugitive. The five children were glad I was there, she said, and they all liked me. Of course I was pleased to hear that.

Tito came mushroom hunting with us and ran back and forth while we walked along the path. He sniffed under each bush and every now and then would start digging in the dirt with his two front paws, never finding anything.

That evening we ate the fresh-picked mushrooms. After supper Antinesca returned with a letter from Liliana. My sister had arrived safe and sound in Florence and had everything ready to send that I had requested. With Antinesca were Giangio and Luisa, who stayed a while to talk while I shaved Gino, who had to go to Montevarchi the next day and wanted to look presentable. It was the first time I had shaved anyone, and I realized it was quite different from shaving yourself. With a brush I lathered up his face and very gently began to shave him with my safety razor. I was scared stiff I might cut him. Imagine what a string of obscenities that would elicit! I did it without a scratch, and instead of obscenities I got profuse thanks. He rinsed his face in icy water and rejoined the conversation, enriching it with his habitual expletives.

We said good-bye to Antinesca and the others, and I thanked them wholeheartedly for bringing my sister's letter and went to bed to shiver from the cold. I do not think I have ever experienced such cold as I did at Poggiarso.

The next day Gino went to Montevarchi, so the rest of the family enjoyed themselves for the day. I got up shivering and consequently only washed myself briefly. I gulped down breakfast and went out to enjoy the brightly shining sun. In order not to miss a single ray, I lay on the top of the straw stack to read my book, with faithful Tito beside me. I felt a physical need for the sun's rays that gradually brought my body back to its normal temperature. I seemed to be in a state of hibernation. Tito stayed nice and quiet next to me, showing me he felt the same pleasure as I did. I had never had a dog in my life and began to see how an animal like this could be good company.

In a little while Tito went to sleep. I could tell by his slow, deep breathing, almost a light snoring, that Tito was sleeping. I tried not to wake him. That peaceful calm meant he considered me one of the family and felt safe beside me.

Later in the morning I helped press the grapes for making *vin santo* and gave a hand with other light chores. In the afternoon Antinesca came with a package of all the books I had requested from Liliana. What a good sister! There was also a letter from her saying that the Germans had not been in our house yet, and everything was as we had left it. I was a little uneasy about how casually Liliana went back and forth to our house in Florence. After the fright Federico's parents had, I was apprehensive when I knew Liliana had to go there.

After Antinesca left we sat down at the table. While we were eating I suddenly heard a thunderlike rumbling in the distance, but the sky was clear without the shadow of a cloud. Looking out the window I realized that the distant thunder was nothing less than an aerial bombardment. On the horizon and in the valley there would be bright flashes and then a few seconds later an explosion. For three-quarters of an hour we were the excited spectators of a shelling taking place in the direction of Florence, which was probably the follow-up of the aerial reconnaissance that had launched the illuminating rockets two evenings before.

The dull explosion of the bombs was like a voice saying: "Enzo, be calm, we are working for you. Soon we'll be there, too." I was sorry for the poor civilians who had their homes destroyed by bombs. It was a great risk everyone ran, including us objects of a blind and pitiless hunt; therefore it seemed imperative for the Allies to hurry up and do what was necessary to end the war as soon as possible.

Gino returned the next day, all cocky. He was in too good a mood. He even started singing, as off-key as a broken bell, which told me things had turned out well for him in Montevarchi. It must have gone *"a gatta,"* as they say here. For a good half hour he even forgot to swear while he gave an accounting of his day—an accounting that I, cautious as I was, considered carefully modified, censuring whatever Erminia did not need to know.

I went to lie down on my pile of straw as usual, with the usual company of my four-legged friend, reading my book. The warm and restorative sun was still shining. I spent the greater part of the day there, until the thought occurred to me that it might be better if I tried to be a little more useful to the family hosting me, beyond the occasional manual labor I showed a willingness to do. I asked Erminia if she would like for me to give lessons to her children who needed some catching up. I was willing to teach almost any subject they wanted. She liked the idea and called in the two boys and Eleonora to give them the "splendid" news. From the faces they made I did not think they were very excited about the prospect, but they had to grin and bear it.

I asked random questions about different subjects and from their very labored and often erroneous replies I realized that for their age they were very much behind in their academic studies. We determined that every day, after they had done the most urgent chores for their father, we would meet in the kitchen and have a lesson. To begin with, I said they needed to improve their reading and arithmetic (something particularly important because Gino was not able to do it and therefore needed his children's help). We could then confront a few basic notions of geography, at least what pertained to Italian territory.

Those children were virgin territory in any field of knowledge, and it would be a source of pride for me to be able to teach them what I could. We set to work. In the beginning there were some rather tragicomic moments around the kitchen table, with Eleonora in tears when her brothers, who were no better than she, teased her for her reading mistakes.

With the passing of the days, by my insisting they read more slowly, I had them acquire greater speed and accuracy. Arithmetic was a harder nut to crack. I had to begin with the multiplication tables, which none of the three knew well enough. After this was digested, we tackled the rest. The most difficult subject was division. But even here, with much patience, we managed to make some progress. While I was giving the three children lessons, Erminia went back and forth from the kitchen to the bedrooms doing her housekeeping chores. Occasionally she would stop to listen to what we were saying, and I noticed that she had the expression of someone who was hearing things she had never heard before. Poor woman, perhaps she would have liked to sit down and learn what I was teaching her children.

I continued to be very careful not to expose myself to the indiscreet eyes of strangers. This required a certain sacrifice, but I had no choice. One morning around ten o'clock, while it was raining heavily, someone knocked at the door. I took my book and ran to my room. It was a hunter wanting to come in out of the rain. The problem was that he stayed in the kitchen until four thirty in the afternoon! I had to put up with my hunger pangs and the bitter cold because there was no way to warm myself in my room. To keep from freezing I stayed under the blanket. I had the suspicion he was a Jew-hunting Fascist who, with the rain as an excuse, had installed himself in the kitchen to wait for me to make my appearance. It seemed highly unlikely that a hunter would stay for more than six hours without wanting to return to his hunting. I know how little the rain deters those who have this interest.

I did not mention my suspicion to anyone. I promised myself to be always on guard and to keep my eyes and ears open—even with my hosts, in case my presence might be undesirable in their house for any reason.

That same day of the hunter two other things happened. First, Santi came to give me news of Federico and his parents: they were well physically, but suffering from low morale because of their great solitude. I promised myself to go there as soon as possible. I talked with him for a long time and asked if he thought I might be a burden to my present hosts. He did not think so, but added that I should be careful, especially with Gino, who was a complicated character. The second event regarded Gino, fresh from a visit with a "witch" of Montevarchi whom he had gone to ask, by way of her "extra-sensory faculties," if their older son was well and where he was at that moment. They had not heard from him for some time, and Erminia in particular was worried about him. The reply from the so-called seer was that their son was well but with the Germans in Yugoslavia. This news was very distressing to Gino and Erminia. I tried to calm their fears as much as I could, giving them hope that the war would soon end and their son would return home. After supper the atmosphere was more serene.

On November 24, my birthday, I said nothing about it to Erminia. I did not want her to feel obliged to celebrate it in any way, which was fine with me. I wished myself another 100 happy years and tried to avoid any melancholy feelings about a solitary birthday by going with Gino and Maria to gather acorns in the woods for the pigs. That day Silvano, their 17-year-old son, went to Montevarchi to do some errands. He brought back a letter from my parents, so I got a wonderful birthday present! He also brought three papers with the latest news. I ate supper with the family and at eight o'clock I excused myself, took my oil lamp, and went to bed with the letter and newspapers. The news from my parents was good. They said they had changed lodging and were better off than before, that our house in Florence had not been disturbed by German irruptions, and that mamma had begun to knit a sweater with the wool I gave her.

The news in the papers was not bad, either. The Germans were getting hit on all sides. Germany was bombed daily by hundreds of Allied planes, and many German cities were a pile of rubble. The Nazi army in Russia had to combat "General Winter," who had become their worst enemy. Thousands of German soldiers froze to death, and those who were taken prisoner by the Russians could consider themselves fortunate. I anxiously searched for any news about the fate of the millions of Jews who were put in concentration camps. A cover of silence hid those horrors carefully from the eyes and ears of public opinion. In my heart I was convinced that the Germans were going ahead with their pitiless plan to totally eliminate my beloved people. They had entered a one-way street and anti-Jewish hate served to keep their minds occupied and distract them from their own tragedy of ruined cities, deprivations of every kind, and thousands of dead and imprisoned soldiers.

The nightmare of what was happening in Hitler's land stayed with me all night long. I dreamed of cadavers piled in the snow, and the next morning I woke up in a terrible state of mind. Outside it was hailing stones as big as walnuts, so I stayed in the house reading next to the fire.

In the afternoon after the storm ended, I went for a walk in the woods with Tito. The funeral march of Beethoven's Third Symphony kept running through my mind. I walked through woods of young oak trees whose leaves dripped rain on me. I was absorbed in my own melancholy thoughts when I heard someone walking in my direction. I moved to a more elevated spot to see who it was. A young man I did not recognize was walking very slowly as though he too were wandering aimlessly about.

I picked up Tito and stroked him so he would be quiet. Leaving the path I was on, I went deeper into the thick woods where I definitely would not be seen. I crouched on the ground, damp from the rain, whispered to Tito to be good, and continued stroking him. He did not whimper, almost as though he understood the situation.

The young man continued walking, completely unaware of my presence a few meters away from him. He passed by and soon disappeared over the top of the hill. I continued my walk, turning toward the house, pleased to have avoided meeting the young man. Perhaps my reaction was extreme and I could have simply greeted him as one routinely does. That would have been the end of it. I had chosen to be wary and avoid any possible danger. Better to be safe than sorry, said the wise man.

Back at the house I ate quickly because company was coming, and I retired to my room. I read *In Dubious Battle* by Steinbeck until nine thirty. Everything was peaceful in the kitchen: Gino's customary profanity, laughter every so often, and the voices of those who were talking about matters of little importance. I decided to leave early the next day and go see Federico. I needed to talk with someone more like myself and of my same faith. With this decision I went to sleep happy and slept soundly, not even noticing when the two boys came to bed.

At eight I got up, shaved after breakfast, and at a quarter to nine I said good-bye to Gino and Erminia, telling them I was off to see a friend of mine and I would be back in time for supper.

I walked quickly; the morning air was fresh and made me feel energetic. The weather was nice again; the sky was clear and a brisk wind blew away the remaining clouds. I was in a good mood, looking forward to seeing Federico and his parents. During my walk I did not meet a human soul, and in an hour, almost without realizing it, I was in the vicinity of Carraino and began wondering how I could keep from frightening my friends with my unexpected visit.

A thread of blue smoke came from the chimney pot, which meant someone was there. I stopped a certain distance from the house to see if anyone might be outside and noticed Federico carrying firewood into the house.

"O' brodo?!" I shouted at him in our customary way. He recognized my voice and special greeting at once. "Oh, you, what are you doing!"

We embraced each other, glad to see each other after so many days, and went straight into the house. Only his father was there with him, because his mother had gone to Florence. I greeted his father warmly and we sat in the kitchen, where they offered me a cup of barley coffee. It was like the good times at Duro. Finally I was able to talk freely about everything that was on my mind, with people who understood perfectly all my problems and anxieties.

I found Federico and his father a little worse off physically. The solitude in such an isolated and gloomy place had left its mark. I felt very sorry for both of them. I began by telling them everything I had done after leaving them at Duro, giving a detailed description of all the family members where I was staying and bringing them up to date about my living in complete isolation from the rest of the world.

They felt the same way. In fact, in that wolf's den it would not have been possible to live any differently.

I informed them of what I had read in the newspapers and gave them the latest news about my parents. In turn, they told me about the life they were leading. Nothing was satisfactory about it, unfortunately. Their total isolation made it very difficult. Provisions for food, news about relatives and friends and about what was happening in the world were very hard to come by, and Federico's mother, because she was a woman and therefore less "visible," had to provide all the necessities. Fortunately, their house in Florence had not been revisited by the Germans, and they had not heard of any hostile visits at Duro.

They spent their long, slow days reading books, playing chess, and taking walks through the woods when the weather permitted. There did not seem to be much difference between their daily existence and mine. Perhaps they were better off because they had each other's company to make them feel less isolated. I told them about Tito and how he was a constant and faithful companion to me. Federico and I recalled the nice days spent together at Duro. It was like watching a good adventure film again. Neither he nor I had the slightest idea what fate had in store for us. Everything seemed so in flux that we did not dare make any predictions. We lived day by day with only one certainty: the important thing was just to live.

I told Federico I had decided to shave my mustache and beard—not as a matter of esthetics or strategy, but only because the long beard was beginning to give me problems with little boils that occasionally appeared on my face.

They asked me to stay for lunch and I accepted with pleasure. Signor Benadì prepared an excellent lunch and I was amazed how at his age he had such energy and the desire to do so much. He was obviously well educated and could discuss any subject. It was a revelation to see how well he coped with the pots and pans. We ate happily and I noticed that after a time Federico's spirit and his father's had noticeably improved. I would have liked to stay longer to prolong that magic moment.

After lunch Federico and I took a walk through the woods. The scenery was thick with plants and blooming with a variety of greens, but much darker and more forbidding than at Poggiarso. A beautiful panorama could be seen from the top of the hill where I stayed: on clear days you could see as far as the Pistoiese mountains and the Valdarno, while Federico was at the bottom of a dark, narrow little valley, with no vista, and you felt constricted by the surrounding hills.

At four in the afternoon I decided it was time to go, because I did not want to return in the dark. I promised Federico I would come back. We embraced, wishing each other good luck. I said good-bye to his father and went away with the sadness one feels when leaving a friend. I got back to Poggiarso a little after five. Every one was in a good mood. Unexpectedly, Gino greeted me very warmly, asking many questions about Federico, where he was staying, and so forth. When I told him how gloomy Carraino seemed in comparison to Poggiarso, I thought Gino seemed relieved. Maybe he had been afraid I had gone to see if I could stay with Federico. I was happy to see that in a certain way Gino was glad to have me there.

The following morning I went through with my plan to shave my mustache and beard. It was a job that took some time, especially since I had no warm water and hated to shave with cold water. Then those bothersome boils jumped out in all their ugly glory after the shave, and I carefully medicated them. I made my entrance into the kitchen with a clean-shaven face and at first no one seemed to notice. Then Erimina suddenly exclaimed: "Oh, Enrico, where in the world is your beard?" I explained the reason for the shave and they all commented about how I looked without mustache and beard. The majority decided it made me look younger. So much the better!

The time was approaching for visitors in the kitchen and I went to finish *In Dubious Battle,* lying on the bed. Fortunately they went away soon and, with my freedom of movement recovered, I went to my customary pile of straw with Tito and my book. This time little Maria wanted to come with us. She begged me to let her turn the pages of my book as I read. "One man's meat," I thought. Then she started playing with Tito. They were so funny romping around like two puppies. It was interesting to see how Tito adapted to Maria's age when playing with her. He clearly realized she was small and closer to him mentally.

Right after dinner I escaped to my room with my book, because it was Saturday evening and some people were coming over. Not only did they make a terrific racket, but at a certain point one of the boys, excusing himself, came to ask for my oil lamp because they needed more light in the kitchen. I gave it to him very unwillingly and remained in total darkness. Good-bye book!

Lying in the dark with my eyes wide open I thought about what I was doing. I asked myself if this voluntary seclusion was right. Actually, what was bothering me was probably bothering my hosts also. Should I face up to it by speaking to Gino, or was it better to let everything take its own course? I decided that for the moment it was better not to muddy the waters with problems that Gino might not even be thinking about. Perhaps my insecurity was making things look blacker than necessary.

How long I might be at Poggiarso was anyone's guess. I paid for my expenses regularly and tried to have as friendly a relationship as possible with all the family members, especially Gino, whose true character I was beginning to put into perspective. He was the classic figure of the *padre padrone,* with the vanity of the "dominant male" in the family circle, thinking he had the right solution for every problem. Consequently he would not allow Erminia or any of his children to express their point of view. This made me unhappy, because I witnessed some absurd arguments where I often saw more good sense in the family members than in Gino himself. However, I was careful not to interfere. Another problem was my personal hygiene. At Duro, Federico and I often went to wash in the open. It was summer when it was something pleasant to do. During the rigid winter it was unthinkable, and I had to make do by using the ceramic basin on the iron stand and the pitcher filled with water heated over the fire. It was a constant coming and going between the kitchen and bedroom, with a little towel around me that served as a kind of Tahitian sarong. Obviously, by washing in this fashion, I made a big mess in the bedroom, with water splashed everywhere. Poor Erminia had to regularly mop up the lake I left behind.

I continued helping out where I could in the fields. One morning Gino pointed out a dry, old oak tree that would be useful as firewood. I took the ax, sharpened the edge with a little file, and when I was satisfied with its sharpness, I set about chopping it down. The oak was very old and large, and must have been at least 15 meters high. Gino had shown me how to cut it in such a way as to make it fall without damaging the younger trees around it.

News from the war fronts continued to be encouraging. The Russians launched a big offensive against the Germans on November 30 and the Allies were doing the same on the Italian front. It seemed they, too, were giving considerable ax blows to the German war machine.

On the morning of December 6, I was peacefully lying on the straw reading. It was a sunny day and less cold than usual, considering the season. Tito dozed beside me. After the daily lesson with my "students," I decided to spend the rest of the day resting in the sun. I was absorbed in reading when Tito suddenly got up and jumped down from the stack barking and running toward the yard. I tried to see who was coming without leaving my refuge and to my great joy I saw Federico. With a joyful whoop I jumped down and ran to meet him. Exuberance, slaps on the back, and all the rest. He looked well and his face told me how happy he was to be with me. We went into the house and I introduced him to Erminia, who offered him something to drink. We talked to her before excusing ourselves to go out and sit on my stack of straw along with the inseparable Tito. I found out that the Germans were intensifying their hunt for Jews and had decreed, through their puppet government of the Republic of Salò, that all Jews had to be put in concentration camps and that their property was to be confiscated and distributed to "needy families." It did not take much imagination to understand that the "needy" were those of the Fascist hierarchy.

Federico said he no longer felt safe hiding at Carraino. Because it was so isolated, they were afraid that if the Fascists discovered where they were they could easily surprise and capture them in their sleep. Furthermore, to live in that sunless place, cold and humid, had become intolerable. His father was seriously thinking about finding a couple of families in Florence where they could hide. If they lived in an area where no one knew them, they might fit in with the local population. That idea did not seem very good to me, but I said nothing.

We returned to the house in time for lunch. Erminia had prepared some excellent tagliatelle with rabbit sauce. I was grateful to her for that sign of regard for Federico. We waited for the whole family to return from their various chores and sat down at the table in a good mood. Gino pontificated in an attempt to make a good impression on Federico. He even temporarily suspended his string of curses, and I must say I missed them: his conversation without *Christs* and *Madonnas* was flat and boring. I let him go on babbling as he pleased. When he finished, the rest of the family put in a timid word and the conversation went along peacefully and pleasantly.

We got up from the table, our appetites satisfied. Federico courteously took his leave of the family and I walked with him for a way on the road. I hated to see him leave. We did not know when we would see each other again. After a couple of big hugs and slaps on the back he disappeared rapidly into the thick woods. I stood there for a few seconds, wondering what fate had in store for us, and I wished him well.

I went back to the house reluctant to talk with anyone. I needed time to think about my friend's visit. It had been too long since I had had someone to talk with about the things that were important to me, someone who could make an intelligent response. Leonora was in the kitchen, just having returned from Montevarchi where she had bought me a newspaper. I glanced over it quickly. An awful thing happened at Badiaccia. Some Fascists had received a tip that a group of partisans were hiding in a cottage there and went to round them up. The partisans, about 60 of them, had reacted immediately. There was a thick exchange of fire during which two of the Fascists were killed; the partisans managed to escape without suffering any losses.

I was pleased with the outcome but worried about the possibility of a bloody reprisal against those poor farmers who had given refuge to the "rebels." This was the fierce law of the "reprisal," instigated by the Nazis in the Europe under their heel.

Badiaccia was not far from where I was staying, so I would have to be doubly careful. I decided not to alarm the family needlessly by telling them what had happened at Badiaccia, so I went on reading. The war news restored my good spirits because the Germans were taking a bashing. When I finished reading I took the paper and tossed it into the fire so no one else would see it.

The next day was Sunday and all the family went to church, including the great blasphemer! My inseparable friend and I were left in charge of the house. I was lying on the top of my pile of straw reading, when my four-legged friend suddenly jumped up barking as he had the other day. I looked in the direction where Tito was going and saw a man about 30 years old, walking with difficulty and stopping often to catch his breath. He seemed in bad shape. I let him come closer into the farmyard without showing myself, the better to observe who he was and what he might want. He was wearing a very shabby bluish military uniform, with a torn sleeve, but no distinguishing Fascist insignias.

The stranger had several days' growth of beard and an expression of someone in pain. I was sure he was not an enemy, so I got up from my "observatory" and greeted him.

"*Buon giorno.* Do you need something?"

He looked up to see where those words had come from. He saw me on top of the straw stack and with a smile that seemed more like a grimace of pain, said: "Yes, thank you. I am tired and would like a glass of water."

As he talked he came closer. Tito concluded he was dealing with a friend and stopped barking. With his tail wagging as usual, he came back to sit beside me.

I slid down and shook the visitor's hand. I must have squeezed too hard, because I heard him moan. I apologized and invited him into the house. By the slow way he went up the stone stairs I realized what poor condition the man was in. I told him to make himself comfortable by the fire and offered him a cup of hot barley coffee, which he eagerly accepted. As I poured out the hot drink, I saw him looking around the kitchen trying to get a handle on the situation. In fact, in that big house I seemed to be the only person, because there were no other voices, and I did not look like a farmer.

He took the cup in both hands to warm them. While he drank I tried to figure out his military corps. Every distinguishing insignia of rank, company, or anything usually attached to military uniforms had been removed. On his wrist was an Omega watch: symbol of a certain social level. His heavy boots were in fairly good condition. He was tall and sturdy.

"What is the nearest town from here?" he asked. He had a northern Italian accent.

"Montevarchi. But tell me, what happened to you? You don't seem to feel very well. Where did you come from? Which service are you in?"

He calmly explained what had happened: he was a fugitive from the air force, where he had the rank of Sergeant Major. The Germans had captured him twice, and twice he had escaped. During his second escape he had hurt his arm on barbed wire that had torn his sleeve and made a deep wound that hurt quite a bit. He had come by stages from Naples where he was attached to the air force and was trying to reach Milan where his family was.

As he talked he became more relaxed and cheerful. I asked him if he wanted me to disinfect his wound with tincture of iodine, and because there was no gauze in the house, I took one of my clean handkerchiefs to wrap around the wound after I had carefully cleaned it. Not the best treatment, but better than nothing. The wound was not very long or deep, nor was it inflamed. He could continue his journey without concern, I thought. I explained that I, too, was a fugitive and was staying temporarily in this farmhouse. I said nothing about being a Jew, pretending to be a military deserter like him. I could see he was pleased. Luckily he did not ask anything about the military unit I belonged to, so I did not have the trouble of telling other lies. Instead, he told me about his many and not too pleasant adventures.

All his military buddies had taken to the bush. Many had managed to cover their tracks, but some of the less fortunate ones had fallen into the claws of the Germans and had been sent in freight cars to German work camps overseen by the Republican Fascists. I asked him if he wanted to stay for lunch. The family would not be away much longer. He accepted without hesitation, poor man. It must have been many days since he had eaten a decent meal. He asked if he could take advantage of my hospitality to shave; it had been a week, and unshaven he looked too much like a fugitive. I let him use all the tools of the trade in my room, while I returned to the kitchen.

When he reappeared in the kitchen he looked ten years younger. He thanked me for the use of my razor and we talked some more about the war situation in general. He could not wait until a stop was put to Hitler's madness; he hated the Germans, but he said nothing that gave me to understand he knew what was happening to the Jews in the concentration camps. Evidently Italian servicemen were kept in the dark about these criminal acts so as not to rally their resistance toward the German domination even more.

When Gino, Erminia, and the children came in they stood open-mouthed at the sight of that soldier sitting next to the fire. I immediately explained the situation and asked Gino if he could possibly stay for lunch, and they had no objection. I must say in regard to the whole family there was a great spirit of hospitality, and this was undoubtedly a sign of their authentic goodness.

While Erminia busied herself at the stove, I let the fugitive tell his story to the rest of the family. They hung on every word. Every once in a while Gino let loose with a solemn oath of admiration for the flyer's courage. They rapidly became friends and the atmosphere grew more cheerful. We had a good meal. My partner in adversity devoured the food with incredible speed and let Erminia refill his plate as soon as he cleaned it. It was painful to watch; he was surely filling up for the next few days!

After the last glass of wine, I asked Gino to explain to the fugitive what road to take to Florence, where he might be lucky enough to find a way to Milan. He thanked the family profusely and I walked with him through the fields to the edge of the woods. Without letting the family see me, I gave him a little money.

"You might have to buy a train ticket; you'll get home quicker that way," I said. I envied that young man a little who was certainly in a difficult situation, but not as difficult as mine. We wished one another good luck. I was pleased to see that now that he had eaten he walked much more quickly and seemed to feel better.

I told Gino and Erminia how much I appreciated their helping that fugitive. They asked if I had been frightened when he arrived, and I replied that I had held my breath for a few moments until I realized he was worse off than I.

In the morning Erminia had to go to Gaiole to do some errands and while she was there, she visited Antinesca and Uncle Vico at Duro. She returned late that afternoon with some unsettling news. First of all, the carabinieri were gone from their barracks at Gaiole and had been replaced by Fascists. It seems the Fascists had no confidence in the way the carabinieri were conducting the hunt for deserters and Jews. The other news, still worse, was that Federico and his parents had suddenly left Carraino. Erminia knew nothing more about it. Of course I was very worried and sent for Santi to get more information. Santi came the next day to fill me in on what had transpired. A friend of the Benadìs had come from Florence to find them at Duro. She warned them to leave because their names were on a list of Jews whom the Germans were rounding up and sending to concentration camps. Federico and his parents left their hiding place immediately and returned to Florence where they had already thought to find hospitality among non-Jewish friends. Santi said he had seen them very briefly when they went to Duro to get some of their personal things and all three seemed very frightened.

Santi did not believe my name was on the list, but I could not have complete assurance that things stood exactly as Santi said. I also learned that Leone Passigli and other members of his family had been taken by the Germans from their villa at San Michele. This threw me for a loop. I knew Leone and his father Goffredo, both very well known in the community in Florence. They had a hosiery factory in Florence and were among the most affluent Jews. I had wondered why, with all the means at their disposal and with all the people they knew in Italy and especially outside Italy, they had never thought about going to the United States where so many of us had emigrated at the beginning of the anti-Jewish persecutions.

I tried to imagine the scene when the Germans, certainly alerted by the Fascists, erupted into their villa, taking them away violently and loading them on a military truck to be taken to an extermination camp. Those must have been awful scenes of fear and violence, and it made my flesh creep just thinking about it. It was the first time that something like that had happened to someone I knew.

After Santi told me all he knew, we said good-bye. I saw Gino walk him to the end of the yard and they talked quietly. I understood at once that Santi was telling him what had happened and that bothered me. Now Gino would worry because his family would be in the middle if by unfortunate chance the Germans came to get me.

That evening no one mentioned Santi's visit. However, I perceived a rather tense atmosphere in the house. I knew that Gino had told Erminia, and from their furtive glances I understood they would have liked to talk to me about it but did not have the courage. I had trouble going to sleep that night, and when I did I had continual nightmares. I awoke in the morning more tired than when I went to bed.

CHAPTER 13

Hiding Out at Enzoli

G ino found the courage to talk to me when I came in the kitchen to eat breakfast. He began with a story that seemed completely invented: a friend of his, a certain Dante, had told him that I was in danger and it would be better if I moved somewhere else. I pretended to believe it and let him go on. He continued: he was very worried for my safety and was afraid that it was risky (always for me, naturally) to stay in his house and he had sent Antinesca to ask her father if he would put me up for a while. The truth, I later learned, was that Antinesca had become worried after Santi told her what had happened to the Benadìs and had asked Gino to convince me to move.

No matter how things stood, it was clearly the time for me to get out of there. Poggiarso was no longer a safe place for me, and I could not blame Gino for wanting me to go. I would have felt the same in his shoes. Luckily for me, Antinesca had shown herself to be more than equal to the situation and if it had not been for her, I would not have had the slightest idea of what to do. I thanked Gino for his concern and assured him that I understood his position perfectly. I would go to Antinesca's father's house as soon as possible.

The only member of the family who seemed relieved by this decision was Gino. He was in excellent humor, while Erminia, Leonora, and Leonetta seemed sad, with a kind of tenderness. Another period of my life as a fugitive was ending and a new one beginning. The daily lessons I had taught not only with patience, but also with satisfaction with my students, were ending. The interminable reading on the straw stack with the companionship of the faithful Tito was ending. And, thank goodness, the dashes from the kitchen when some guest was about to arrive and reading in the weak light of the oil lamp attached to the headboard were also ending.

As happens every time we have to leave people or places, I felt a part of me break off and remain at Poggiarso. I would certainly remember them in the future, as they would remember me. After all, we had all run the same risks.

I had been at Poggiarso from November 8 without a break and now, after more than a month and a half, I had to change my lodgings again. Gino's character aside, the women were sweet and protective, treating me like a son and big brother. What more could I have asked?

Beppe told Antinesca they could keep me for 20 days. It was not long, but I had no choice. My only hope was that after I was settled things would take a turn for the better and I would be able to stay a few more weeks.

That atmosphere of deep sorrow hovering about the house did not agree with me. I was already downhearted enough. I decided that Christmas day, the last day before my move, I would spend with my old friends at Duro. I wanted to see them again and return to the spirit of the times when Federico and I were together. I told Erminia of my idea and asked her to let Leonora and Leonetta come with me to eat supper with the Brogi. She had no objection. Beppe's son and Antinesca's brother, Costantino, would come with us also and take me to my new lodgings the next day.

So the four of us set off happily toward the lovely places where I had spent the end of summer. I seemed to be reliving my life backward. The two girls had put on their Sunday best. I had no decent clothes to show off and had to be content with what I had. The important thing was to spend a happy evening with old friends without too much gloom. And that we did.

It was getting late and I did not want the two girls who had come with me to get too tired, so we left the Brogis and went to see my friends at Duro. I could not leave without telling them good-bye. We pulled Sergio, Marina, and Uncle Vico out of bed, where they had been sleeping like rocks. All three came into the kitchen in their nightshirts and started up the fire. We sat on the famous benches inside the fireplace, where Federico and I had spent so many evenings. I felt very nostalgic! When they offered us something to drink, we accepted, of course. They would have been offended if we had not. The wine and the warmth from the fire made us even more exhilarated, and we joked around for a good half hour.

Now it was really getting late: one o'clock in the morning. With a thousand hugs and kisses, we said good-bye and Leonetta and Leonora and I took off. It was cold, but the road sloped steeply upward and the walk warmed us up. In spite of the exertion, we talked constantly, and Leonetta confessed that her father was happy to have me leave, and not only for the danger I represented. He did not want to give up his freedom. He felt that his hands had been tied by my presence because every time he wanted to invite friends over for a game of cards Erminia would tell him not to let them stay too long so I would not have to stay shut up in my room. I also learned from Giulia that when things had started to get a little awkward with her father, Leonetta had offered to go stay at Montevarchi with an aunt so I could stay at Poggiarso. That way I could use her ration of wheat because what the family had at their disposal was not enough for an extra person. I was moved by this generous gesture and said so to Leonetta, who laughed it off, saying it was not true. But I knew it was.

We reached the house around two o'clock. The night was very still and cold, but not a breath of wind stirred. In the black sky the stars shone with a flickering but intense light. I kissed my sweet party companions good night and we all went straight to bed.

The first thing I did the next morning was write a postcard to Liliana, informing her I was moving. We had devised a kind of secret code for our correspondence. I addressed my postcards to the owner of the house where Liliana was hiding with papa and mamma. I wrote as if I were Erminia, with all the appropriate female adjectives, and signed her name. If by chance my cards should fall into the wrong hands, they would seem like an exchange of news between two women.

I wrote that I was "changing jobs" and that I was going "to work for another family." I assured her that everything was going well and I was in excellent health—it was enough to relieve their minds, or almost! For the rest of the morning I packed my suitcase and backpack. I had accumulated so incredibly much I had to fill a second suitcase. I sent Leonetta to the butcher nearby to buy some meat because there was no telling what the food situation would be in the new house. Among rabbits, chickens, and pigeons, Loretta brought back seven carcasses that I wrapped in a bundle.

After I finished packing, we sat down at the table for a big farewell lunch. Leonetta's twin, Loretta, joined us—she was a large girl, married to a farmer some distance from Poggiarso. We quickly struck up a friendship. In spite of all we had eaten the previous evening, we were hungry. Our spirits were rather high, each one for different reasons, and in some cases for opposite reasons. Gino was happy because a stifling weight on his freedom had been removed, and I was happy because I hoped to have a better kind of life in the house where I was going. Perhaps the women in the house were a little less elated. Maybe they were sorry I was going away so soon.

Toward four in the afternoon Beppe's son Gosto arrived, the boy who would accompany me to my new house and help with my baggage. We had to leave the second suitcase because I had a very heavy backpack in addition to the package of meat. Gosto could not handle a second suitcase with one on his shoulder. Antinesca would bring the second suitcase in a day or two.

I saluted each member of the family: first Gino, who even wanted to embrace me ("no harm in kissing an enemy good-bye," I said to myself); then Erminia, with tears in her eyes, and Leonetta and Leonora, without undue emotion; then little Maria, who asked if I would be back to give lessons; then Silvano and Mario, my two bedmates, who shook my hand vigorously.

I loaded the backpack on my shoulders and carried the package of meat in my hand. Gosto heaved my suitcase on his shoulders and down the hill we went in the direction of Valdarno. Tito, my sweet, faithful companion of so many tranquil and solitary hours, trotted along beside us, and every once in a while he looked up at me as if to ask what was going on. I think he must have been very bewildered by the unusual activity. We walked quickly down the descending path and were soon far from the house. I stopped, bent over him, stroked his muzzle gently, and told him he had to go back home now, pointing in the direction of the hilltop. He seemed to understand, although he was not much inclined to obey, and continued to jump on me and lick me. Then I clapped my hands hard and yelled sternly: "Go home, Tito!" This time he obeyed, going back up the path. When he turned a couple of times to give me tender looks, I stood still with my arm outstretched and a stern look on my face (it was an effort), pointing the way home. Finally convinced, and perhaps disappointed, he took off running up the hill.

Gosto and I started up our hike again. Now the path was no longer descending, so our pace slowed. The more we walked, the heavier our baggage became. It soon grew dark, but luckily Gosto knew the paths like the back of his hand. If I had been alone I surely would have been lost. In spite of the fact that I had an excellent guide, going through those thick, dark woods was anything but easy. My hiking boots hurt my feet, and then we had to cross streams of different widths, and in the darkness I could not see where to put my feet on the rocks. To keep from slipping in, I decided that the simplest thing would be to walk in the water. So for the rest of the time I walked with my feet squishing around in boots full of water.

Around seven thirty we thankfully reached our goal. I was tired and sweaty in spite of the cold. My new house was in a locality called Enzoli. In the dark I tried to get oriented. The house was pleasantly situated halfway up a hillside. Thick chestnut woods surrounded it, which meant we were at a high altitude. Interspersed with the chestnut trees were enormous tufts of yellow broom corn. An excellent hiding place, was my instinctive conclusion.

Things were less than flourishing around the house, suggesting these farmers were rather poor. We were welcomed by Gosto's mother, Settimia, by his father, Beppe, and by his sister, Alivarda. (I have often wondered where these Tuscan country folk find such names.) Settimia was a large woman of medium height, with her gray hair pulled back and tied at the neck. She had prominent, almost masculine, features—a typical countrywoman. Beppe was a little man, smaller than his wife, with a fiery red face probably caused by his liberal imbibing. He was balding and tried to comb what little remaining hair he had over his pate, making some incredible swirls and counterswirls. His mustache resembled Hitler's. A fall from a chestnut tree had left his arm impaired. Because of this he could not do everything that needed doing and often had to be helped by his wife or Gosto.

Beppe was a man of few words, and he expressed those few in a primitive fashion. His hands shook continually, evidently a sign of his alcoholic condition. Unlike Gino, Beppe did not curse, because Settimia strictly forbade swearing. She did everything possible to control her husband's behavior. Besides his immoderate love for alcohol, he had nearly been institutionalized after becoming violent and threatening the family with a pruning knife.

Alivarda was a tall slip of a girl, 14 years old, with a mild, sweet nature and small, delicate, but not beautiful features. She wore short skirts that left most of her long legs uncovered, revealing the thorn scratches she got in the woods. She had developed early, as did all the country girls, even though she was almost without breasts. Gosto was about 16. Thin, taller than his father, with bright eyes in an expressive face and a tuft of brown tousled hair, he was almost always smiling and had a nice disposition. A mixture of his father and mother, he seemed to take the best from each.

I noticed that, aside from Beppe (who had difficulty in speaking and could not be understood when he did manage to blurt out something), the rest of the family expressed themselves well enough. They did not use vulgar expressions and carefully avoided the kind of suggestive subjects so common in other houses. Finally was Venusta, another daughter who lived in Montevarchi, where she worked as a maid in a Fascist's house. I was not thrilled by this proximity to the Fascist element. The idea that Venusta might let something slip about the man her family was keeping in the house at Enzoli was unnerving. I promised myself to speak frankly with the girl the first time she came to visit her parents.

After the introductions and pleasantries, it was time to eat, and I hurriedly washed my hands in the stone sink in the kitchen. After putting my backpack and suitcase in a corner, I gave Settimia the package of meat. I told her to use it as she saw fit for me and the family. I noticed at the table that everyone sat straight except Beppe, who leaned sideways because of his arm. Everything was already on the table and we ate quickly. That suited me, because I was anxious to take off my water-soaked boots and socks; I did not want to catch cold.

Gosto took me to his room, which was also to be mine. We would sleep in a medium-size bed with a gray canvas mattress filled with dry corn shucks. It was the first time I had seen such a mattress—all hills and dales with the occasional thin piece of cornstalk poking through the canvas that would surely bother our sleep.

The roof was low and supported by wooden beams upon which the roof tiles rested. I had not the slightest doubt that one would suffer the cold there in the winter and the heat in the summer. The walls were covered with lumpy stucco that at one time must have been white but now was an indefinite color, dominated by gray cobwebs. The furnishings of the room were spartan, speaking euphemistically. There was only one chair, the usual ceramic washbasin on a stand with a pitcher, and little mirror hanging from a long nail in the wall. A kind of coatrack was on the other side of the room. Air and light came from a shutterless little window. Here, too, no electricity, no running water. The only comfort, if one can call it that, was the "priest," as the Tuscan peasants call it, that Settimia put in the bed each evening, consisting of a terra-cotta pan filled with coals from the fireplace. The warm pan hung from a hook inside a kind of dome constructed of strips of bent wood that kept the blankets from burning. This warmed the bed before I crawled in and helped compensate for the uncomfortable mattress, the most miserable I have ever experienced.

The rest of the house was in more or less the same condition. The kitchen followed the common plan, except that the furniture was more modest. The large fireplace was completely blackened by years of smoke, and the "andirons" for holding the burning logs were two long stones about 60 centimeters apart. A large iron suet-coated chain with a hook hung down from the chimney. On the hook was a copper pot for boiling water for a variety of purposes: cooking, washing oneself, washing clothes, and so forth.

In the bedroom I managed to get my boots and socks off and returning barefoot put everything near the fire to dry, careful not let them all be reduced to ashes. While sitting in front of the fireplace to warm my feet and legs still numb from the water and cold, I thought it only right to bring up the conditions of my staying there with Beppe and Settimia.

To avoid an embarrassing situation, I started by saying I would pay them 25 lire a day in exchange for my food and lodging. Their eyes opened wide in unison with their mouths. Their reaction was completely unexpected. They said it was too much and they would be satisfied with less.

Because I had already mentioned the amount it seemed miserly to reduce it, so I told them I would rather stick with my offer than give up that minimum of comfort and good nourishment I had been accustomed to. The couple was happy and said I would always be welcome in their house. Another example of how money talks.

I felt encouraged because it seemed an auspicious beginning for a stay that I hoped would be longer than the original 20 days Beppe had planned. Excited by the prospect of all that money, Beppe suddenly became very loquacious. Yet, his tongue could not keep up with the speed of his thoughts, and he said things I had difficulty in deciphering. Evidently the wine drunk at supper began to have its effect. Beppe realized that talking took too much of an effort and decided to remain mute, leaving Settimia to hold up his end of the conversation. After a while his head lolled on his chest and he slept like a baby.

I stayed to talk with Settimia and Gosto, recounting some of my previous experiences with other families and my intention to lead a normal life with them, in a way that did not interfere with their routine. I asked if among their friends who visited them there were any Fascists, or worse, Nazi sympathizers. They assured me they were all anti-Fascists. I then spoke of their other daughter, Venusta, who was a maid for some Fascists in Montevarchi. I said I would like to talk with her because I was worried about her relations with those people. Settimia agreed and promised she would ask Venusta to come as soon as possible.

In the meantime, Beppe started snoring and often nearly slipped out of his chair. Settimia and Gosto took him under his arms and, without disturbing his slumber, put him to bed. It seemed the time had come for me to go to bed also, after such a tiring but generally a very positive day. To get to my bedroom I had to cross through the master bedroom, which was not very convenient, especially if I had to get up to go to the toilet. But it was not necessary that night. In fact, seeing that the "priest" had adequately warmed Gosto's and my bed, I crawled under the blankets, making the corn leaves squeak scandalously under my weight, and slept like a rock.

When I woke up the next morning, Settimia brought me a pitcher of water to wash with and I was astonished when I discovered it was hot. I had not expected such treatment, which up to that time I had not received. Because of the polar temperature in the room I particularly enjoyed my wash, but not before I thanked my benefactress for such a "warm" thought and expressed the hope that the gesture would be repeated every day.

While I was eating breakfast, Beppe came in after taking care of the oxen. The tipsiness from the night before was completely gone, and he began a long discourse about his arm and shoulder, which had been bothering him for some time. I did not understand where this was going, but he soon came to the point. "Antinesca told me you studied to be a doctor and you cured people at the first place you stayed. It would be a big favor if you'd look at this shoulder that gives me so much trouble."

I hurriedly explained I had not "studied to be a doctor," even though that had been my intention, but Signor Benito Mussolini had not allowed it. However, the desire to cure people had never left me, and what I had done for some people was dictated only by a little knowledge of hygiene and some experience in first aid.

"Anyway, let's see what I can do for you," and I added, "without guaranteeing anything."

I had hardly finished speaking before he pulled off his shirt and undershirt and stood there bare chested waiting for me to give him a "checkup." The pain was located in his shoulder and part of his left arm just below his shoulder. I took a little talcum powder I had with me and began slowly to massage all the sore muscles. While I massaged him, Beppe would occasionally let out a moan of pleasure, like a cat purrs when it is petted. Evidently the massage was giving him some relief. After his muscles were well warmed by the massage, I took his wrist and had him make some slow movements up, forward, and back. He did not seem to have too much trouble moving his arm. I "prescribed" several days of rest and made him a kind of sling with a strip of cloth that went around his neck to support his arm comfortably. I promised to massage him twice a day until he was healed and asked him to buy some camphorated alcohol, useful for massages, and some talcum powder.

Beppe could not thank me enough and said he felt better after the first "treatment." Good. One more reason for being welcome in his home.

I continued this physiotherapy conscientiously every morning and evening for about a half hour each time, and after two weeks, my patient considered himself nearly healed. I must confess I had not anticipated such a rapid and positive solution.

The news of Beppe's recovery spread swiftly, and I had to deal with different cases like a real doctor. First, a farmer who lived nearby arrived to show me a lump that had appeared on the back of his neck. I had never seen anything like it and I did not have the slightest idea what to advise that poor man who had put himself in my hands with such blind faith. I began by carefully washing with soap and water that fiery red infected area and in doing so I could see that his neck had not been washed for weeks. Then I disinfected everything well with alcohol, and over the inflamed part I spread Antipiol, which I took everywhere with me. I told him to buy another tube of Antipiol to continue the treatment and to keep it covered with a clean handkerchief tied around his neck. He told me that after washing, disinfecting, and applying the salve it burned less and he went away happy and satisfied.

The next day he returned for a second treatment and brought with him one of his children, a boy about 15 years old who also had two boils on his neck full of pus. I cleaned and disinfected them, after giving them a good scrub with soap and water. The inevitable Antipiol, two little bandages on the neck, and I sent them on their way satisfied and full of unending gratitude. Poor people, I said to myself, they think I performed miracles without realizing that if they washed more often they would not have these problems. In about a week both father and son were better, and every time I saw them I asked if they had washed their necks and everything else that day. They swore they would never forget to do it.

In the course of this "free health clinic" a neighboring farm woman of about 30 came to me to complain that her hair was falling out. It did not seem to me that she had lost much hair judging by the thick mop she still had. Anyway, I remembered that one time our family doctor had said that very often patients came to him with only imaginary ailments and that to make them happy he would prescribe medicine that would neither harm nor help. I adapted to the situation and told the good woman to wash her hair twice a week with shampoo and not with laundry soap as was her custom, and with every washing to massage in some "Petroleum," a hair lotion I had sometimes used. I never saw that woman again and consequently never knew the results of the treatment I prescribed.

My little efforts also brought me nutritional rewards. The farmer I had cured, as well as his son, came by the house occasionally to bring me eggs and even a chicken. I gave them to Settimia to use for the whole family.

When the weather was bad I stayed by the fire to read the books I had brought with me. I began a series of Pirandello's novels that kept me occupied for weeks until the weather improved and I went out for walks through the chestnut woods. I found a hill higher than all the surrounding ones from which I could have a 360-degree panoramic view of breathtaking beauty. I saw the whole Arno valley dominated by snow-covered Pratomagno. I could see a piece of Vallombrosa and the decline of the hills almost as far as Arezzo. But the thing that thrilled me the most was that from my observatory I could see the squadrons of Allied Flying Fortresses that came from the south of Italy and dropped their bombs on the train tracks and the industrial centers of Valdarno. At first it would sound like the distant rumble of thunder. Then the rumble would slowly become more distinct and I would recognize the unmistakable sound of a hundred airplane engines quickly coming nearer. I tried to count the number of planes and at times they were more than 100. Then all at once, as if obeying a single command, from every Fortress would fall bomb clusters. As they descended, the shiny bombs gleamed brightly like mirrors in the sun's reflection. Then I saw plumes of black smoke and, after a few seconds, came the explosions. It was an unbelievable spectacle. Only once during these incursions did the counterdefense enter into action with little explosions of white clouds, too low to hit the Allied planes.

News from my family was very infrequent. Gosto brought me a letter from Liliana that had been sent to Poggiarso. She told me she also had started giving lessons to some children where she was. She gave me some good news about Gianna who was still in hiding nearby. Papa and mamma were well and had a friend of the farmer's who worked in city hall make all three of them false documents. This way they would not worry if they had to show their identity cards. I wrote her a quick response.

I learned one day that some English prisoners who had managed to escape from a German concentration camp were hiding out in those parts. I tried to find out where they were, but there was no way to get precise information. Obviously the prisoners did not want their hiding place to be discovered, so they moved constantly from one place to another. Because they slept out in the open, it was easy for them to continually switch locations.

Realizing my search was going nowhere, I returned to daily reality and gave Gosto a hand, cutting firewood in the woods with an ax and a pruning knife. I liked doing this kind of work, especially in the winter when it is harder to work up a sweat. We brought the oxen and cart into the woods and loaded up the largest pieces of wood, which we then split into smaller pieces for burning in the fireplace. With the rest of the firewood, Gosto began to build a pit to make charcoal, which he did with expertise. I watched closely in order to remember each particular step, realizing it is easier to do than to describe.

After the stack of firewood was covered with dirt from the woods in the form of a dome, Gosto bored holes into it, starting at the bottom. Then he set fire to the wood in the circle. This began to burn slowly and at first a thick white smoke came out of the holes. Gradually the smoke became more dense, and when it was a transparent blue color, Gosto bored another row of holes inside the dome. When some white, thick smoke began to come out of the second row it meant that another, higher, layer of wood had begun to burn. Then Gosto closed the first row of holes in order to keep the wood underneath from burning. And so he continued up to the dome of earth. We let it cool and after a few days we took down the dome of dirt and removed the charcoal, which we put inside some barrels that the oxen brought to the house in the cart. Now Settimia woul have charcoal for her kitchen stove.

I tried to make myself as useful as I could, such as by taking the couple of dozen of sheep to pasture. Every evening Beppe milked them in order to make small cheeses. Then, when the season was right, he rented a ram to provide lambs that Beppe used partly for eating and partly for raising.

I was happy to be involved in this more relaxing life, busy with various activities, with no fear the neighbors would see me. They were coming to visit us more and more frequently. There was a boy who said he knew how to play the harmonica. He was not such a remarkable musician in my opinion, but his little tunes were enough to accompany the rather awkward dancing of some girls who came to spend the evening with him. His harmonica also allowed them to show off some songs typical of the Chianti region, whose origins certainly went far back in time. The songs were not so bad, except that they were repeated endlessly by those warblers with a limited repertoire.

Anyway, the evenings were pleasant and I made friends with all the farmers in the neighborhood. They all knew I was hiding from the Fascists and Germans and we had an agreement that if, heaven forbid, they saw or heard about any individuals or groups snooping around, they would tell me at once in order to give me time to hide in the woods. It was not a 100 percent sure solution, but at least it gave me an extra bit of peace that certainly did not hurt.

As she promised, Settimia wrote a postcard to Venusta, saying that she did not feel very well and would like her to come home. After a few days Venusta appeared, the only member of the family I still had not met. She arrived one noon on a Sunday, after asking her employers for two days off to be with her parents. Venusta was about 20. She was not tall. In fact, she was the shortest in the family. She had beautiful, long and wavy, dark brown hair. Her face was pleasant enough: shapely nose and large beautiful eyes. Her expression was sweet and she laughed easily. I would say she was the best looking of the whole family. You could see she was fond of Gosto and had a similar character. She was respectful toward her mother, but less so with Beppe, probably because of his drinking.

I introduced myself and outlined my situation, which she had already heard about from her sister Antinesca. Her cordiality made it easy for me to broach the subject on my mind: the family she worked for. I explained my fears that she might accidentally let it slip that her parents were harboring a fugitive, with consequences that could be disastrous, not only for me but also for her entire family. I could never let their lives be jeopardized because of me.

My little speech had the hoped-for effect. The situation bothered her because, aside from the fact that she lived with a Fascist family, the danger that the Germans might discover me was real. I agreed and assured her we had taken all possible precautions to keep this from happening. She asked me to let her think over the whole situation calmly and we would talk about it the next day.

We changed the subject and went on to discuss more pleasant things. Working with a middle-class family had made Venusta more refined. She was astute enough in her own right, and one could tell she was in contact with quite a different world from her own. She told me one of the sons of the family where she worked had been courting her for some time and was doing all he could to get her into bed. She had always refused, and he had occasionally become violent, and once had even slapped her. I asked her why she stayed there under those conditions. The parents of that crude young man were good people in spite of their political ideas, and Venusta needed to work because that was the family's only income. It was painful, but I had to admit she had no choice. At least, I suggested, she could speak to the boy's parents and let them know how things were. It was up to his parents to make him behave.

For the two days Venusta was home she did not sit around idly but helped Settimia with the household chores while I went out into the fields with Beppe and Gosto. Beppe's arm continued improving and gradually regained its normal use.

Tuesday afternoon Venusta got together the few things she was taking back with her. As she had promised, she talked to me about the problem of keeping my presence with her family secret. She was sure of herself: she would never let it be known that I was there. About this I could be certain. Anyway, she was not at all sure she wanted to work in Montevarchi because almost every day the Allied bombers came and she was very afraid. Many people had already left Montevarchi for the country. She would stay as long as she could hold out, and then if the situation became intolerable, she could come back home, resolving both her problems and mine. Gosto and I walked with her part of the way and then Venusta and I parted like old friends.

The weeks went by quickly. I was perfectly settled into the work routine of the little farm. I had chores that I performed automatically each day, such as taking the sheep to pasture for three or four hours, making the chaff for the oxen and giving them their fodder mornings and evenings, and making several trips to the well each day. The rest of my time I spent reading or talking with Gosto and Settimia. It was once more difficult to communicate with Beppe. After the enthusiasm aroused by the payment of 25 lire a day and by his arm being cured, he grew more silent and taciturn, even with his family. He was almost completely excluded and no one paid much attention to him. I did not feel obliged to initiate conversation with him, either: I would not have known what to say.

In the evenings, Beppe was almost always in a state that varied from slight intoxication to real drunkenness. As long as he stayed within the limits of alcoholic euphoria it was tolerable; he could enter in the conversation of the rest of the family with some stupid, senseless comments. And then he would remain silent, ignoring the discussions of the others. On the other hand, if he got very drunk things changed for the worse. Beppe would hold forth with his stuttering speech without beginning or end. Gesturing with his good arm, he would rise on his unsteady feet and amplify the concept, if such it can be called, of what he had said. We would all listen to him in silence for a bit without even trying to understand what he was saying. At any rate, it would have been impossible to understand him because his tongue stuck to his palate and what came forth was nothing more than indecipherable gibberish.

Soon we would take up the subject again where we had left off, ignoring Beppe. That was when the real torture began. Realizing he was being totally ignored, and balancing as well as he could, Beppe would get up again and this time begin to cuss a blue streak. Strangely enough, his curses were perfectly understandable. He would shout and threaten death to each member of the family in turn. If all of us did not know he was drunk out of his mind we would have taken off like scared rabbits. Instead, Settimia and her children did not turn a hair. They would take him by the arm, one on each side, and literally lifting him from the floor (he was small and lightweight anyway), they would carry him to his room and put him to bed fully clothed. It was a scene that had its humorous side: here was this little man kicking in the air and continuing to swear while his wife and son, unperturbed, removed him from the room. In bed, as if by magic, he would fall into a profound sleep and snore until the next morning. When he awoke the next day he remembered absolutely nothing of the scene in which he played the leading role.

It was hard living with someone like that. I mentioned it one day to Settimia and asked her if in the past Beppe had ever followed through with the violence he threatened every time he got drunk. She said that only once had he taken up a pruning knife, but she had managed to get it away from him. She added that sometimes they had thought of putting him away for a time in a hospital to get him detoxified, but then they had always dropped the idea in the hope that he would at least cut back on the amount of wine he drank each day.

From my point of view, he was a walking time bomb that might explode at any moment, involving me too. I felt he was a real danger I could not take lightly.

Every Sunday morning I settled up with Beppe. I paid him the 25 lire allowance plus anything extra that Settimia had to buy just for me. Oddly enough, the biggest problem was with bread. The amount of grain each farmer could keep for his own needs was limited, and my presence did not simplify the problem. Settimia always cooked enough food, especially homemade tagliatelle and lasagna, but I was a voracious bread eater. The ration card I brought with me had expired, and in order to satisfy my needs I had to buy a good eight kilos of wheat every week from some farmers Beppe knew. Luckily, I always found them amenable.

Beppe bought one of those little pasta-making machines for Settimia to make various kinds of pasta. She would work up the dough and then with the machine she made (especially for me) tagliatelle, spaghettini, and other kinds of pastas.

One day, a country woman came to our house carrying her two-year-old child. I had never seen her before. In fact, she came from a rather distant house. She came up to the kitchen and asked Settimia if she could talk to Enrico. Settimia pointed to me and introduced me to the woman. I asked her what she wanted and she said she wanted me to look at her baby who a few days before had accidentally sat on a nearly red-hot fireplace stone. The baby's bottom had been completely bare, as is the custom in the countryside, and the hot stone had severely burned one buttock.

Before coming to me the woman had tried to treat the burn and relieve the baby's pain by applying some fresh cow manure. My first impulse was to tell her that she was crazy, but I refrained.

"And then?" I asked. "What other remedy did you try?"

"A poultice of herbs, lard, and eggs."

"And you think your child can be healed with all these disgusting things? It's a miracle if it's not already infected."

I made it clear to the woman that I did not take any responsibility for her son's cure for two reasons: first, because I was not a doctor; and second, because the child's wound could very well be infected, in which case he would have to be treated in a hospital.

Very unwillingly, I steeled myself to look at the poor child. The mother undressed him so I could see the disaster. The burnt surface was covered with a yellowish dry scab.

I decided to see what was going on underneath the scab. If it was infected, I would send the mother and child directly to the nearest hospital. I asked Settimia to boil some water for 20 minutes. After the sterile water had cooled a bit, I soaked a cotton ball in it and rubbed the scab until it softened. Then, very gently, I began to remove the top layer. A noticeably thinner layer remained over the open wound. The poor child began to cry with pain. Eventually, I discovered that the area was not infected. Naturally, the skin was still inflamed from the burn, but a trip to the hospital was no longer necessary.

I dried the wound with some gauze and left it open for a few minutes. Then I took the famous tube of Antipiol and made ample use of this miraculous salve. The little boy was not crying any longer, a sign that the burn had stopped hurting.

I told the mother that I would have to medicate the child twice a day, and that she should change his underpants daily. And I told her not to touch the wound for any reason.

Every morning at nine and every evening at seven, the woman returned with the child and I checked his wound and the surrounding area. Each time it was less inflamed, a sign that it was healing. I reapplied the Antipiol and sent them home. To my great satisfaction, by the end of the tenth day the entire wound was covered by thin, rosy new skin. Now that the danger of infection had passed, I told the mother that she no longer needed to bring the child to me and showed her how to apply the salve. It is impossible to describe the mother's joy. She wanted to pay me, but of course I refused.

One afternoon toward the middle of February Venusta came home with two large suitcases. They were so heavy I wondered how she managed to carry them. Clearly she had returned for good. She went into the kitchen and fell exhausted onto a chair. The poor girl was sweating and out of breath. She told us that she had quit work because the continual alarms and bombings had made life unbearable.

The family she worked for was leaving for a village beside Pratomagno. I was happy about her decision. One less danger to worry about.

Settimia and Beppe were also happy. They would have to get along without the money their daughter made, but they would have her help around the house and in the fields. At that time we had begun to spade the rows of vines, prune them, and tie the bent branches. I put to good use my experience gained at Duro under Santi's tutelage. Venusta gave a hand at pruning the vines and came with me to watch the sheep in the afternoon. We spent three or four hours together while the sheep grazed, and she told me what had happened with the young man who had courted her and wanted to take her to bed. There were some stormy scenes that ended with nothing more than some buttons torn off Venusta's blouse. I noticed that while she recounted these episodes, she described them slowly, with the most graphic details, as if wanting to excite my imagination. I have to admit that it worked. I had no reason not to believe what she said, and therefore I listened without making any comment or asking indiscreet questions.

The days began to slowly lengthen. Spring would be here soon and nature would awaken from her winter lethargy. That prospect put me in a good mood. My hiking boots that had gone many kilometers and dug many hours were beginning to show signs of wear. The upper parts were fine, but the soles were in bad shape. If Santi were here I would have had him resole them. I asked Beppe if he could send Gosto to Montevarchi to have them resoled by a cobbler there. Gosto took them down the next day and in two days they came back with such nice soles they seemed new. I spent 150 lire but I would be able to walk for some time longer in my old boots.

The evenings were more pleasant than usual. Beppe seemed to be drinking less, and consequently never surpassed a light buzz. Very likely it was Venusta's presence that affected his behavior, as well as Settima's strong admonitions. I often played cards with him while the women gossiped among themselves, and Gosto read for the umpteenth time the *Giornalino di Giamburrasca* I had given him. Occasionally a farmer would come to visit who had electricity in his house and was able to listen to Radio London in the evenings. He was a well-informed young man and passed on the latest war news he got from the English newscasts.

I could not wait for the war to end. I thought of the five years I had lost by the institution of the racial laws. They should have been the best years of my life, the years that form a young person's character, when he falls in love, and builds a foundation for the future.

All this had been denied me. Not only that, but I had had to run away to avoid being sent to a German concentration camp, with the fear and continuous tension it brings. I was tired of vegetating without anything promising and constructive to do. I was surviving and that was all—too little for a 21-year-old young man full of ambition. If in 1938, when the anti-Jewish persecutions began, they had told me that I would have to live as I had for the last five years, I think I would have shot myself in the head. But the instinct to survive is strong and makes us adapt to the most extreme situations. This happened to me and to many others.

Sometimes I looked in the mirror while I shaved and realized how day after day I was neglecting myself and my appearance, conforming to the level of the decent people who had taken me into their homes at their own risk. On the one hand, becoming like them made our living together much easier; they considered me one of their own. On the other hand, I felt as though I had thrown away what I had learned from my parents and my schooling and reading. Such observations left me depressed.

Antinesca came to visit with good news about her in-laws, Santi and his family, and about the Benadì, who were hidden in a friend's house in Florence. Along with this good news she brought the sad news that the Germans had taken away our rabbi, Nathan Cassuto, and his family. I was deeply distressed and at the same time it made me aware of how fortunate I was to be able to survive and avoid the destiny of my poor fellow Jews. I also had to thank heaven that my family was still safe and sound, which was nearly miraculous, considering the atrocities that had been and were still taking place. So I took control of my nerves and resigned myself to spending a few more months (I hoped it was a few) in those conditions. After all, I was eating, sleeping and staying with people who liked me and kept me safe.

I continued to help Gosto with work in the fields and to watch the sheep a few hours a day with Venusta. This had become more a pleasant habit than work. Every once in a while we had to interrupt our conversation to run after a sheep that had taken off for the mountains. Talking with her was relaxing. We could talk about anything. She would question me about the oddest subjects and I would do my best to give her honest answers. Sometimes I had to give up because I did not have the answer to her question.

One day I asked her if she wanted to do something for me.

"You only have to ask. Of course I'll do it."

I have no idea what she was thinking, but certainly not what I asked. "I'd be very grateful if one of these days you'd take a letter to my parents. That way they can have news about me, but more importantly, they could meet a member of the family where I'm staying."

"That's all?" she asked. "That will be a cinch. Go ahead and write your letter and I'll deliver it personally."

I gave her a hug and thanked her, telling her that since it was a long trip to make by bus I would naturally pay all her expenses. She agreed without argument.

That evening at supper I told Beppe and Settimia what I had arranged with Venusta and neither of them had any objection. In fact, Beppe said he would be glad to go with her. That seemed a little odd since Venusta was more than capable of traveling alone. Perhaps Beppe was curious to meet my parents and Liliana and also to show them the real custodian of my virtue. I said nothing, only exchanged meaningful looks with Venusta.

I waited until Sunday to devote myself to writing the letter. I did not want it to interfere with my agro-pastoral activities. After lunch I began to write and quit around nine in the evening, stopping occasionally to flex my cramped fingers. Some 26 pages were the result, in which I recounted in detail everything that had happened since Liliana had accompanied me to Poggiarso. The secret writing code we had invented restricted what I wanted to say, consequently I had to leave out a lot of things that might be too compromising. But I was satisfied with my effort and gave the envelope to Venusta, asking her to tell my parents everything she knew about me—my activities, the state of my health and spirits, and so forth. I also asked her to try to persuade Liliana to come back with her, so I could see her again and learn about everything important to me. I said not to insist if Liliana seemed unsure because I did not want to urge her to take a risky trip against her will.

Venusta assured me she would follow my instructions to the letter, and I had faith in her honesty and good sense. She and Beppe, in their Sunday best, left early in the morning in order to reach Montevarchi in time to take the bus for Poppi in the Casentino. After a visit of two or three hours, they would have to take a return bus to Montevarchi in the middle of the afternoon to be home by evening for supper.

I got up at five to see them off. The stars shone bright in a cloudless sky and it was not cold. They would reach Montevarchi in plenty of time to catch the bus. I did my morning chores, helping Gosto, and went to watch the sheep in the afternoon. I missed Venusta and our long chats, an indication I was definitely not a misogynist, because I liked the company of women and felt uncomfortable without it.

I tried to analyze my feelings: I liked Venusta for her simplicity and the ease with which she expressed her feelings and goodness. She was like a little sister, and I was constrained to keep our relationship on the level of affectionate friendship, avoiding any deeper involvement for either of us. While I watched over the little flock grazing peacefully, I thought about what was going on at Poppi between my ambassadors and my family. I was pleased with my idea and hoped Liliana would accept my suggestion to come visit. I also hoped that Beppe would not talk nonsense just to try to appear important.

I stayed with the sheep until dusk before starting to walk back slowly to the house; after checking to see that all the sheep had come back with me, I shut them in the pen and went in the house. While Settimia prepared supper, I sat beside the fire with Gosto. On the chance that Liliana might also come, Settimia was making fresh pasta and rabbit sauce. I kept looking at my watch and imagining where they would be. I was feeling too anxious to sit still and fiddled with the logs burning in the fireplace.

Finally we heard people in the farmyard. I immediately recognized Liliana's voice and jumped up, followed by Gosto. I ran to meet them, now coming up the stairs. I was sure Liliana would not disappoint me. I embraced her, happy to see her after so long. I hugged Venusta and Beppe also, who had brought her back. She looked very well, even a little heavier. She brought a small bag just right for an overnight stay.

Because it was late we all sat down at the table and did honor to Settimia's hard work. The meeting with my parents had gone very well and both had been happy with my idea. We sat around talking for a while, but we were all tired from the long day and we soon went to bed. Liliana slept with Venusta. The next morning we got up early, had a noisy breakfast together, and Beppe excused me from work that day.

It was a wonderful day: the air was cool, but it felt like it would warm up as soon as the sun rose higher. I took Liliana by the arm and together we walked through the chestnut woods. I besieged her with questions, particularly about papa and mamma. The last time I had seen them was on that fateful September morning when Federico and I left on our bicycles to go to Chianti five months ago. I had never been away from them for such a long time. They were both well and perfectly adjusted to their new life. Mamma spent many hours reading books and newspapers out loud to papa. Then the two of them would take short walks in the nearby woods. They were very apprehensive about Franco and me. It was understandable that they would be worried about Franco because none of us knew where he was. News from the Red Cross filtered through with great difficulty, and for months we had had none. They had been noticeably relieved about me after Beppe and Venusta had fully informed them of all my activities. One of papa's constant worries was not being able to provide for his family. Although all his children were adult and self-sufficient, the family income had been reduced to zero until, hopefully, both papa and us children could take up the slack after the war.

Liliana said there were days when papa got in a really bad mood and mamma had to bear the brunt of it. The farm family they stayed with were very hospitable and did everything for their well-being. Of course, they were without running water and electricity and this was the only serious problem. Liliana gave lessons to the little children of the neighboring families, so part of her day was occupied constructively.

We talked about our future for the thousandth time. It was natural for our thoughts and plans to be projected into the future. The past and the present had little to offer us. As soon as the war front passed the Valdarno, I wanted us all to be together to wait for the liberation of Florence. Then Liliana and I would go see what remained of our house and the things we left. After we saw that everything was all right, we would have our parents come. From then on we would roll up our sleeves and start to work at anything, just to earn some money. To judge by the way the war was progressing in Italy, we would not have to wait more than six months. That was not very long when we thought of the many difficult years in the past. We felt encouraged after making concrete plans. Now it was up to the Allies to work as fast as possible to help us put our plans into action.

The bus that would take Liliana from Montevarchi to Poppi left around three in the afternoon. We ate with Settimia and Venusta while the others worked in the fields. Liliana packed her small bag and Venusta and I walked with her in the direction of Montevarchi. When we saw we were close to the first village, Venusta and I would turn back. I embraced Liliana and gave her all kinds of advice and recommendations. We made a date for the future liberation.

CHAPTER 14

The Fourth Hiding Place: Consuma

The only one who did not seem totally satisfied was Beppe. In the last few days he had become more taciturn. The pain in his shoulder and arm that had almost completely disappeared had come back, and when I offered to give him more massages he said, strangely, there was no need for it. "The pain will pass by itself."

That seemed odd. The first time I had proposed my "cure" he had accepted enthusiastically and, in the end, had seemed grateful. I felt that he was brooding about something. However, his behavior was no different from usual. Either he would sit peacefully by the fireplace in a pleasurable state of intoxication or, in the more serious cases, would be carried to bed where he fell dead asleep.

His reserved attitude toward me was something new. I spoke about it with my confidante, who said she had noticed the same thing. According to Venusta, every day her father was becoming more jealous of the close relationship between us and of our long conversations while we watched the sheep. He did not want his daughter to talk to me about things she did not tell him.

Neither of us liked this and we began to fear that one day Beppe would explode violently, as he was apt to do when drunk. I dropped the matter of the shoulder massages. That was his tough luck. It just meant he would be in pain. I felt on edge and began to watch his behavior. It bothered me to have to be careful of his every word and move. The other family members behaved normally. The problem seemed exclusively Beppe's.

It was toward the middle of April 1944, and Venusta and I had taken the sheep to pasture, as usual immersed in our conversation, when we heard Beppe yelling from the house. We could not understand what he was saying. It was too early for him to be drunk, so he had to be yelling for another reason. Then we caught a few words. One of the sheep had returned to the house alone, separated from the rest of the flock, and Beppe was furious because we were not watching the flock carefully enough.

We rounded up the other sheep and took them back to the sheepfold. When we arrived, Beppe started to quarrel and fight with Venusta. He let fly everything he had kept bottled up. He accused her of being a whore, saying she had left her work at Montevarchi so she could carry on with me. He said the sheep had run away because we had been too occupied with our dirty business. He swore, insulted, and blasphemed.

I told Venusta not to reply to the insults and I did not say a word to him myself. While he continued shouting in the farmyard, I quietly told Settimia that I would leave that very evening. I would leave before her husband did something drastic. I begged her not to tell him until the next morning. Tears came to her eyes and she made excuses for her husband. She was quite aware that he was jealous of his daughter and that there was no truth in the slanderous accusations. She was sorry that my stay with them had to end so abruptly and badly.

I consoled her by saying that sooner or later I had expected Beppe to explode as he had, in fact, that afternoon. In the final analysis, I preferred it that way. It would have been worse if Beppe had vented his rage by reporting me to the Fascists to have me hauled off.

Settimia fixed supper as usual. A heavy silence hung in the room. I noticed that during the supper both Gosto and Settimia kept filling his glass with wine. I understood at once that this was the only way to neutralize him and allow me to leave without creating some further family tragedy. None of us had much appetite, so the supper ended quickly. As foreseen, Beppe was soon in the grips of a somber state of intoxication. Settimia and Gosto calmly hoisted him to his feet and carried him off to his bed, where he immediately began snoring.

Released from danger, we got busy packing my things. It was not possible to take everything with me. I did not need the heavy clothes because it was already spring and the temperature was very pleasant. I took the things that still looked decent. Everything that would not fit into my backpack I put in a burlap sack, along with my boots and toilet articles.

Settimia, Gosto, Venusta, and Alivarda stood around watching what I was doing without being able to say a word, and I was even less loquacious. My baggage ready, I looked each one in the eyes without saying a word. I had to leave those decent, good people who had protected me, and who were subject to the violent nature of the head of the family now in his room snoring like a bear. He had broken the enchantment of a nice sojourn and with a single blow he had annulled the generosity of the family that had risked its own neck to save mine. It was as though I had become an orphan overnight and had to look for another family willing to take me in and be endangered like those I had to leave.

This time Antinesca would not be able to help me find a new arrangement. I was alone, with the few resources at my disposal, without the slightest idea of where or to whom I might turn. I did not want to ask hospitality from any of Beppe's friends I had become acquainted with while at Enzoli. Doing that would not eliminate the possibility of Beppe reporting me to the Fascists, something he might do in revenge for my depriving him of those earnings by leaving his house.

"I know how bad Antinesca will feel when she hears you had to leave. Why do not you let her find you another place with some family she knows?" It was Venusta's trembling voice that broke the silence. I looked at her. In her eyes I read sadness and affection.

"You're right. She'll feel very bad, but I don't want her to run a risk in finding me a new place to go. When Beppe found out, he'd have it in for her, too. All I can do is count on my lucky star and hope it leads me to the right door. Up to now things have turned out all right. Let's hope they continue in the future as well."

I was absolutely determined not to let Beppe and the others know where I ended up. My voice was firm, excluding any possibility I might change my mind. I thanked Settimia for all her care and promised her when the war was over I would come back to see her. I gave her some money to cover my expenses for the last week and a little extra to buy whatever she pleased. I embraced her and kissed her on both cheeks. I did the same with Gosto and Alivarda.

I started to say good-bye to Venusta when she stopped me, saying: "No, not here. I want to walk with you for a bit so you won't get lost." I did not dare refuse. She would be offended, and also I really could not orient myself in the dark of night to see in which direction I was headed.

"All right. If you really want to go with me for a bit, that's fine with me. But not for more than half an hour." She nodded, understanding completely that I did not want her to know where I would go to ask for hospitality. I asked Settimia to thank Beppe for what he had done for me and to tell him I was sorry I left without saying good-bye. After all, Beppe had taken me willingly into his house and I owed him the same gratitude that I felt toward the rest of the family.

With my backpack hoisted on my shoulders and the little burlap sack in hand, I left with Venusta, waving good-bye to those good people. We descended the stone steps rapidly and went into the dark woods. The backpack was very heavy, and the other little sack threw me off balance, so I asked Venusta to carry it. We continued walking hand in hand. I was sorry to have to leave that girl with whom I had spent so many pleasant hours. I knew I would miss her.

"I'm sorry you're going away," she said after a few minutes of walking hand in hand. "You don't know what it has meant to me to have known you. I can't believe what my father said to us. If we had really done what he accused us of doing I wouldn't feel as humiliated as I feel right now. I'm surprised you didn't fight back. He deserved it. We didn't do anything bad, and he acted like a crazy man."

"You're right," I answered. "I should have made him eat those stupid things he said. You must understand, though, that under the circumstances almost anything I might have said would only have made it worse. I couldn't let that happen. It might seem selfish to you, but put yourself in my shoes. What would you have done?"

Venusta said nothing. We continued walking in silence for a few minutes. Her hand squeezed mine tightly. We stopped. She turned to me and looked in my eyes. In her look were all the things she had wanted to tell me during the times we were together, which she had kept to herself. I pulled her slowly toward me, took her in my arms, and we kissed. We made up now for all the scandalous things Beppe had said with a long, liberating kiss. We were happy to be kissing, confident we were doing nothing wrong.

We continued walking in the direction of the Valdarno. We felt great. We were liberated from all the taboos, free to express ourselves and do what seemed best. A new sense of intimacy took over that made us happy. I thought that now it would be easier to leave Venusta. I realized that in all these past weeks together I had repressed my natural attraction to her and in the last half hour I had given free rein to my feelings, although with a prudence the situation imposed.

We reached a point from which we had a panoramic view of the very wide valley opening at our feet. The night was illuminated by a bright moon, and although it was not the first time I had seen such a sight, I was once again filled with admiration.

"It's time you went back home," I said. "It's nearly midnight and I don't want you to be too late. Settimia will worry. I'll go on alone. Anyway, I know where we are and it will be easy to find the right road."

Venusta did not reply, but threw her arms around my neck, and we kissed for the last time. My thoughts turned instinctively to the last kiss I gave Gina many months before. I gave her a gentle caress and said: "Go on home and be a good girl."

She smiled with her eyes full of tears and, after handing me my little sack, turned her back and without another word started back on the path. I was not sure in which direction I wanted to go. All around were cultivated fields and vineyards, immersed in total silence broken only by a dog barking in the distance. I noticed a wide, white road, undoubtedly a main road with traffic. It was advisable to stay off that, so I headed in the opposite direction and found a narrow country lane without the sign of an automobile and I followed it for a while. Sooner or later I would run into a farmer's house.

A large house appeared that had more the aspect of a farm consortium than a simple farmhouse. Inside a shed was farm machinery of every kind, a motorcycle, and even an old automobile—a dilapidated but still functioning Balilla. I decided it was not the right house for me. It was too easily accessible by motorized means, and above all more than one family must live there to manage that arsenal of farm machinery. I also noticed that around the farmyard were two very large piles of straw, and I remembered hearing some farmers say that a large pile of straw in the farmyard meant that the farmer living there was a Fascist or close to it, because an anti-Fascist tried to produce as little wheat as possible. Consequently the amount of straw would be skimpy. Taking this into consideration, I crossed the farmyard as silently as possible and went on in search of a more suitable house.

It was getting late, and worried about having to knock on a farmer's door at some impossible hour, I stepped up my search. Another house came into view. It was very small and probably belonged to the big farm I had just seen. To judge by its exterior, it could have a bedroom and kitchen at the most—too small to put up an extra person. Changing directions, I took a path that descended steeply into the valley. I reached an area with wide, deep cracks in the earth that seemed like canyons made by centuries of running water. I had never seen such a landscape, so unreal in the bright moonlight.

I walked along the edge of one of these canyons when suddenly the roof of another house appeared. It was isolated from the surrounding territory and I had not seen any important roads in the neighborhood that could lead to it. I stopped to observe it closely. It was a perfectly square building, on two floors. There was a large farmyard with a small pile of straw (an encouraging sign). The lower outside walls were stone, topped by red bricks. It must be rather old. There appeared to be about three bedrooms. It had no electric wires, which made it even more isolated.

Encouraged, I moved closer. All the windows on the top floor were open. From one of them I distinctly heard snoring. The wooden front door was large and thick. Under the shed there was some farm equipment, a couple of plows and a harrow, but little else. No tractor. This meant they worked the land with oxen. In fact, from a little window on the ground floor I heard the strong breathing of oxen inside their stalls.

The house had the characteristics of what I needed. I decided to wake up the snorer. It was 12:30, late, but not too late. In order not to wake up the whole household, I walked around the house and stopped under the window the snoring came from. Usually when someone snores that loud he is of a certain age, I thought. I clapped my hands twice. The snoring stopped abruptly. I had taken the first step.

"Hey, you in the house," I said loudly enough to be heard, but not too loud. Then I cleared my throat and coughed a couple of times. Through the open window I heard a man's sleepy voice, "Someone's outside." A woman's voice spoke something I could not hear. I coughed again to confirm that someone was outside.

A short time later a man looked out the window. He seemed to be around 50 years old. "What do you want?"

"Excuse me for waking you at this hour, but I would like to speak to you for a minute, if you don't mind."

"All right. I'll come down."

I heard him mutter something to the woman and then I heard footsteps on the stairs and saw the weak light of a flickering oil lamp descending. In the meantime

I went around to the front door. I put my backpack on the ground. While I was waiting for the door to open, I hoped and prayed I had happened on to the right house.

The sound of an old bolt sliding, and the door opened. The man of the house appeared: thin, medium height, dark gray, thinning hair. He had a kind expression. He was wearing a pair of trousers that he had obviously tossed on in a hurry and an undershirt with half sleeves.

"I'm very sorry to wake you at this hour," I repeated. "I heard you sleeping soundly!" I added with a smile that asked his pardon.

He stood listening to me half amazed and half incredulous. However, he did not look angry.

I continued. "I am in a rather difficult situation, because I'm hiding from the Germans." I had decided to get right to the point. From the reaction of my interlocutor I saw immediately that it was to my advantage.

"Come in," he said in a calm voice. "You don't have to stand in the doorway." I noticed that when he spoke he lisped his *s* in a way the Tuscans call a *lisca*.

I came into the large entry hall with a number of doors. Oil lamp in hand, he led the way up a stone stairway. We reached a little open door off a very large kitchen. He had me sit down in a chair before the fireplace. On the andirons two large pieces of wood were slowly burning out. The farmer took a poker and stirred the fire. The two pieces caught fire again and the room became illuminated by the flame.

I introduced myself as "Enrico." He said he was Bista and we shook hands. He took another chair and sat next to me by the fireplace.

"Tell me about yourself," he said. "But first, would you like something to eat?"

To tell the truth I was a little hungry. "Thank you, but never mind. It's not the time for eating."

"Don't worry about that. Stella!" he called in a loud voice. He waited a moment, and after getting no answer, he went to a door that must be his room and woke his sleeping wife. He returned to the kitchen and, as though apologizing, said: "You know, women sleep sounder than we do."

Stella appeared in a minute. She was a thin, short woman, also with dark gray hair pulled back. Her small face was set off by two small, bright eyes. From her skin, wrinkled and brown from the sun, you could tell she was used to working in the fields as well as the house.

I stood up and shook hands as we introduced ourselves. Bista spoke up: "Fry him two eggs." Stella took a little pan with a very long handle from a nail on the wall near the fireplace. She put it directly on the burning stump, took two eggs from the *madia,* broke and dropped them into the pan where they began to sizzle. While they fried, she took a plate and fork from the sideboard and cut a piece of bread.

She let the two fried eggs slide from the pan onto the plate and handed it to me with the greatest simplicity, as if it were the most natural thing in the world. For me it absolutely was not. I had plummeted into their house in the middle of the night, pulling them out of bed, and in less than ten minutes I was there with two fried eggs and a piece of bread on a plate. And I still had told them nothing about myself, beyond the fact that I was in hiding. Incredible people, I thought. I never dreamed I would get such a welcome as they gave me.

I thanked Stella profusely, who in the meanwhile had taken a chair and was sitting next to us, and I began to eat those splendid eggs and at the same time to outline my situation. I realized I was with two people who certainly were not Fascists and to whom I could tell everything about myself without fear. I said I was a Jew, that for eight months I had hidden with different farmers and that they were the fourth family I had asked for hospitality.

While I talked, Bista and Stella listened silently, nodding occasionally. Bista lit up the butt of a Tuscan cigar. He smoked it slowly, every once in a while drawing in a mouthful and letting the smoke come out in a white cloud. They were both very attentive to what I was saying. I did not want to keep them awake too long, because I knew they would have to get up at dawn. I concluded by saying that I hoped they could keep me until we were liberated by the Allies and that I was prepared to pay for their hospitality, even though my economic resources were not too flourishing. I said I would do everything I could to help with the work in the fields, which was becoming heavier with summer coming on. I added that I realized that they were risking a good deal if the Germans or Fascists discovered me. I wanted them to think over what they would be doing before giving me an answer. I stopped talking and waited.

Bista and Stella exchanged looks. Stella only made a motion of assent with her head. And Bista said: "All right, Enrico. As far as we are concerned you can stay until the English arrive. Don't worry about the money. The important thing for us all is to stay alive. If there is enough food in the house for five, there must also be enough for six. We have a son, Dino, who was a prisoner in Africa. Now he's in an English military camp. You'll take his place."

I could not believe my ears. Such simplicity, such generosity, so spontaneous and sincere. Mentally I thanked my Lord for what was happening. I shook Bista's and Stella's hands and thanked them for such goodness. They burst out laughing. "But what do you expect?" Stella said. "We'll pretend we have another son," and so saying motioned for me to follow her to her prisoner son's room.

"This is his room. Bring your things here. Tomorrow you can get settled."

I entered the room that was to be mine. I could not believe that after so many months of having to sleep with others I at last had a bed all to myself. Not wanting to wake the other family members, I quickly took leave of Stella and Bista. I thanked them again and took one of Bista's small oil lamps, closed the door of my room and undressed in a hurry, slipping into "my" bed.

For a few moments I gazed at the ceiling and surroundings. I still could not believe what had happened. Thinking back over the moment when I first noticed the house from the edge of the canyon, making a flashback of all the sequences, I seemed to be looking at an adventure film. Everything had happened in such a rapid and incredibly simple way, like a mosaic that is put together piece by piece. What left me more surprised than anything was the simple way it had happened: the immediacy of Bista and Stella's decision was unreal, as though they had recited a script memorized for months. If the same scene had happened with people of a much more elevated social level, it certainly would have had a more complicated, studied development, with an uncertain outcome. The level of humanity of these simple people was extraordinary. I looked all around my room: the usual iron bedstead painted black, a dresser with an oval mirror, on one side of the bed a nightstand with marble top, a chair on the other side, and the inevitable washbasin with ceramic pitcher under the window. A coatrack hung on door. Very white walls and ceiling: proof I was in the house of clean people.

My inspection over, I declared myself fully satisfied to be in that house and, blowing out my lamp, I fell asleep at once without waking until the next morning when I heard subdued voices coming from the kitchen. They were all women's voices. I listened for a minute, trying to make out what they were saying. I could only glean they were talking about me, since the name Enrico was often mentioned. Periodically I heard a low laugh. Then absolute silence.

I remained stretched out in the bed. It was of normal size and therefore quite comfortable. With arms and legs outstretched, I enjoyed the total relaxation for a few minutes.

I put an end to these meditations and decided to get up. I looked at my watch: it was ten o'clock. I jumped out of bed, slipped on my trousers, and looked in the three drawers of the dresser to see if the things I brought would fit. As I imagined, the drawers were full of the son's things. I closed them and decided to wait for Stella to empty them, as she said, to make room. I put on shoes and socks, kept on a cotton undershirt. I opened the door and went into the kitchen. Not a soul. I looked around and got a very pleasant impression of the ambience. Someone had set the table for my breakfast: a large coffee cup and a plate with three slices of bread and a little marmalade, a bowl of sugar, and in the fireplace near the fire, a small coffee pot from which came the good smell of roasted barley: my coffee!

I filled my cup with that blackish liquid, dropped in four spoons of sugar and began to eat the bread and marmalade with gusto. While I ate I looked around with interest: the walls were clean and white in here, also. The floor was made of bricks, some broken because of their age. However, they were obviously freshly mopped. The dining table was large, with two drawers and four turned legs, probably of chestnut. Standard *madia*. The usual sideboard dominated the longest wall, with the customary photographs inserted in the glass doors: Stella and Bista in wedding attire, the three children when small, and a photo of a robust young man who must be the prisoner son.

While I was taking a close look at the photos a voice behind me said: "*Buon giorno,* Enrico. I'm Dina." I turned around and found myself facing a rather short, sturdy girl, with a nice, open face, thick brown, curly hair, a ski nose, and two small eyes like Stella's. She was smiling.

"*Buon giorno,*" I replied, extending my hand. "I'm happy to meet you. I was looking at your family pictures, and I think this is you as a little girl," pointing at a little girl with a great cap of curly hair.

"Yes, that's me. Now I'm a little bigger," she said with a silvery laugh.

We shook hands energetically. She motioned for me to sit at the table.

"I've just finished an excellent breakfast," I said. "I do not know who I should thank for having fixed everything so nicely. The marmalade was excellent, and the coffee, too. As you see, nothing is left on my plate."

"My sister Delia fixed your breakfast. She's in the fields now with mamma and daddy, but in a little while they'll come back for a snack. You know, every morning about eleven we have a light snack that keeps us going until suppertime. We start work these days every early in the morning when it's cool.

"Want some more coffee?" She picked up the coffee pot that had begun to smoke.

"Yes, thanks. I'll have half a cup. I'd like to ask you to be less formal and call me *tu* instead of *lei*. In the other houses they always addressed me with *tu*."

"All right, Enrico, that's what I'll do."

We sealed our agreement with a smile. She was certainly a very nice girl and conversed easily, not the least intimidated by my presence in the house. The energetic way she moved denoted a strong constitution. We sat for a few minutes while I sipped my second serving of boiling coffee.

I asked where I could find water for washing. She said they went to the well with a *mezzina* to get whatever water they needed. They all washed with cold water these days, but if I wanted to heat it, I could do so in the pot hanging on a chain in the fireplace directly over the fire. I got the picture, and standing up, I asked: "Where is the *mezzina*?" She pointed at a copper bucket near the door, on the floor. "And the well?"

"You'll find it just outside the front door, on the left side of the house."

I attached the copper bucket to a hook on the rope hanging from a pulley above the well and the bucket fell into the well with a thud. I let it fill and pulled it up by the rope, dripping water from the sides. I removed it from the hook and took it into the house.

Dina was busy cleaning the crumbs I left on the table.

"See how fast I did it?" I said, and went into my room with the bucket of water and brushed my teeth and washed my face, neck, and chest from waist up. The cool water whipped up my energy. I carefully combed my hair and put on a clean shirt. Now I was more presentable.

Dina was putting away the plates and cups from breakfast. She asked me some questions about the previous months hiding out with other farm families. She wanted to know what they were like, what I did during the day in order not to die of boredom, and other unimportant things. She spoke in short sentences, hurriedly, in spurts. She had a very distinctive manner of expressing herself.

I tried to answer all her questions without going into needless detail. In turn, I asked her about herself and her family. I found out a grandmother lived there. I had not been aware of her existence. She was always the first to get up in the morning and left the house to do lighter tasks. I would meet her before long when she came back. According to Dina, her grandmother moved through the house like a ghost: she almost never spoke and did everything in the greatest silence. When she did not have anything to do she retired to her room. Her favorite occupation was mending the family's clothes and knitting socks.

Dina was about 20 and had been engaged to a local boy for a couple of years. They were waiting for him to get out of the army and for the war to end. Then they would be married.

Her brother Dino, who was three years older than Dina, had been a prisoner in an English military camp for a long time. Occasionally they got word about him from the Red Cross. He was also engaged, to a local girl named Dina. I got the feeling that there was bad blood between the two Dinas.

Delia was the youngest sister, 18 years old. She was not engaged yet and was like the family pet. I met her a little later when she came in from the fields. The Nepi family had lived in that house for generations. Different brothers worked at farming on neighboring farms. The farmhouse where Dina's family stayed was called Consuma. It was not very large, but adequate for their family. It belonged to a man in Montevarchi, and the Nepi family worked as tenant farmers, with two oxen for working the land, a pig, chickens, and rabbits, but no sheep. Since they were practically on a plain, the work of plowing was comparatively easy. There was a nice vineyard that produced some excellent grapes for the wine Bista made from them. They had many different kinds of fruit trees that provided them with their excellent marmalade.

While Dina was recounting all these details, the rest of the family made its noisy entrance. I could hear them coming up the stairs toward the kitchen, so I got up to meet them. The first to enter was Bista. I went up to him and shook his hand. He asked if I had slept well and at my affirmative answer he nodded and sat down at the table where he immediately poured himself a glass of wine. He enjoyed it, clicking his tongue from time to time. Obviously Bista was a man of few words. No problem.

Right after him came the grandmother, Stella, and Delia in descending chrono-logical order. I shook hands with all three in the same order. The grandmother had to be over 80, but was still in pretty good shape. Her back was bent, perhaps from the thousands of kilograms she had carried all her life. Her face was full of wrin-kles, as was reasonable for her age and continual exposure to the elements. Her full head of hair was completely gray. She said a few words of welcome that I did not completely understand because of the few teeth still remaining in her mouth. I replied courteously to her few words and she went directly to her room, as Dina said she would.

I turned to Stella and thanked her for the nice welcome the previous evening, for the two eggs, and above all for letting me use her son Dino's room and bed.

"I had a wonderful sleep," I said. "Such a good sleep that I didn't wake up before ten this morning. The bed was very comfortable and for the first time in many months I was able to sleep in a bed all alone, without the company of other males!" They all started laughing and made ironic comments, as might be expected.

Finally I said hello to Delia, shook her hand and said: "I'm Enrico, as you know. I hope that we can be informal with one another, as Dina and I are. Dina told me that you fixed the breakfast that was ready on the table. Thanks so much. It was exqui-site. I'm so happy to have met the whole family, including the smallest, so to speak." Delia blushed and started laughing at my joke. In fact, she was the tallest in the fam-ily, even though the youngest. She was a very beautiful girl: she had blond hair down to her shoulders in two thick braids, and her blue eyes were very bright and intelli-gent. She had a milk-and-honey complexion with cheeks already burnt by the early spring sun. Her sweet and spontaneous smile showed two rows of small white teeth. She was more slender than Dina, though well developed in all the right places.

"All right," she replied. "That means I'll call you *tu* also. I'm glad you liked the breakfast. I'm glad you can stay in our house."

Now that I had met the whole family I already felt almost a part of it. I was happy to be in the midst of simple, direct people of few but clear words. I was sure the parents' political ideas as well as their stability would allow me to live peacefully. I asked Bista what he advised me to do in regard to outsiders. I told him about my previous experiences with farmers and asked him to be very honest with me, because I did not want to complicate the normal life of their family and the relationship with their friends and relatives.

Bista took a while to think about it and then he said: "I think it's better if you behave as one of the family. Among our friends and relatives there's no one who would harm you. They are all like us. In fact, it's better if they know we're hiding someone, so in the case of any danger, they could warn us at once."

This sounded reasonable and I thanked him. I found out exactly where their house was situated in relation to the towns. It was near the road going from Moncioni to Montevarchi, about a 40-minute walk to the latter; however, it was far enough off the road to give me peace of mind.

The next question was what kind of work I could do to make myself useful. I told Bista what I had done in the past and said I was ready to learn anything new. He said I could certainly be of use since they had lost Dino's help and that put more responsibility on the shoulders of his wife and two daughters. He added that in time the most pressing work would be the wheat harvest and threshing, something I had never tried, but Bista thought I could easily do. I insisted on compensating them with a fixed daily sum for my maintenance: it was the least I could do for their hospitality, not to mention the danger they were running because of me. Both Bista and Stella unequivocally refused to discuss it. To help me escape capture was their sole objective. All the rest was unimportant.

I cut it short by saying: "All right. We won't fight over it. It just means that, God willing, when we all make it through this trying time and everything returns to normal, I'll find a way to make it up to you." And with that the argument was closed.

I asked Stella to show me where I could put my few things and she immediately emptied two of the three drawers. In a few minutes I had put away my things, liberating them from the suffocating "arms" of my backpack.

While the family had their frugal snack I, who had just had breakfast, kept them company. Between one mouthful and another they took turns asking me questions about my family, where we lived, what kind of work my father did, how many of us were in the family, and so forth. I answered fully, but without going into unnecessary detail. Naturally most of the questions came from the women. As Bista tranquilly ate he followed what was being said. At the end of the meal he pulled out a cigar and began to calmly smoke, polluting the air around him. Dina and Delia made a few timid protests, but Bista did not seem concerned: he continued smoking as though it were nothing.

I enjoyed the rapport between the parents and daughters: it was based on reciprocal respect, without any resentment and with tolerance for the others' ideas—a true democracy. Bista finished his cigar and slowly got up from the table, motioning for me to follow him outside. We went to the farmyard and he showed me his tools. They were few, essential, and kept in good condition. He showed me the stall with the two sturdy white oxen peacefully munching their brunch—excellent help for working the land. I caressed them both under the neck, which they stretched out to enjoy with eyes closed. I told Bista I would enjoy working with those sweet animals at the first opportunity.

We went along a little path that skirted the woods of young oaks. Bista had brought a spade for me, and when we came to rows of vines that had already been pruned and tied, Bista gave the spade to me and said: "If you want to work you can help me turn the dirt on these vines. Don't be in a hurry, go easy, or you'll soon get tired out."

He was right. When I worked on the plain at Sesto I had learned to do things with a slow but even rhythm, without tiring myself too much. I took the handle and began to dig on one side of the row while Bista dug the other. We proceeded in tandem and I saw at once that I could keep to his rhythm without fatigue. We worked like that for a good hour without saying a word.

The spade Bista had given me to use was a very good one: it had a sharp blade that entered the soft soil easily; the handle was perfectly smooth and did not hurt my hands. I had learned to spit on my hands occasionally to grip the handle better, as I saw Bista doing also.

"Now let's have a drop of wine," he said. We sat on the ground. Bista had a bottle of wine and two glasses he had taken from the kitchen. He filled them both and handed me one. I slowly sipped that ruby-colored wine. It was still young but had an excellent perfume. I swallowed it without any problem. I liked it a great deal and besides taking away my thirst it gave me energy.

"More?" Bista asked.

"Yes, thank you. It's really good."

"Go easy because wine is treacherous. While you are drinking you don't feel anything, but afterward it gets you in your legs."

While he refilled my glass, I answered: "Should the worst happen, I'll stretch out by the vines and have a nap."

We resumed our digging with the same rhythm and in fact my legs did feel a little heavy. I tried to hide it, because I did not want to appear to be a weakling. Out of the corner of my eye I saw he was watching me as I dug. He may have sensed I had slightly slowed my rhythm, but he said nothing and pretended not to notice. I liked Bista. He was a man of incredible calm. His few words were a sign he preferred to think more and talk less, the opposite of most people. His words were concise and to the point, but he managed to say all he wanted and made himself understood. He was a clear demonstration of the saying about the farmer: "rough shoes, fine brain." I knew we were in basic agreement. These thoughts made me feel good. I was happy to have found a family like this one. It was a real stroke of good fortune.

We kept digging for another good hour. When we came to the end of the row Bista planted his spade in the ground. I did the same. He leaned on the handle and wiped his brow. "That's enough digging for today. Now I'll go take care of the animals and then I have to go to Montevarchi to get Stella some things."

"All right," I said. "Do you mind if I help you with the oxen? I'd like to work with them. I like them."

"No problem. I'll show you what has to be done."

We slowly returned to the house. The sun was still high enough, but I could already tell the sunset would be beautiful. As we walked Bista pointed out the boundaries of the farm. It was a portion of land well defined by rows of poplars and tall hedges. There must have been around five or six well cared for hectares in all, not bad for one family. There were no weeds or sections of unplowed land. It was obvious Bista loved his land and it gave him good harvests in exchange.

We put the spades in the toolshed and entered the stall. With pitchforks we removed the straw that was soaked with urine and dung, which we carried to the manure pit. Then we tossed on fresh clean straw that was kept at the edge of the farmyard. With that the oxen would have a soft clean bed to sleep on at night.

I made the chaff with fresh grass mixed with hay. We filled the trough with fresh fodder and gave the oxen water that they drank as though they would never stop. Each time they raised their heads from the pail their mouths dripped water that they licked off with their long rough tongues.

When the oxen were taken care of I asked Bista if I could stay and pet them for a while. "Go ahead, but be careful not to spoil them too much. They are worse than dogs. They take advantage of someone who likes them."

I stayed with the oxen for ten minutes caressing their foreheads and under their necks. I could see they enjoyed the attention that they probably rarely received from someone with other things on his mind and too little time at his disposal. Now and then one of the two would let out a low moan of pleasure that amused me. I loved to do what I was doing: the work on the land, the contact with these animals that made the cultivation of the land possible with their enormous strength, seeing the produce that is used for one's own nourishment grow from one's own work. All this fascinated me. It was like returning to a primitive life when man could survive only by working the land.

After this dangerous time had passed and normality was restored, I would like papa to buy a little land with a house where we could spend time. My imagination was galloping into the future. That was a good sign: it meant the present did not worry me too much, thanks to Bista and his family.

I was immersed in my thoughts when I heard the familiar distant thunder. Allied bombers were coming to eliminate obstacles for the advancing troops. I ran from the stalls and on the horizon I saw airplane shapes flickering with the sun's reflection. It was a large formation proceeding implacably over a vast tract of sky. They communicated a sense of power, flying through the hundreds of little anti-aircraft clouds without changing course a centimeter. As they approached Montevarchi (coming from the south) the sound of the engines became louder. It was an extraordinary concert. This was the first time I had witnessed a bombardment so near. It was like being on the front row of a terrible and exalting spectacle. I called Bista, Stella, Dina, and Delia to come. Bista and Stella looked out the window while their daughters ran outside to join me in the farmyard.

The planes were almost over our heads. The symbols of the Allies painted on the wings and fuselages were clearly distinguishable. I waved my arms and jumped around like a crazy man. "Who knows," I thought, "maybe they'll see me and know I am welcoming them."

Suddenly I saw bomb bays open under the planes and clusters of shining bombs began to fall. At first they looked very small, but as they fell whistling toward the earth they grew bigger and more frightening. Immediately afterward large columns of smoke rose from the ground and explosions ripped the air.

After their arsenal was empty of bombs, the Flying Fortresses continued their imperturbable flight. Only then did I notice that during the whole operation there were many small planes flying above and below the bombers: fighter aircraft that would have protected them from attack by German fighters. Those, however, were completely absent. The only defense was the anti-aircraft artillery that luckily did not hit a thing.

Like magic the spectacle came to an end. The planes went on their way, perhaps flying toward other objectives still further north. We continued to hear strong explosions, probably from oil tanks they hit. Heavy black smoke filled the sky.

Dina and Delia were also excited by the spectacle, even if it was not the first time it had happened. They asked me what the blue star with five points under the wings of the bombers meant. I said it was the emblem of the American air force. They thought it had something to do with the Communist star. "No, that one is red," I told them.

For a while we stood looking at the columns of black smoke that were growing larger at the base instead of smaller: the fire was expanding. The more German oil that burned, the less there would be to run their tanks and trucks.

We went back to the house. In the meanwhile Bista had changed his clothes and was ready to go do some errands for Stella at Montevarchi. "Stay away from the fires," I warned. "And if possible, find out what damage the Allies did with this blitz."

Bista nodded as he descended the path that led to the main road to Montevarchi. I sat on a stone step by the front door and began to watch the sun fall slowly behind the hill. The sky was flaming red. I loved that particular moment when dusk takes the place of the luminous daytime sky and puts on a show that has always enchanted me for its infinite variety of colors. There is an American song that says that the best things in life are free. Sunsets are one of these things.

While I was admiring that wonder with my mouth half open, Dina came up and sat on the same step. "What are you doing, Enrico, dreaming?" The little shock brought me back to reality.

"That's it," I said. "I'm in ecstasy admiring the sunset. I've always loved sunsets, and I can't stop looking until the sun disappears completely over the horizon. It's stronger than I am."

Dina started laughing. "I didn't know you were such a romantic. If you don't have anything else to do, why not come with me to make a little fodder for the animals? I forgot to do it this morning and if I don't do it now there won't be anything to give them to eat tonight."

Reluctantly I got up and followed her to the toolshed. We took two sickles and a big basket to the alfalfa field not far from the house. We cut for about a quarter of an hour until the basket was full. I handed my sickle to Dina and with her help hoisted the basket on my shoulder. We dumped the grass near the pile of straw. By now the sky was dark blue and the early star already shone in the sky. It was time to go in the house.

I washed my hands in the kitchen sink and rinsed my face. It had been my first day at Consuma. All together I had put in a good day's work and felt satisfied. Stella was fixing supper with Delia's help: pappardelle with rabbit sauce and steamed rabbit with potatoes. I could not wait to sit down at the table; I had worked up quite an appetite.

They sent me to the well to get a bucket of water, which I did in a flash. I poured the water into the pot that hung from the chain above the burning logs, stirred up the fire, and sat by the fireplace to watch the women busy around the stove. I was anxious to hear from Bista what damage the bombing had caused. I liked the idea of being so near the war front and being able to follow its progress.

Stella had already made the pasta dough that morning and now she cut it into wide strips to toss into the boiling water. But before she could do that she had to wait for Bista to come back so the pasta would not be overcooked. I asked Stella about their local friends and those in Montevarchi. I wanted to get a general idea of the kind of people I would eventually meet. For the most part they were farmers like the Nepi family who lived on the adjacent farms. At Montevarchi they knew three or four people outside the farming business. One of these was a police marshal. That made me curious. I wanted to know what he did, and more than anything, what his political leanings were. Stella vouched that he was anti-Fascist without the shadow of a doubt. He had helped some partisans escape after they were arrested by Fascists. He was very reliable and I would soon meet him because about once a week he came to their house to get provisions. This piqued my interest: I could get news about what the Germans and Fascists were doing in regard to the Jews.

Stella asked me to tell her something about my life with the farmers where I had stayed before. I told her about my different experiences, the work I had done, my activities as "doctor," the differences in habits and behavior between one family and another. I added that as a first impression the Nepi family seemed far above average and I felt as though I had known them for many years. I could see this pleased her. She blushed and ducked her head with a slight smile of satisfaction.

Like a ghost, the grandmother floated into the kitchen. I had completely forgotten she existed. I stood up and greeted her: "Buona sera, nonna, how are you? Did you have a nice day?"

"Like poor old people!" she replied.

I stammered out a conventional phrase just to keep the conversation going, but she gave no sign of having understood. She crossed the kitchen, shaking her head as if commiserating with herself, and went to the floor below.

Stella said: "Don't let it bother you, Enrico. Grandmother's always like that. She hardly ever speaks to anyone. Now she's gone downstairs to take care of her favorite hen that lays one egg every day."

Delia was giving a hand with the cooking. With a wooden spoon she gave an occasional stir to the rabbit pieces cooking in tomato sauce inside an earthenware pot. Every time she lifted the lid the smell stimulated my already ravenous appetite even more.

Finally we heard the front door open and footsteps coming up the stairs. "It's papa," Dina said. Bista entered the kitchen with the package of things Stella had asked him to buy. He put it on the table and his first words were: "What a mess the Americans made. The firemen are still trying to put out the fires that are burning everywhere. They hit three freight trains carrying oil tanks that are still exploding one after another. People are afraid to go near. The tracks between Rome and Florence are damaged and it will be several days before they are back in service. The Germans run back and forth with their trucks and no one knows what they intend to do. It's a big confusion and they say some Germans were injured and killed."

I rubbed my hands with delight and asked Bista about the townspeople so near that turmoil. He said many wanted to get out of Montevarchi and that the Germans were scouring the countryside for any kind of food they could get their hands on because evidently their supplies were running low.

That news did not please me much. They could push as far as Consuma, even if motor vehicles could not come this far. It would not take any more than a lost soldier wandering around on foot and meeting up with me to set off a series of events I would do anything to avoid. I decided to talk this over with Bista the next day.

All of us, including grandmother, sat down at the table. A table full of happy people. We ate and drank, even finding time to talk between one mouthful and another. The most loquacious were Dina and Delia, then Stella, and at a far distance,

Bista. It was quite as though grandmother did not exist! She ate what was put on her plate without making the slightest comment about anything.

When supper was over Bista and I sat by the fireplace. Stella and the girls cleared the table and cleaned the kitchen, and the grandmother, as usual, disappeared at once. I asked Bista to wake me up in the morning as soon as he got up. I did not want to seem like a do-nothing. I was tired, and excusing myself, I took an oil lamp and retired to "my" room. I was asleep in a minute and slept soundly until morning, when Bista knocked on my door. I did not know where I was. I replied with a kind of grunt and after looking around the room I came back to reality.

I got up quickly, had a makeshift wash, and joined Bista in the kitchen in time to have breakfast with him. I remembered that I wanted to talk over the problem of the Germans wandering around the countryside. I broached the subject at once and explained my fears. Bista did not seem too worried. "Anyway," he said, "if you're uneasy about it, the best thing would be for us to make a hiding place in the woods, where you can go at any time and sleep there at night, if necessary." That seemed like a good solution, and I suggested that if Bista did not mind we could find a place together that very morning.

After breakfast we left the house to go straight into the woods. We stopped after a few meters where the vegetation was thickest. "This will do fine," he said, and taking the scythe he had brought with him, he began to cut bushes to clear a space large enough for me to lie down. In less than a quarter of an hour Bista had finished the work. With some dry leaves he made a kind of soft mattress covering the small clearing. All around young oaks formed an almost impenetrable cover.

I was pleased and thanked him, adding: "Let's hope I never have to use it."

Then we went to the row of vines at the place where we had stopped the day before and began digging with the same rhythm, without talking. It was still early and the air was sharp. After a bit of shoveling I warmed up. That day went by more or less like the one before. I did my chores: oxen, fodder, water from the well. My relations with all the family grew stronger and more friendly and the girls began to joke with me. The jokes were somewhat on the suggestive side, but always well meaning and never malicious.

The Allied planes continued their systematic destruction of the German supplies on the front lines. Now, when I heard the rumble of engines I barely looked up and only then to see how many planes there were. One morning I noticed the Flying

Fortresses were flying lower than usual. Perhaps they had sighted some well-hidden objectives that required a better look. Because of the large number of low-flying planes the anti-aircraft artillery seemed to go crazy. They shelled relentlessly and the little clouds of exploding projectiles made the sky look like a colander. Unfortunately one of these shells struck an Allied plane that peeled off from the others, leaving a tail of smoke. It made a sharp turn, coming dangerously low. It was an awful moment for me: suddenly I saw first one, then two, and finally three white parachutes open in the sky and slowly float down. The plane, abandoned to its destiny, continued to fly, descending slowly. At a certain point a huge ball of fire engulfed the plane and immediately afterward it exploded. The fire had reached the gasoline tanks and bombs still on board.

All around the explosion it rained large and small metal pieces, scattering over a wide area. I was afraid for a few moments that the three parachutists might have been injured in the explosion. When the sky cleared of smoke and flying objects, I saw that the parachutists continued to slowly descend and the three men seemed unharmed. I watched them until they disappeared behind a hill. The Germans and Fascists were certainly already on the alert to hunt them down. How I would have liked for at least one of those men to escape and find his way to Consuma. I would have had someone to hide with and wait for the war front to pass through. Thinking it over later I realized that had this really happened I, and Bista's whole family, would have run an enormous risk because we would have been involved in the German's search, ending with our falling into their hands.

Some pieces of the plane fell nearby and I told Bista I was going to see if I could find something in the woods. I went into the thick growth and walked around without any precise point of reference, moving the branches aside with a stick. After a good half hour of searching I had found nothing, so I changed direction, always careful not to go into the open or too far from the house. I rummaged around with my stick until I smelled something like burning paint. I soon found under some leaves a kind of gray tube, about one meter in length, out of which protruded a very shiny, silver-colored steel cylinder. I found what I had been looking for but could not imagine what it could be. I picked it up very gingerly, first of all assuring myself that it was not hot and that it was not a bomb or something like it. It seemed to be the mechanical part of a hydraulic system that made something close or open.

I heaved the wreckage onto my shoulder and returned to the house. It must have weighed 20 kilograms. How strange to be touching an object that until a few minutes earlier had been part of an American airplane, made in America for the destruction of the German army. I had come into contact with a piece of freedom. Even if it were useless now, it was still a great symbol to me. I carried it up to the house and showed it triumphantly to Bista and the women. They all started making the strangest conjectures as to what part of the plane it could be. Bista wanted to be certain it was not an explosive device, so looked it over closely. When he was sure, we brought it into the house and leaned it in a corner in the kitchen to show to relatives and friends.

That evening the only topic of conversation was the three American flyers. Bista tried to find out something about them the next day when he went on errands to Montevarchi. My fear was that the Nazi Fascists might hurt these men in revenge for the bombings. Although international conventions did not permit such actions, those delinquents could not be trusted. We sat around talking for about an hour and I retired to my room early with my faithful oil lamp. Once in bed, I was unable to sleep for quite a while. I could think of nothing but what those three men were doing at that moment. Maybe they were being interrogated or tortured to get information. Maybe they were hiding in the woods and the Germans were on their trail. I would have liked to help them. Finally I slept, but had nightmares all night.

The next day was Sunday, and I promised myself to sleep as long as possible, to recoup a little of the sleep I had lost by getting up so early to help Bista in the fields. I was awakened by voices that were now familiar and looked at my watch: it was ten! At least I had had a good night's sleep. Stretched out, immobile, I looked at the ceiling. Through a crack in the shutters a blade of bright light filtered. "It must be a nice day. Today I'll take it easy and enjoy the sun," I promised myself.

Among the voices coming from the kitchen was one I did not recognize—a man's voice, with a decidedly southern Italian accent. It was the voice of someone used to speaking with authority. Perhaps it was the marshal come to have a morning visit with the Nepis.

I tried to hear what they were talking about, but they were all speaking at once and I could not make it out so I decided to wash and get dressed before going into the kitchen. I opened the window and the room was inundated with splendid sunlight. The air was perfumed and slightly biting. "What a beautiful world!" I exclaimed under my breath and stretched in front of God's glory. It is incredible how sometimes the shining sun, the perfumed air of spring, and a good night's sleep are enough to put one in a state of grace. I left my room in a good mood, greeted the whole family, including grandmother, and with an inquiring expression on my face, greeted the visitor.

Bista made the introductions: "This is Enrico and this is our friend the *maresciallo.*" I shook his hand. "Pleased to meet you," we spoke simultaneously. I sat at the table where my cup was waiting to be filled. I began to eat my usual breakfast while without preliminaries the marshal began to interrogate me. "Occupational hazard," I thought, while I answered all his questions calmly. At any rate I had nothing to fear. He tried to be as casual as possible, even though sometimes the tone of his voice betrayed his true business.

After he had satisfied his curiosity, I began to pose some questions. I asked him to tell me about the time he helped the partisans who had been captured by the Fascists. I also wanted to know if a band of partisans operated in this zone and what kind of things they did. I asked him if he knew anything about the three American flyers who jumped from their burning plane yesterday. I asked him if it was true that the soldiers of the Wehrmacht were grabbing up food from the farmers' houses of this area and, according to him, what was the probability of their coming to Consuma.

He answered all my questions exhaustively. Those partisans he had helped had fallen into a Fascist trap after they had blown up a munitions depot. They were handed over to the local police while waiting to be transferred to the German police. The firing squad would surely have been their sentence. To free them, a fake partisan assault on the police was enacted with the police being subdued. The whole staging, of course, was arranged in a way to make it seem authentic.

The partisan band that had operated in the area moved north, now that the front was very close and the Allied aerial bombings were doing an excellent job of destroying the German war machine without the need for partisan support. This pleased me. Any partisan action would be followed by reprisals, with the systematic rounding up of everyone they could find in the whole countryside. That was something I wanted to avoid.

The news about the three American flyers was not so good. All three had been captured. From what he knew, however, the Germans treated them with the respect due prisoners of war. They had been immediately picked up by a Wehrmacht truck and taken to the nearest command. All three were in good condition. They would have to spend some months in a prison camp, after which, when the Allies won the war, they could return to their homes. They were lucky to have been able to jump from the plane before it exploded.

As for the Germans scavenging the farms, that was unfortunately true. I should avoid any contact with them whatsoever, the marshal said. If a man of my age were not in the Italian army he would be treated as a fugitive in hiding, if not a rebel. Because there was no way to know in advance where the Germans would go in search of food, it was essential to keep our eyes and ears alert, and in case of danger I would hide in the place in the woods Bista had made for me. By now I considered this inevitable and to hear it confirmed by the marshal did not affect me much.

I wanted to take a walk and enjoy the springtime that was rapidly approaching, and I asked Bista and the marshal if they wanted to walk with me. They agreed. We promised the women we would be back in a couple of hours. Bista led us up a hill to enjoy a wide view of the valley. From the top I was able to take in all the Valdarno. Montevarchi seemed close enough to touch. Too close, it seemed to me.

We could see San Giovanni Valdarno and the massive Pratomagno dominating the valley. In the distance, sounds of military trucks coming and going on the state road that went from Arezzo to Florence gave me the idea that in a car I could be in Florence in half an hour and find out what had happened to our house and see all my things I had been separated from for what seemed an eternity. It would be a suicidal undertaking, without any practical result. However, there was something less difficult that I could do. I asked the marshal: "Listen, if I wanted to know what had happened in my parents' house in Florence, do you think it would be possible for you to take a look without creating suspicions? Naturally, I would pay all the expenses for the bus and any other necessities. It's just to satisfy my great curiosity."

He thought it over for a moment, and then said: "I have to go to Florence on business in a few days. If you'll give me the address of your house, I'll go by and find out how things are. You'll see it's undoubtedly occupied by someone whose own house has been destroyed by bombs. Don't get your hopes up too much."

I gave him our address on Via della Cernaia and the name of the concierge who could give him information. I was prepared for any kind of news, even the most negative, so he need not worry. The thought that someone would be able to give me news about Florence was exciting: almost a preview of the longed-for moment of my return home. I could not wait until the marshal had gone and come back from the mission I had just given him. I envied him his freedom to move from one city to another. An ordinary citizen would find it very difficult.

We strolled around the fields of other farmers. Bista said he wanted to stop with the marshal to see a brother-in-law. I preferred to be alone and went back slowly toward the house, immersed in my thoughts about the marshal's trip to Florence.

I reached the house around one o'clock. Stella almost had lunch ready. I said that Bista had gone to visit a brother-in-law but that he would be back in time to eat. I stayed outside to enjoy the sun, sitting on the stone steps. Delia came out to get some well water. When she came back I asked her if she wanted to get some sun while we waited for Bista. After she took the water to the kitchen she came right back to sit and talk. I still had not found an easy way to talk to her. Delia was more reserved than Dina, and I noticed she was never the first to initiate a conversation.

I wanted to give her the opportunity to open up to me, to ask me questions, and at the same time to give me the possibility of asking her some. Delia asked me about my family, about our life in Florence, if I had a fiancée, what plans I had for when I returned to Florence. The usual things. I answered all her questions without neglecting any details. I told her I had been in love seriously only twice, but that I had never had a true and proper engagement. That seemed to satisfy her. As for the future, I still did not have a clear idea. Probably I would try to work with my father.

Then it was my turn for questions. I did not ask Delia if she was engaged, because the day I arrived Dina had told me that she was not. I asked Delia if she was happy with her life, if she ever wanted to live in a town like Montevarchi instead of staying in the country all her life. She liked her life, the work in the open air, being with her friends and relatives, and she did not feel the desire to be in a town like Montevarchi except for an occasional trip with her friends to do some shopping. Delia was the one to bring up the subject of a fiancé. More than one boy had shown an interest in her, but she had never allowed anyone to court her. None of the boys she knew interested her enough, and she thought they were too immature. It was still too early for her to tie herself sentimentally with anyone and she wanted to continue being what she was, a daughter. She was very attached to her parents and sister, something obvious by the way she acted around them. She said she was happy that I had come to Consuma and that I wanted to talk with her. Then she asked point blank: "Enrico, do you think I'm pretty or ugly?"

I began to laugh. "What kind of question is that? Of course you're pretty!"

Delia blushed and bowed her head in shame at the question that had revealed her whole character: candid, sincere, and modest.

Then she wanted to justify herself: "I asked you because no boy has ever told me and it would make me happy to hear it."

"If that's the only reason," I continued, joking, "you can ask me once a day. The answer will always be the same."

In fact, she was a pretty girl: the picture of health and a sweet nature.

Our colloquium ended with the arrival of Bista and the marshal. We all went in the house and sat at the table for the customary Sunday dinner that never ends. When we got up it was almost three in the afternoon. The marshal went to the cantina with Stella to get the provisions he had come for. He filled his basket and before leaving us for Montevarchi he told me: "Enrico, in a week you'll have the news you want." I thanked him.

He delivered the news himself, along with another pressing concern. But let us take it in order. He went to Via della Cernaia and asked for Rosita, the concierge of our building. He told her who he was: a marshal of public security. This information immediately threw Rosita into a panic, and when he asked her what had happened in the apartment from the time the Tayars had had to leave, Rosita became totally distraught. She was afraid the marshal was looking for us and calmed down only after he told her he knew me and that I had sent him there to get the information.

Our apartment, as the marshal predicted, had been given to a family of refugees, after which a Fascist had taken possession of it in the name of Party, and he had taken away everything, selling off what he could. Right now a family of refugees from Livorno was living there. No bomb had damaged the building. Rosita was very anxious for us and hoped that we would return to Florence soon. The marshal asked if the Germans had come looking for us, and no one had. Undoubtedly they knew that we had taken off at the first sign of danger.

This report was disturbing. I was sure that when we returned to our house we would not find it as we left it. But to learn that a Fascist had taken everything made my blood boil, especially when I thought of how unhappy it would make my parents. It would be particularly hard on my father. Never mind, I thought, it just meant we will have to start rebuilding our life in Florence from the ground up. Everything was lost that my father's work and my mother's self-denial had accumulated, but the important thing was for the family to be saved.

CHAPTER 15

Carlone

What had made the marshal return was something terrible that had happened in Florence. A few evenings before, at the Logge del Porcellino, there had been an argument over nothing between a Fascist and another man, a certain Carlone. Most likely the two had been drinking. Carlone shot the Fascist dead and ran away.

Carlone was a Communist and had found immediate refuge with one of his comrades, but because the Fascists were looking for him he had to find a hiding place as far from Florence as possible. The marshal had come to ask Bista if he could put Carlone up for a few days. It was a matter of giving the police responsibility for the case to keep it from the Fascist squads. This way Carlone could save his skin, because if he were arrested by the Italian police he would be treated as a simple murder suspect and transferred directly to an Italian prison.

It was not up to me to decide, so I kept quiet. I could not help thinking, however, of the possible repercussions if Carlone came to hide in Bista's house. It was one thing to give hospitality to a Jew who was hiding only because he was a Jew, without ever hurting a fly. It was quite another thing to give hospitality to a man who had killed someone in a fight, with the aggravating circumstance that the victim was a Fascist.

Not only the Fascists were hunting Carlone to revenge their comrade, the police also wanted to capture a murderer, without taking his political beliefs into account. Things were growing very complicated for all of us. I could see that the marshal's request left Bista very perplexed. I compared his reaction now to what it had been when I pulled him out of bed in the middle of the night a few weeks ago. Now he was weighing very seriously what was going through his mind. It was clear he did not want this Carlone in his house, but he did not have the courage to refuse him what he was giving me.

In the end he had to agree, but he added: "Look, if I do it, I'm doing it because you asked me to. I've never let a murderer in my house and I don't want to start now. But please make it clear that this man's comrades must find him another place as soon as possible, because I can't risk keeping him for more than a few days."

As Bista spoke, it was obvious that he was very upset by having to accept something definitely against his better judgment. The marshal thanked him and said he would bring Carlone himself in a couple of days.

It made the whole family depressed. Poor Bista did not know how to defend himself from the women's attacks. The nicest name they called him was a "twit." I felt I should side with Bista by defending his decision as something he could not avoid. I admitted that if it had not been for my presence, he would have had no problem saying no to the marshal, and I praised Bista for the stipulation he had made about limiting Carlone's stay to only a few days. When he arrived I would go sleep in my hiding place in the woods for two valid reasons: first, because I did not feel like sleeping in the same bed with a killer; second, because I would be safe if the police or Fascists should come in the middle of the night to arrest him.

The women objected. "He can go sleep in the woods, not you, Enrico." Stella blurted out. "Do you think I'd be happy to know he was sleeping in my son's bed?"

To calm the waters I suggested we wait until Carlone came, to see if he might offer to sleep in the woods instead of me. If he did not, well, never mind. It was no problem for me, particularly now that the nights were no longer cold, and the idea of sleeping under the trees was almost beginning to appeal to me.

"Who knows, I might meet someone interesting!" I said jokingly. And with that the debate was closed, but I saw that the bad humor continued to snake around. For the time being the women had signed a kind of silent armistice, but sooner or later the discussion would surface again. The atmosphere in the family was very heavy, so palpable you could cut it with a knife. They reluctantly communicated in monosyllables. Bista, poor man, let off steam by smoking his cigar, polluting the kitchen as never before. The two girls avoided any discussion. Every so often Stella could not keep from tossing some barb at Bista, who would make a slight gesture and remain silent.

It seems paradoxical, but relieving the atmosphere were the Flying Fortresses that arrived in truly massive numbers to unload their arsenal. They came in successive waves, one after the other, without interruption, and they flew much higher, perhaps remembering the plane that had been downed by the anti-aircraft artillery.

The noise of the engines was like continuous thunder broken only by ground explosions and lightning. It seemed like the end of the world. The Allies must have discovered some large German troop movement along the Valdarno, either by truck or train, and their continual aerial blitzes were destroying war material and interrupting the replenishment of troops on the front line.

We went out to observe that pandemonium. The German losses must have been enormous and my happiness infected the others. The day ended better than it had begun. We decided that after four or five days at Consuma, Carlone would be encouraged to find another hiding place. At the same time Bista would ask the marshal to arrange a police arrest.

Two days went by before the new guest arrived. He came late in the evening, after supper. We were all in the kitchen talking about nothing in particular when we heard the marshal call from the farmyard. Bista went to the window and invited the marshal to come on up with the guest. Carlone was a big heavy man, with dark skin, but not like someone who had been in the sun. It was a strange color, almost gray, which must have been the color he was born with. He greeted us in a deep voice and sat on the bench next to the marshal. He kept his head down, almost as though ashamed to look us in the face. I felt a little sorry for him in spite of everything.

For two days I had everything ready to move to my hiding place in the woods. In a bag I had put a woolen blanket, a pillow, and a flashlight they bought me. Everything else I had left in my room, where I hoped to return soon. Given the late hour and the fact that I did not much want to talk to Carlone, I stood up after a few minutes and said: "Fine. Good night, everyone. I'll retire to my private room in the hotel nearby."

I picked up my bundle, and with a wave I left the kitchen and hurriedly went to "the hotel." The hiding place was not hard to find with the flashlight. I spread the blanket over the mattress of leaves and put the pillow on top of it. I took off my shoes, lay down, and wrapped the blanket around me. I turned out the flashlight and for the first time tasted the pleasure of sleeping under the starry skies. I lay on my back with my hands behind my head to contemplate that splendid view of a billion stars shining brightly in the clear sky, framed by the tops of the young oaks surrounding me.

Looking up, I thought: what I was doing would not be considered so unusual by the many hundreds of thousands of people in the world who sleep in the open every night. And with this mild temperature it is anything but a tragedy. Winter would be less pleasant, I had to admit.

The mattress of leaves was soft enough and the blanket was large enough to cover me from my nose to my toes. I was so happy with that hiding place I decided to stay there day and night. The less I stayed in the house, the smaller the risk I would run of some unpleasant encounter. To this could be added my lack of interest in talking with the new guest. I could ask one of the girls to bring me something to eat for supper, while at noon I could eat a snack in the fields with them. Of course, I would continue to work with Bista and the girls without ever going near the house. I was sorry for those who would have to put up with Carlone alone, but it would only be a matter of a few days, or at least so I hoped. I closed my eyes, and after taking two or three deep breaths in that flower-perfumed air, I slept.

The twittering birds, engaged on their morning activities, woke me. It was six o'clock. I folded the blanket and put it in the sack with the pillow and covered everything with branches. I stayed for a minute to enjoy that particularly magic moment. In spite of the peculiar billet I felt rested. The first rays of the sun filtered through the tender green oak leaves. The air was slightly cool but full of the intense perfume of moss and earth. I heard nothing other than the chirping and fluttering of birds in search of insects. Thus isolated from the world, I might as well have been on a deserted island in the middle of the ocean.

I stretched my cramped limbs and got ready to face another day. Bista and Stella were already eating their breakfast when I joined them. Whispering, I asked how it had gone with Carlone. Bista gave a negative shake of his head and signaled we would talk later in the fields. We quickly finished our breakfast and I followed him to the work awaiting us.

While we walked he told me about the previous evening. The marshal left almost immediately, promising to return in a couple of days. They were left alone with the guest and no one had the courage to initiate conversation, not knowing what to talk about. They offered him a glass of wine that he tossed down at once.

Stella then showed him the bedroom, and he went in with his small suitcase. He did not even take the trouble to ask where I had gone to sleep in order to make room for him. Obviously he had not caught my sarcastic remark about the "hotel."

I told Bista about my idea of staying in the fields all day and in my hiding place at night, without eating supper in the house. He was of the same mind. "I'd like to do it, too," he said. I consoled him by reminding him it would just be a few more days.

We sprayed the vines with a hand pump and cut alfalfa for the oxen, each of us preoccupied by his own thoughts. Bista had many more worries than I did. Poor man, he had been living a peaceful farmer's life, with nothing more to worry about than watching his wheat grow, when two bricks fell on his head: first me with all my problems; then Carlone with that disaster he had caused. To tell the truth, it was too much.

We worked all morning without seeing another soul. Toward noon Delia came with our snack. We all sat under a mulberry tree to eat our frugal meal. Bista asked Delia what was going on in the house. Carlone got up around nine, ate breakfast, and stayed in the kitchen to talk with Stella. He asked if it would be possible to have a newspaper with the local news of Florence. Maybe he wanted to see if there was something about his crime. Stella told him that the only way to have a newspaper was for someone to go to Montevarchi to buy it, which meant a half hour each way. She did not think that with all we had to do in the fields it would be possible for anyone to make the trip just to buy a newspaper. He had to wait until someone went to Montevarchi on other errands. He seemed put out, but Stella pretended not to notice. Then he left the house, saying he was going to take a walk in the woods. "Let's hope he gets lost!" Bista said.

Delia added that Carlone was very withdrawn, with crude ways, and she could see he had a hot temper as he amply demonstrated in Florence. He did not inspire any sympathy or compassion. She would also be glad to see him go as soon as possible. Before he left the house he returned to his room and came out with his right hand in his trouser pocket: without a doubt he had a pistol in his hand, because she could see its shape through his trousers. This had bothered her because he was the kind who would not think twice about shooting; seeing that he had already killed one man, he would not have any problem killing another.

This information did not please Bista, either. "I do not want anyone in the house with a pistol in his pocket," he said. "Tomorrow I'm going to the *maresciallo* and telling him to take this pest off my hands." The situation could become even more dangerous, I agreed, if by chance there was a shootout while some family member was present.

I had never seen Bista in such a bad mood. He looked glum and had difficulty eating what Delia had brought. I, on the other hand, did honor to the snack and tried to soothe Bista, saying it was right for him to talk to the marshal and to Carlone himself about the pistol, and to do it without irritating the undesired guest, given his rather violent nature.

I told Delia I would spend the days in the fields and nights in my hiding place in the woods and that this would mean more work for her to bring me supper in my new "lodgings." She did not bat an eye and said it was right for me to avoid the undesirable guest and it was not any problem for her to bring me my food in the woods.

We finished the snack and Delia returned to the house to help Stella. Bista and I wondered what Carlone would do all day. Considering his rather cold rapport with the family, it did not seem likely that he would stay in the house to make conversation. Therefore, the only alternative was for him to wander around the countryside, with the risks that entailed.

After about an hour of work, Bista said: "Enrico, I'm going to Montevarchi to talk to the *maresciallo*. Until I get this thing with the pistol cleared up, I won't be able to do anything."

"All right," I replied. "Go ahead, and remember to buy the paper for Carlone. That will keep him quiet for a while."

Bista left and I continued to work alone. After a short time Dina came to give me a hand. Bista must have told her to keep me company. I asked her what had happened with Carlone. He had eaten lunch and then left with barely a word, not thanking anyone. He only said he was going out to get a breath of air. Not much for someone who was treated as an honored guest. I told Dina to keep me informed about things and let me know what Bista had to say after he got back from Montevarchi.

I returned to the house with Dina to say hello to Stella and get a book to read while I was in the woods resting between chores. I had not read for some time. The many things to do to get settled with a new family had not left me time for reading. I returned to my hiding place and immersed myself in a book I had left half finished. I had found an old friend again. I only hoped that in his wandering Carlone would not stumble onto my refuge. I was not in the mood to make small talk with him. Instead, Bista came to find me as soon as he got home. His face was less tense. He had talked with the marshal. It was true that Carlone had brought a pistol with him, against the wishes of the marshal himself. He had done it to defend himself from a possible punitive mission by the Fascists. It would be a question of a day or two at the most and the marshal would be ready for the police arrest. He would come himself to Consuma with his colleagues and it would be done so as not to cause problems to anyone. In the meantime we had to pretend nothing was happening and keep Carlone as calm as possible.

I was very happy at the prospect of soon returning to my normal life in the bosom of the family. Bista also had recovered his usual good humor. He had bought the newspaper and given it to Carlone who began to read it hoping to find news about the business that interested him, but found nothing.

The sun was quickly falling behind the horizon when Delia brought a basket with my supper, or rather, two suppers. Delia had decided not to let me eat alone. I appreciated this courtesy that could only spring from a truly nice person. We spread out a large tablecloth and settled down to eating the good things Stella had fixed. It was very pleasant: we were completely alone and I felt like I was having a luscious picnic with a very sweet girl. The hour was especially romantic, with the sun just about to give us one of those fiery sunsets I adored. There was nothing romantic about our conversation. We were both in an excellent mood because Carlone would be going away so soon. We joked and said many foolish things throughout the meal. I felt as if I was with a dear friend who had given me a sense of well-being and optimism. I told her so and thanked her for everything she was doing for me.

When we finished eating, the sun had been swallowed by the hills on the horizon. The sky had turned dark blue and only in the west was a long silver stripe of the dying day visible. I told Delia it would be better if she went home. We stood up, put the few dishes in the basket, and said good-bye. Instinctively, without even thinking about it, I gave her a light kiss on a cheek and said: "I'm so happy you stayed to eat with me. Thanks, Delia." In spite of the growing darkness I saw Delia turn red from my unexpected gesture. She kissed me back and said: "Ciao, Enrico.

Good night. Until tomorrow," and ran off as if she were afraid I might ask her to stay longer.

I sat down and thought about what had happened under the spell of Delia's happy and casual chatter. I wondered if I had not been out of line to give her that innocent kiss on her cheek. However, it had been an impulse of the moment and not a calculated act, nor did it have ulterior motives. It was simply a demonstration of my affection and gratitude for what that sweet, good girl did for me.

I pulled my blanket and pillow out of the sack. With the help of my flashlight I fixed everything as I had the evening before. Just to be more tranquil I made a little inspection of the surrounding woods. Everything was normal: the birds were getting ready for the night with their families. I heard their subdued chirping. A light wind advised me to make sure the blanket was carefully wrapped around me to avoid catching cold. I lay down on the bed of leaves, put out the flashlight, and said good night to the whole world.

That day no Allied plane had flown over the Valdarno. Why not? This thought was followed by another, more pressing, thought. With everything that had happened over the past few days, I had not remembered my parents or Liliana. The next day I would write them a card. With this decision sleep came over me until I awoke to chirping birds. I lay still to enjoy that blessed state for a few moments. Another radiant day was getting ready to dawn. The air was tepid; the wind from the evening before had died down.

I remembered that I had to write my parents. I was convinced Liliana would not visit me again until Tuscany was liberated. What news I was able to hear, though very indefinite, indicated that the Germans were continuing their retreat to the north. As far as news about the Fascist and German hunt for Jews, I only heard that the two large factories of Montevarchi, La Familiare and the Cappellificio Rossi, which produced felt cloches for hats, were requisitioned by the Fascist government. In fact, both factories belonged to two Jewish families: La Familiare belonged to Nino Donati, father of my dear friends Rosina and Lazzaro, while the Cappellificio Rossi belonged to the Loria brothers. Luckily, no one in the two families was taken by the Germans.

I got up and made ready to return to the house. From a distance I saw Carlone come out and walk in the direction of Montevarchi. Good, I would not have to meet him. The whole family, including the ever-silent grandmother, was around the table having breakfast. My clean, white cup was there waiting. I greeted the whole crew and sat down with them, immediately asking how supper had gone the evening before and where Carlone was going so early in the morning.

Supper had been peaceful enough. Although few words were spoken, Carlone managed to put together a short speech of gratitude for their hospitality, clearing the atmosphere. He asked who I was and where I went to sleep each evening. Bista told him I went to stay with some of his relatives for the time Carlone was there. He did not seem very convinced of that answer but pretended to believe it. During supper he drank a lot and went to bed early.

That morning Carlone seemed to have something urgent to do and that was why he left the house. Bista thought that perhaps he wanted to call the marshal from a public phone. He seemed suddenly to have made an important decision that morning. We all hoped it was a decision to leave. After breakfast I had my usual quick wash. I felt a great need for a thorough bath, but that would not be possible until my room was free. I took a postcard from my backpack and wrote a few lines to my parents, putting them at ease on my account. I gave it to Dina, asking her to please mail it the first time she went to Montevarchi or Moncioni.

We wondered why the Allies had not bombed the Valdarno the previous day. According to Bista, only one small reconnaissance plane had surveyed the area. Perhaps they wanted to make an exact inventory of all the damage the bombing had done the preceding week, in addition to identifying the objectives still to be destroyed. I fervently hoped the Flying Fortresses would start up again soon.

I took advantage of the fact that Carlone was not in the house that morning by visiting my oxen friends. For several days I had not seen them and I missed them. I went through my usual routine: replaced the old straw with that fresh and clean, gave them food and water, mixed the fodder for their next meal, and lingered a few minutes to stroke the two giants' faces and underneath their necks. When my duty visit was over, I went with Bista and the two girls to do the daily chores. I cut some alfalfa for the oxen, while the others spaded and fertilized the vines.

It was around 11 in the morning when we heard the far off rumble of approaching Allied planes. That was sweet music to our ears! My morning prayers were about to be granted. We stopped working and ran to the hill that gave us the best view of what was happening in the valley. An impressive number of Flying Fortresses were coming at a high altitude in perfect formation, seemingly slow and irrepressible.

The anti-aircraft artillery fired wildly, without making the formation move a meter or hitting a single plane. Below the bombers a couple of dozen fighter planes dove about, and with every machine gun on board they fired enormous quantities of shells that evidently sliced some military convoys moving in the valley. When the fighter planes came down at breakneck speed, they made a sound that tore through the air like an animal screaming.

When the fighter-plane carousel ended, I saw the usual shimmering bombs fall from the Fortresses, and explosions came one after the other as black smoke rose to the sky. I wondered what was left of the German war machine to destroy. We stayed on the little hill until all the Allied planes disappeared and then returned to our chores accompanied by the dull thud of the explosions; however, we could not help looking up every once in a while to see if other planes were coming. But for that morning the show was over.

Stella came to inform us that Carlone had returned and was asking for Bista; Carlone would probably be coming to the fields to look for him. That was a good reason to stop what I was doing and retire to my hiding place to read. After a few minutes I could hear Carlone's voice calling Bista, and Bista answering him. Then I could tell they had met up with each other, but I could not hear what they were saying, so I continued reading.

More or less at the same time as the previous day, while the sun was slowly setting, Delia came with the supper basket. This time she brought only one for me. Not wanting to embarrass her I did not ask her for an explanation. Perhaps that innocent kiss on her cheek had disturbed her and made her afraid of an involvement she was not ready for. I thought it only reasonable and pretended not to notice anything.

Delia spread the tablecloth on the ground and put my supper on it. I watched her as she did it, noticing her cheeks were rather red and that she kept her head down. When she finished I thanked her with a smile and, touching her lightly on the arm, I said: "You are very dear, Delia, and I appreciate what you are doing for me. I'll always remember these special moments. Because of your goodness and your family's, I can believe in the goodness of humanity again. If it weren't for all of you, who knows what an awful mess I might be in now."

As she listened to my words her cheeks grew even more red. She looked at me, and simply said: "Enjoy your supper, Enrico. I'll come back later for the basket."

She turned and walked back quickly toward the house. I ate everything Delia brought me but could not enjoy it as much as I had the previous evening. I missed her company. I put everything carefully back into the basket and remained sitting on the ground with my back against an oak tree, waiting for Delia. It was getting late and I could not understand what was keeping her. When it was nearly dark I heard some uncertain footsteps coming near. I flicked the flashlight two or three times to show Delia the direction. Finally she came and sat on the ground to tell me what had happened. After Carlone talked with Bista in the fields, he went to the house until dusk. He was very agitated and what he said did not make much sense. He talked about "putting an end to it," "betrayal," and things like that. Perhaps after his phone conversation with the marshal, he realized the moment had come to let himself be taken by the police without an argument. That would certainly be the beginning of his problems, but fewer than he would have to face if the Fascists were to arrest him. He sat down with the family for supper, but ate little or nothing. While the others were still eating, he got up and said he was going outside for a breath of fresh air.

The reason Delia had been late coming to get the basket was that she did not want to run into him in the woods and preferred to wait for Carlone to come back to the house. Because he was so late coming back, Delia decided to dash to my refuge.

She had just finished telling me what had happened when three shots made us jump. They came from the woods, but in an opposite direction from the house. Instinctively Delia grabbed my arm in fright. We sat still, listening. We heard some excited voices coming from the same direction as the shots, Carlone's among them. Then silence, except for retreating footsteps.

I told Delia to wait until everything was quiet before going back to the house. We remained sitting with our ears strained to catch what was going on. In the distance we heard the sound of a car starting and taking off in a hurry. After several more minutes we heard footsteps crossing the farmyard and I recognized the marshal's voice calling Bista from the farmyard. It was clear what had happened. The marshal had come with reinforcements to arrest Carlone and take him by car to Montevarchi. Now he had come to tell Bista that the operation was over.

"Come on, Delia, let's go to the house," I said. I took the basket in one hand and pulled Delia along with the other. We entered the kitchen as the marshal was explaining what had taken place. My heart was pounding and from the pulsations in Delia's hand I could tell her's was too. We sat down with the others and listened.

The marshal was very calm and in his conspicuous southern accent told how that morning he had received a telephone call from Carlone asking if there was any news. There was big news, the marshal had told him: the Fascists were looking for him more determinedly than ever and had sworn to make him pay dearly. Therefore, it was in Carlone's interest to turn himself over to the local police who, by arresting him, could guarantee him the protection of an Italian prison, avoiding a worse fate. Carlone was indignant and said he had been betrayed.

At this point the noncommissioned officer became stern: Carlone was free to choose what he wanted to do, but he should leave Consuma because the police were coming to arrest him the next day. If he did not accept that solution he would have to hide out in the brush and would be caught by either the police or the Fascists in less than 24 hours.

That afternoon Carlone called the marshal again, agreeing to give himself up to the police. He was instructed to be at a certain place far from the house, to avoid involving the family. When Carlone had gone to talk with Bista in the fields, it was to tell him about the first phone call with the marshal and to ask Bista if he could stay for a few more days; to this he had received a decided no.

"And those shots in the woods a while ago?" I asked, joining the conversation.

"That was all Carlone's idea. As soon as he saw us coming to arrest him, he ordered us to stop and threatened to kill himself if we made a move. With his revolver in hand, he suddenly turned and disappeared into the woods and fired shots to make it seem he had attempted suicide. We knew at once that he had not shot himself because if that were the case we would have heard only one shot. He wanted to create a little confusion with that silly scene. That's it in a nutshell."

Carlone let himself be arrested without any resistance. He handed over his revolver to the marshal and got in the car with the other policemen, who took him directly to a security cell in Montevarchi. The marshal had come to explain everything to the family and to thank Bista and Stella for their help. He also thanked me for giving my room to Carlone and for sleeping in the woods for three nights. I replied that I would sleep in a treetop rather than share the bed with that kind of rhinoceros.

The marshal took the prisoner's things and quickly left. I was exceedingly happy and so was the rest of the family. Bista took a flask of wine and filled the glasses.

We toasted our restored freedom. I toasted my restored bed! The good humor that had left us for three long days returned. We made jokes about Carlone's stupid and ineffectual scene and made some predictions about what would happen to him, but most important, we decided that from then on we would not talk any more about him—a vow we scrupulously maintained.

Stella went into what was again my bedroom, opened the window to air out the stink of Carlone's cigarettes, and changed his sweaty sheets and pillowcase with fresh ones. I was very grateful to her for that thoughtfulness. I would not have dared ask her, but I would not have been able to sleep on the same sheets as he slept on.

It was the end of a nightmare for us all. Bista swore that he would never give hospitality to anyone else again, but that was a vow destined to be overturned.

I stayed up for a while longer to enjoy the tranquil atmosphere of the house. Surprising us all, grandmother emerged silently from her room and had a few lapidary words to say: "I didn't like that man much. He made my flesh crawl." And with this she fell back peacefully into her habitual silence.

I said good night to everyone, excusing myself by saying: "I can't wait to jump back into that nice big bed," and I disappeared from circulation. In the wink of an eye I was undressed and under the sheets. It did not seem real. I remained immobile to enjoy the sensation of my body, centimeter by centimeter, all its weight abandoned on the soft mattress. I dropped off to sleep and did not wake up until the next morning. Thinking I was still in my hiding place, I could not understand why the birds were not singing and flying over my head.

The prior evening I had told Stella that in the morning I would like to have a good wash and would appreciate a pail or two of hot water. When I went into the kitchen there were already two pitchers full of hot water. I greeted Stella and Delia, who were there (the others had already been in the fields for an hour). I took the two pitchers and closed my door. The bathing was a little complicated but entirely satisfactory. I made a big lake on the floor with all my rinsing, but never mind, I would mop it up myself. I shaved carefully, changed my clothes, and fresh as a rose I entered the kitchen where my usual cup was waiting for me with open mouth.

CHAPTER 16

Jim

Before going out into the fields I looked after the two oxen and asked Delia if she was also coming out. She had to help Stella and would come out later to bring us our snack.

Jauntily I strolled out to join Bista and Dina. "Better late than never," Dina said as soon as she saw me.

"That bed is too comfortable," I responded. "It's your fault for making me sleep in it!" And at that I started digging with them.

"When do we start working with the animals?" I asked Bista.

"After we harvest we'll use them to carry the grain to the farmyard for threshing, and then we'll use them to plow the field to get it ready for the new planting."

Which meant I would have to be patient for a few more weeks before taking the oxen out of their stalls. I was anxious to start working with them.

Toward noon Delia came with the basket full of the usual good things and all four of us sat in the shade and ate and drank happily with a good appetite. What luck to find such good and friendly people. I considered myself very fortunate.

The air had become warmer and after eating I went to lie down in the shade to rest. Bista and the girls did the same. He took out his faithful cigar and began to peacefully smoke, a sign the storm had passed and he had returned to his proverbial calm. Bista announced that he would go to Montevarchi that afternoon to do some errands for Stella, and I asked him to buy me a newspaper to find out what had happened the day before with the Allied bombings.

A little later he went to the house and I stayed in the fields with the girls. We continued working a short distance from each other so we could talk at the same time. It was clear they were very relieved that Carlone was gone. They too had been afraid that at any moment he could do something foolish with that revolver. When someone has killed once it is a short step to killing again. Aside from the final scene in the woods, nothing bad had happened and everyone was pleased and happy.

We finished the day's work and walked slowly back to the house. Every so often we stopped, still talking, as if we wanted to extend as long as possible that magic moment of the approaching twilight, staying outside under the immense sky, breathing in the sweet odors suddenly liberated in the evening air.

Back at the house I took care of my two oxen friends, giving them fodder for the night and staying a little for my usual blandishments. It had become an inevitable ritual for me as well as for them.

Bista came back just in time for supper. He had bought me the newspaper and before going to the table I gave a quick glance at the headlines. I promised myself to read it carefully after I went to bed. I was still savoring the pleasure of having the bed to myself again.

I asked Bista if he had heard any news in town. He had stopped in to see the marshal, who told him that transferring Carlone from Consuma to Montevarchi had not been without its excitement. He had become violent during the short trip and wanted the policemen to let him go. Luckily they had handcuffed him so he was not able to do any harm. He was put immediately into a secure cell waiting for the judge to have him transferred to a prison in Florence.

The Fascists had found out, to their annoyance, that the police had captured their prey and that they had been outmaneuvered. The case could be considered closed: no mention had been made of the three days Carlone spent in Bista's house. Officially he was hiding out.

We ate very happily, and I excused myself and went to bed to read my newspaper. Something very tragic had happened in March. The Germans shot 335 hostages, 75 of them Jews, in reprisal for some Germans killed by partisans. The massacre had taken place at the Fosse Ardeatine, in the suburbs of Rome. Otherwise, nothing extraordinary seemed to be happening in the world, at least according to what was printed in the paper. The war news was naturally filtered by the censor, but even so, it was clear that the Nazis were going from bad to worse.

What had happened at the Ardeatine struck me in the pit of my stomach like an awful physical pain. For me it was as though it had happened yesterday. I had not heard about it because of my total isolation from the world around me. I damned the Germans for all the atrocities they were committing against so many innocent and defenseless people. Unable to stop the destruction of their war machine, those savages took revenge on hundreds of helpless people like those poor Jews they cut down in the ditches. I felt the despair of those families as if it were mine.

Would the day ever come when the Germans would pay for all the evil they were doing in the world? Would there ever be a *redde rationem* for the murderers who so pitilessly exterminated a people for the mere fact of adoring the One God, the God of Israel?

I became extremely angry and frustrated because I could not fight those evil people who blindly followed that madman Hitler. I hated them with my body and soul.

I could not calm down, and after putting out the oil lamp I continued to toss and turn for at least two hours without going to sleep. I prayed the Lord to save my people from more death and suffering, to protect my dear ones, and to inflict terrible punishment upon the Germans for what they were doing. This calmed me a little and after a while I slept but had terrible nightmares all night long.

The next morning I awoke in a bloody mood and when I joined Bista and Stella in the kitchen they were quick to notice.

"What happened, Enrico? Are you sick?"

"No," I replied. "I feel bad about something I read last night in the paper."

I explained about the Fosse Ardeatine. I let loose everything I had bottled up inside against the Germans for many months. I told them what I knew about the concentration camps, the gas chambers, and all the atrocities that had been per-petrated by these people for years. They had trouble believing such things could happen.

Stella had tears in her eyes. In silence she took my hand and stroked it in an effort to calm and console me. I understood they could not find words to speak. It was as if they felt in some way responsible for what the Germans were doing. I was sorry to see them so mortified and said that luckily such wicked people did not exist in Italy, and that if it were not for good and generous people like them, I would have ended up like so many of my fellow Jews.

That outburst was good for me. Slowly I cooled down and ate breakfast with them. I apologized and asked them not to say anything to Dina and Delia. No use upsetting them, too.

One day followed another. My ties of affection with that family grew stronger. I felt like their son and brother.

News from the war front continued to be favorable. The Allies were slowly moving northward from the south of Italy and were approaching Rome. The Germans were retreating slowly, burning the land as they left. The Allied planes hammered incessantly behind the German lines, decimating men and supplies.

The time for harvesting the wheat was approaching, one of the most onerous tasks of the season. We got up early to work in the cool hours of the day. The whole family except Stella, who had the house to run, participated in the harvest. For a few days some strong and willing young men of neighboring families came to give us a hand.

One morning toward ten we were busy cutting the wheat when I heard Bista, who was working about 50 meters away, call out: "Enrico, come here." Stopping work, I went over to him and saw that he was with a rather oddly dressed stranger, a sturdy young man with blond hair, wearing some kind of military uniform. My first impression was that he was a German soldier. Then, after a closer look at his uniform I realized it was a different color than that of the Wehrmacht.

Bista said: "See if you can tell what he wants. I can't understand him. He doesn't seem like a German."

I took a good look at the soldier: he was a mess. His uniform was dirty and torn in several places. He had abrasions on his face and other parts of his body and dried blood here and there. Standing close to him, with the sickle still in hand, I saw him look at me with suspicion and some fear.

"What do you want?" I asked him in Italian.

"I am a British soldier and I need help."

I heaved a big sigh of relief and shook his hand enthusiastically. Patting him on the back, I said: "Don't worry, you're among friends. I'm British myself."

His face lit up in a big smile and he could not stop shaking my hand. I told Bista the fellow was an English soldier and he need not worry.

The soldier's name was Jim Foxall, he belonged to the British 8th Armoured Division, and he had been in a German prison camp at Fara Sabina, near Rome, for several months. Because the Germans were retreating to the north, they had dismantled the prison camp and were transferring all the English prisoners to other prison camps in Germany. Along with other English soldiers, Jim had been loaded onto a freight train, and while it was traveling toward Milan, he and a friend decided to try to escape. The train made long stops, and during one of these they cut two boards from the wooden wall of the freight car with a knife. They waited until the train went through an uninhabited and woody area and then slipped through the small opening and jumped. They landed head over heels on the stones supporting the tracks and ran in different directions. As he rolled down the slope covered with large, sharp rocks, Jim received painful cuts and bruises all over his body. The German guards who were crouched on the cars to watch the prisoners saw them and fired some machine-gun rounds that, happily, missed their mark. The convoy stopped and the guards got off the train to search for them, but they soon gave up for fear that during the stop other prisoners would try to escape through the same escape hatch.

Jim hid in a ditch full of water covered by reeds, and he stayed there until he heard the train start up again. He walked a long time across wheat fields, trying to avoid the local inhabitants. And now he was here with us, at Consuma.

He said he would just like a drink of water and to wash his deepest cuts, if possible, and then he would continue walking to reach the front lines of the 8th Armoured Division, now not far from Rome. I explained the situation to Bista and asked his permission to take Jim into the house to wash and disinfect his wounds and let him collect himself a bit.

In his usual calm manner, Bista gave his permission and added that maybe Stella could also fix something for Jim to eat. I looked back on a similar scene that distant April night when I had arrived at Consuma. Why should this be any different? I told Jim what Bista had said and I will never forget the expression on his face. Perhaps he thought he was dreaming. He thanked Bista in English and shook his hand.

I took Jim by the arm and as we walked to the house I asked him if he would like to stay there for a few days until his injuries were at least partially healed. I explained my situation and how the Nepi family had been wonderful to me. I added that as far as his lodgings were concerned we could both make use of the same bed. While I talked I was thinking it was foreordained that I should continue sharing my bed! This time I would do it very willingly, because he was a fugitive like me. My suggestion seemed to please him, so I told him to leave it to me.

When we reached the house I called to Stella from the farmyard and waited for her to come to the window. I did not want to frighten her by dropping into her kitchen with a stranger in that condition. Stella looked at me and then at Jim. Her hands went to her head, and *"Gesù mio!"* she exclaimed. "What did he do to get in such a condition?"

Still speaking from the farmyard, I explained very briefly what had happened and told her that Bista said it was all right to bring him into the house. As we went up the stairs I could see he was in pain and I helped him into the kitchen.

Stella came over to us. "Look at the poor thing. Come here and sit down." She talked to him as though he could understand what she was saying. I invited Jim to sit down and asked Stella please to give him a glass of wine, and if possible, fix him something to eat.

In an instant two "welcome" eggs, of happy memory, were cheerfully frying in the usual pan. Then Stella put a plate and fork on the table, and inviting Jim to sit on the bench, she slid the two eggs from the pan onto the plate and cut him a nice slice of bread.

Jim devoured it all quickly as he looked around the room with an incredulous expression. He had never been in a Tuscan farmer's house, and I do not think he had ever expected to be.

I enjoyed watching him savor that first taste of freedom. After so many months of hard life under the Germans, he could relax, feeling surrounded by people disposed to helping him hide from those hunting him. No one understood better than I what was passing through his mind.

I acted as interpreter for him with Stella, who wanted to know how he had managed to escape from the freight train. As he told his story for the second time, I noticed that Jim was becoming more sure of himself. To get over his fears it was obviously necessary for him to talk about them.

When the three-way dialogue had ended, I asked Stella if she would mind heating up a little water so Jim would wash in my bedroom where he also could shed his torn and dirty clothes and put on a pair of my underwear, a shirt, and a pair of trousers.

Afterward I set about medicating his cuts and abrasions, which seemed less serious after he had washed off the dried blood. I carefully disinfected all the injured areas and over the deeper wounds I put some sterile gauze and tape. When my work was finished he did not look so bad.

Jim felt refreshed, especially after Stella's snack. I took him on a tour around the farm, showing him my oxen friends, the granary, the shed for tools and storing hay. In the meantime Bista had come home with Dina and Delia for their morning snack, and we found them all together in the kitchen happy to see how much better Jim looked than when we first saw him.

"He doesn't seem like the same person," Bista said. "Ask him how he feels and what he intends to do."

I repeated Bista's question to Jim. I already knew what Bista had in mind when he asked the question. It was obvious that, good man that he was, he would end up inviting Jim to stay at Consuma for a few days, at least until he had recovered his strength. Jim replied that as soon as possible he wanted to return to the vanguard of the English 8th Army and be repatriated to Birmingham, his hometown where his family lived.

To which Bista replied: "I think it would be better to stay here for another few days until he feels better. Then, if he wants, he can go join his friends. However, he needs to be very careful not to get caught again by the Germans or Fascists."

I translated it all to Jim with a wink. He replied promptly and enthusiastically, thanking Bista and Stella. I offered to share my bed with him in order to cause the least trouble possible. Everyone was happy that Jim would stay with us and Bista forgot the solemn vow he made a few weeks ago that he would never again give hospitality to anyone.

Even the girls were happy to have this new guest. Doubtless the fact that he was an English soldier who had escaped so dramatically from the hands of the Germans made him interesting. There was the language problem, but I noticed that when we spoke Italian Jim could understand what we were saying. He explained that when he was a prisoner at Fara Sabina he had learned a few words from the Italians working in the camp.

I would say he understood almost everything. So much the better. With a little effort he could make himself understood without my help. I told everyone to try to make him understand and to urge him to speak Italian as much as possible.

Stella said she would give Jim some clothes that belonged to Dino, so I would not have to deprive myself of any of my already spare wardrobe.

We all ate around the big table, and even Jim did well in spite of what he had already eaten. Then I advised Jim to go rest a little, after all the excitement of the day. He did not have to be begged and went to crawl into bed, falling asleep at once.

We stayed in the kitchen to discuss the day's big event. Dina and Delia asked if I knew whether he was married. I did not know but I would ask him soon. It is amazing how when women meet someone they quickly try to find out the details of the person's life, especially if the person is male. I asked jokingly if they had set their cap on Jim. They dodged the question by saying that such a question was only logical.

"Certainly," I replied, "for two young women, the question is almost obligatory!" And for the entire afternoon, while we harvested the grain, I continued to tease them about it.

Bista asked me what I thought of his idea of inviting Jim to stay. I said I was in total agreement, and in fact I was very happy to have the company of the new guest. What a difference between Jim and the Carlone of a few weeks ago. I added that it would be very nice if Jim stayed at Consuma until the day the Allied troops arrived.

Jim soon became the VIP and everyone wanted him to tell about his war adventures. He soon became accustomed to being around people who spoke only Italian, and he made daily progress in speaking the language.

I had no trouble sharing my bed. We both snored like two bears, therefore we did not bother each other. However, those in the adjoining bedroom might not have slept so well. We became very close friends. He taught me some English war songs that we sang all the time, and with Dina and Delia we formed two couples and spent many hours talking and joking. Jim also began to help Bista in the fields.

We finished the wheat harvest and finally the big threshing day arrived. With a huge tractor they towed the large harvest machine to the farmyard. Finally Bista allowed me to yoke the two oxen to the big cart that had stood idle for months.

My job was to guide the two oxen back and forth from the fields to the house and vice versa, after we loaded up the cart with the bundles of wheat we had cut, gathered, and tied. I was very glad to be able to work with my oxen friends. They had learned to recognize me during all my visits to clean their stall and feed them, so were very docile and obedient. I had a stick to prod them to walk, and I learned to let them turn and go back by pulling the two ropes that ended with a kind of double iron hook threaded through their nostrils. That year the wheat harvest was very good, and with the cart we formed a great pile in the middle of the farmyard.

Some farmer friends also came to give a hand with the threshing. Otherwise we would not have been able to keep up the frenetic rhythm of the machine that de-voured the ears of wheat, spitting out grain on one side and straw on the other.

The grains of wheat were immediately put into burlap bales, tied, and stacked in a pile. With the straw, under Bista's careful scrutiny, four or five people formed a round straw stack. In the center they planted a tall pole that served to support the large dome of straw, besides allowing it to be perfectly circular.

The activity was frenetic and noisy, a great clamor of voices, a mighty clanging of the old machine, and an unbreathable dust cloud coming from the grain as the machine chopped it up. We dripped with sweat from the exertion and the sun that beat down on us. To slake our thirst Stella prepared some *vinello* made from wine diluted with water. If she had given us pure wine to drink I am sure we would all have been drunk in no time flat.

It was like a great festival. In the fervor of the threshing there was a continual exchange of rather rough jokes between the sexes, which had been part of the game for centuries. The high point of the agricultural kermis was the supper. No one ate during the day because the threshing had to be finished by evening so the machine could be moved at dawn to another farm.

The finished straw stack was of monumental size, a perfect ogive. Bista, who directed the operations, was proud of it. The wheat was baled and carried by back to the granary. The farmyard was cleared of all encumbrances, and the women swept away the residue of the threshing and got the long table ready.

More than 20 of us sat down at the table around seven o'clock. The sun was still high because of daylight saving time. One dish appeared after another without pause and the platters were cleaned like lightning by that hungry crew.

This time pure wine flowed into the glasses with all its 11 percent alcohol and everyone felt its effect at once. The women were more sober by nature, but the men showed the effect of their libations in different ways, according to their person-alities. Most were very happy; only a few got melancholy or drowsy.

Jim was quickly inebriated. Obviously he was not used to drinking so much strong wine, and I was not much more accustomed to it. We began to sing our En-glish military ditties at the top of our lungs and expected the others to join in. Everyone had a good laugh, and it was a wonderful evening. One of Bista's relatives, a young man in his twenties, brought a harmonica with him and began to play different tunes and we sang the songs we knew the words to. When we did not know the words, Jim and I, all inhibitions gone, joined in with a chorus of "da-da-da-da." We made an unearthly racket but enjoyed ourselves immensely. I had not let myself go like that since I left Florence. I must have felt the moment was coming when we would be liberated from the Nazi-Fascist nightmare.

Before long some of the young people started dancing in the middle of the farm-yard to the harmonica music. Jim was quick to take Dina's hand, and they began to dance. I invited Delia to do the same, not that dancing on the loose stones in the farmyard was the easiest thing to do. However, for me it was delightful, after such a long time, to hold a pretty young woman in my arms. I could tell Delia liked dancing with me and we all continued in this fashion for half an hour.

It got late and the guests began leaving one by one. In the end only the family remained. We sat outside at the long table illuminated by two acetylene lamps and talked over the events of the day. Bista was very satisfied with the good harvest and was already making plans for the work in the fields we would have to do over the next few weeks. I reserved plowing with the oxen. Sold! Jim did not know what he was capable of doing, so he did not receive a specific work assignment. He would be Bista's helper.

Jim's injuries were completely healed and he had begun to put on some weight with Stella's abundant meals. His Italian was improving and he could make himself understood very well. He liked Dina, and the feeling was reciprocated, as we could tell by their long conversations during work breaks.

The aerial bombardments continued with the regularity of a metronome. I wondered what was left standing in the Valdarno, after that incessant rain of bombs. Every time some "city" friend came to Consuma I asked for news about the Allied advance that was continuing, but very slowly. Because Rome had been declared an open city, and Vatican City was in its center, the Allies could not do any kind of shelling, so their offensive was notably hampered. In spite of all that, however, it was going well and there was the feeling the Germans were preparing to leave the capital.

Finally, on June 4 the good news arrived: Rome was occupied by the Allies. People went mad with joy and the Americans entering the city were welcomed as liberators. Lucky Romans, I thought. How joyfully the more than 10,000 Roman Jews must have greeted the Allied troops. Unfortunately many could not participate in the great celebration, because deportations from Rome had been particularly heavy. And there was the matter of the Fosse Ardeatine.

Less than 200 kilometers separated us from the Allied vanguard. On the one hand, Jim yearned to join up with the British 8th Army, but on the other hand I could see that his friendship with Dina had become very deep and it would be difficult for him to leave her.

We were thirsty for details about what was happening in Rome after the flight of the Germans. Unfortunately, Fascist propaganda blocked any news of the war from getting through, and only fragmentary news was brought by friends who listened to Radio London.

We had barely recovered from our exuberant happiness at the fall of the capital when, on June 6, the Allies landed on the beaches of Normandy with their enormous forces. I hoped that opening another important front in Normandy would not lessen the Allied thrust in Italy. For Jim and me this was a top priority.

The excitement of what was happening did not keep me from my chores. I had to plow a big area where we would plant the wheat, and I worked at it all morning with the oxen without interruption.

Around noon I would stop to take the oxen to the stall to drink and eat. The sun beat down strongly and both the oxen and I needed to rest in the shade for a little while to cool off.

At sunset Jim and I would talk about what we had done that day and as sure as anything we would end up discussing what we planned to do the moment we were liberated. One evening he said he had something important to tell me and we went to the woods. Jim had difficulty getting started because he did not know where to begin. I came to his aid: "It's about Dina, isn't it?"

"Yes. How did you know?"

"Even a blind man could tell that!"

So he opened up to me. They were in love. Dina had broken her engagement and wanted to marry Jim at the end of the war and go live with him in Birmingham.

He asked me what I thought and what I advised him to do regarding Bista and Stella. I told him I was very happy for them and I was sure it would be an excellent marriage. I advised him to speak calmly with her parents, who certainly would give their consent. Destiny had brought them together and they had to help complete the work.

We embraced and I wished Jim a long and happy life with Dina. I have always believed that each of us has his own book in which his whole life is written. It is called "destiny," and we cannot escape it. It was destiny that made Jim jump off the freight car headed for Germany; it was destiny for him to end up on Bista's farm. To have jumped off the train even 30 seconds sooner or later would have taken my friend who knows where to what other fate. Instead it had happened the way it did, thanks to a generous destiny and to a generous farmer. A mosaic of large and small events was crowned by a happy marriage.

I could not help analyzing what had happened to me during the recent years and what had happened to so many of my fellow Jews who had been taken away to German extermination camps and killed there without mercy. I felt a sense of guilt about the good luck that had saved me from such a horrible fate. On the other hand, I reflected on how even in a normal situation, in the most peaceful times, some people are destined for a long and happy life in good health, and others die young after great suffering. Therefore, I decided that instead of feeling guilty, I should give thanks to my Lord for all His blessings.

The next day Jim brought up the subject with Bista and Stella, who did not hesitate to give their consent. It was now "official" and the whole family celebrated the event with a glass of *vin santo*. Even grandmother said (a few) congratulatory words for the occasion and emptied her little glass. Dina was radiant and there were expressions of affection and congratulations all around.

Jim wanted to give Dina the customary engagement ring, but because he did not have a lira to his name he had to postpone it to better times. He just had to wait until the end of the war and get all the papers necessary for the wedding.

Practically overnight Jim had become part of the Nepi family. Everyone treated him with respect, both in the radius of Consuma and in the larger circle of relatives. For everyone it was a matter of just pride to have a young Englishman from Birmingham in the family, and Dina made no secret of it to her girlfriends and relatives about how privileged she felt compared with other girls. To go live in one of England's largest cities, where no one spoke Italian, was certainly a big adventure for someone like her who had never gone more than a few dozen kilometers from the house in which she was born.

Now it was Dina's turn to learn English, as Jim had learned Italian. Jim and I decided that every day we would try to get Dina to learn a few English words. It would be an enormous help for the day she moved to England.

The euphoria over the event lasted for many days. The unending topic of conversation was how Dina would be in that distant land, what she would do, and what kind of people and customs she would find. Certainly, for someone who was accustomed to working in the fields in the open air from morning to evening, it would be a big change to become part of an urban center like Birmingham.

Dina had begun to grow restless because the war was going on so long. She, like Jim, could not wait for it all to be over so they could start their new life. I told her to relax, that anyway there was nothing she could do to make things move faster. I advised her to enjoy this engagement as much as possible and to try to do it in such a way that Jim did not run any danger from the still ferocious Fascists.

The Allies had left Rome behind and were continuing their northern advance. The British 8th Army would be coming across the Valdarno; the prospect of being liberated by the English was a happy one, because Jim and I would be able to get to know them without any problem.

The Germans seemed frantic and the retreating troops turned violent, raiding the farmers' houses to grab all the food and other supplies they could. They were very dangerous because practically every soldier did whatever he pleased without any restraints.

We decided to hide most of the food, leaving a minimum of things to eat in the house so that if the Germans came to clean us out they would have something to take. If they found absolutely nothing they would certainly be suspicious and capable of any brutality until they found what they were looking for.

Jim and I tried to stay clear of the house. It would be absurd to let ourselves get taken just as the war was about to end. I continued working with the oxen. The heat became more unbearable and we began work early in the morning and stopped around ten or eleven when it started getting really hot. The oxen snorted more than usual, and so did I.

Jim and I had our snack in the woods to avoid being surprised in the house by the Germans. Dina and Delia brought food for the four of us, and we enjoyed it together in the open under the young oaks. It was a pleasant and relaxing break in the day. Every once in a while Dina and Jim exchanged some tender caresses and Delia and I snickered. For Bista and Stella, Jim was already a son-in-law and among the three were signs of warm affection.

Luckily, the Germans never came to raid the food at Consuma. One day everything grew quiet as if by magic. The distant rumble of German trucks traveling at great speed were not to be heard. It seemed as if the war had ended overnight.

This silence lasted only a few hours. Suddenly loud explosions came from the south. Then we heard a long ominous hissing above our heads and finally more explosions, but this time from the north. We were exactly on the strip of land where there were no more Germans and the English had not yet arrived. That hissing came from big guns the English were shooting at the retreating Germans.

Certainly liberation was only a matter of days, but we were going crazy with the suspense and replicating our disquiet were the explosions of guns and the whistle of projectiles that went all day and into the night. A consolation was the fact that the aerial bombardments had moved far to the north and in the distance the explosions sounded very muted.

We got news that the 8th Army was proceeding slowly but surely along the Valdarno and had already liberated Arezzo, but several days went by without much change. It seemed that the English were catching their breath and consolidating the progress made before continuing their advance. We kept waiting for something to happen at any moment. The fear of being taken by the Nazi-Fascists was greatly reduced, yet we still remained watchful for anyone who might come near the house.

Had the two parties agreed to take a break and limit their exchange of fire? No troop movements or armored vehicles were to be seen. We continued to be on a no-man's-land waiting for a new master.

I killed time by working; however, my mind was a thousand miles away. I was thinking about what I would do after the English troops arrived. Perhaps I would introduce myself to the first officer I saw, explain my situation, and put myself at his service. I yearned to make myself useful in any way that might speed up the Allied victory. I thought they would need interpreters they could trust and useful information about German troop movements. After so many months of inactivity, in which my only worry was saving my skin, I had come to the point where I wanted to move, to push on, to do something useful for myself and others. I wanted, in my small way, to hasten the defeat of the Germans in the hope of saving other Jews from extermination in concentration camps. It would be enough to save even one of those poor deportees.

Jim, on the other hand, contrary to his earlier aspirations, was no longer so anxious to rejoin the British army. Should he do so, he would be sent back immediately to England, or in any case, made to rejoin his original detachment, which was probably now fighting in some part of Italy. He was now more interested in staying peacefully with his fiancée so they could enjoy a quiet time together. For him it was like a vacation, being nourished and coddled by everyone—not a bad deal. Therefore, when I told him of my wish to introduce myself to the first English officer I encountered, he begged me to leave him out of it, and not to let anyone know he was hiding out as an ex-prisoner of the Germans. I promised to do as he wished.

The Allied artillery fire was coming closer, although it was difficult to judge the distance. Those deafening blasts were sweet music to my ears. One morning when the shelling had reached a greater intensity than usual, we heard a motorcycle roaring across our fields, coming toward the house at top speed.

It raised a big cloud of dust and bounced dangerously on the uneven surface. On the motorcycle was a soldier in the unmistakable British uniform. He wore the classic helmet of His Majesty's army and the khaki-colored uniform. He was wearing high motorcycle boots and big goggles. A large pair of binoculars hung around his neck and a little transceiver on his shoulders, on his belt a pistol, and around his waist a cartridge belt. He looked like a cowboy from the Tom Mix days. I thought I was seeing a mirage.

When the soldier reached the farmyard I ran to him waving my arms in greeting. Trying to overcome the noise from his cycle, I yelled: "Welcome! Finally you are here!"

He looked at me in surprise, the same surprise I had read on Jim's face the first time I met him.

"It is good to be here," he replied. "Who the hell are you, anyway?"

We shook hands vigorously. He turned off the motor and took off his goggles. White dust covered his face, leaving a clean mask in the place of the goggles. He was tall and robust with an open, smiling face, and I noted he was a sergeant major.

I replied to his question by explaining I was a fugitive Jew and English and had been in that house for several months. In the meanwhile Bista, Stella, and their two daughters had come out and the soldier shook the hand of each, saying: "Happy to meet you."

Jim had made himself scarce by going to hide in the stall. I invited the soldier to drink a glass of wine, but he did not accept. I could see he was in a hurry and had important things to do. He thanked me and said he had come on a reconnaissance mission to determine the German military locations and to direct the firing of the British artillery.

He asked where he could find a hill that would give him a view of the entire valley. I told him to leave his cycle in the farmyard and follow Bista and me to the hill where we had watched the bombardments so many times.

He took what he needed with him, and we walked to the observation point. With his powerful binoculars he slowly began to scrutinize the whole valley. As he looked he pointed out the places where he would have the artillery fire converge.

When he was finished with his preliminary work he started up his transceiver and began to communicate with the artillery batteries of his company. He gave the calculations for the various objectives—all incomprehensible to me. A shot from one of the heavy guns landed on the concentration of military vehicles. The soldier transmitted: "You got them. Give them murder!"

At this command an inferno of shelling broke loose and completely destroyed the vehicles. Dense columns of black smoke rose toward the sky: they had hit a fuel truck.

The soldier stayed for a little to evaluate the damage and gave the colleagues of his battery a detailed report. Then he took up his careful observation of other objectives through his binoculars and gave some new calculations over his microphone. It was a replay of the first routine: a trial blast, "Give them murder!" And down came another hail of shells.

I was excited. It did not seem real that I had been able to help that sergeant do his job. I felt like part of the English army!

This work went on for a good half hour. In the end the sergeant realized there was nothing more to shell. He transmitted his final message in which he said he would be returning to the base after he drank a glass of wine with some "friendly farmers."

We came down off the little hill that had served as an observatory and headed toward the house. While we walked I asked him his name and how many kilometers the front line was from us.

"My name is George. The front lines are just seven miles away. What's your name?"

"My name is Henry," I replied, and asked him how many days he thought we would have to wait before being completely liberated. According to him not more than two or three days, depending on German resistance. He planned to come back the next day and bring some fellows from his squadron for a little celebration.

The whole family was in the kitchen when we got there. I was sorry Jim could not be there to talk with his fellow soldier. Stella invited him to rest a little. He took off his vest and helmet and rolled up his sleeves. He washed the dust off his face with cool water and, thanking the family, said he felt much better. We sat down at the table and Bista filled six glasses with the best wine he had in the house. Even grandmother had to come see what an English soldier looked like.

We warmly toasted the health of the Allied army and the freedom regained after so many years. I kept asking myself if it was real or the figment of my imagination. It did not seem possible that we were sitting and drinking with a young Englishman and that all our fear and suffering of the past five long years was about to end. I was so happy I had to give Bista, Stella, Dina, and Delia a big hug. I even hugged the soldier; it did not seem right to leave him out. He started laughing, I imagine because he was not used to such emotional displays.

I remembered Jim who was hiding in the stall and left the kitchen without saying anything. I told Jim what had happened and asked him if he wanted to come to the kitchen and meet the soldier. He thought it over and then decided to come up. He could not bear to miss our celebration.

I went ahead of Jim into the kitchen and before he came in I said to the soldier: "You are going to meet someone now. But before you do, I want your word of honor that you won't mention this to anybody."

He was very surprised by my request and gave it some thought before answering. I assured him there was nothing to fear and that it would be a nice surprise for him. Finally he said: "All right, I give you my word." I called Jim and he came into the kitchen with his face as red as a beet and tears in his eyes from excitement.

He went to the soldier with his hand outstretched and greeted him in typically military jargon that did not require explanation. The two embraced warmly and began a constant stream of chatter. Jim told him about his engagement with Dina and the reason he did not want the soldier to reveal his presence in that house. He told him what Bista and his family had done for both of us. The soldier thanked Bista and Stella in English for saving Jim. He shook both their hands and promised he would try to compensate them for their generosity.

In the meantime he took a package of cigarettes and chewing gum from his vest pocket and gave them to Bista and the girls. He promised Jim he would keep his secret, but advised him not to wait too long to present himself at some command, or else he would be considered a deserter or worse.

He could not stay too long because he was due back at a certain time. He promised to return the next day with a couple of friends and he would bring some things for the family. We walked with him to the farmyard and watched until he disappeared in a cloud of dust.

We talked about nothing else for the rest of the day; the experience did not seem real. Jim was happy, and he and Dina discussed the best course to take. He was rightfully worried about having to report to an English command. He thought that if he did it without waiting too many days, perhaps they would understand his situation and allow him to stay with Dina; or the worse hypothesis, they would let him reenter the ranks and give him a special leave to return to Birmingham with Dina and marry her.

In the morning Stella baked a cake in honor of the English visitors. We attended to our daily chores rather unenthusiastically, keeping our ears and eyes open for their arrival.

At about the same time as the previous day we heard the drone of motors and saw the familiar cloud of dust. This time both the noise and the dust were much greater. We stopped what we were doing and ran to the farmyard.

Three soldiers came roaring up on three motorcycles. The same scene was enacted as on the day before. They got off their cycles, and after greeting everyone, went directly to the hill and began to look through their binoculars at what was going on in the valley. Only Jim and I went with them. We told the others it would be better to let them work unhampered.

Also this day, calculations were transmitted by radio, trial shelling ensued, and: "Give them murder!" with everything that followed. It was just as exciting for me to take part in that show for the second time. The artillery fire that spewed tons of shells on its objectives, the thick black and white clouds that rose after the objectives had been hit, were like weights lifted from my stomach. I would have liked that bombardment to go on forever.

When they finished their work, the three soldiers communicated to their command that they would be slightly late in returning. Permission granted. We all returned to the house.

An incredible ovation was waiting for them by friends and relatives from neighboring houses. Each person celebrated in his own way with the three soldiers, with endless pats on the back and hugs. They were treated like true liberators, as they deserved. Given the large number of people, Bista decided that instead of coming into the house, the party would be held in the farmyard so everyone could take part.

George and his two friends had come loaded with nice gifts for Bista and his family: cigarettes, chewing gum, chocolate, sugar, coffee (the real kind, not roasted barley), pipe tobacco, tea, cookies, and an amazing thing that made the women delirious: nylon stockings! It was the first time we had seen that kind of stocking and the women were ecstatic over that new silklike fiber, lightweight and transparent, but much stronger. There was general jubilation in seeing, after so many years, so many wonderful things and in such quantity that left everyone astounded.

Bista distributed cigarettes, chewing gum, and chocolates among the guests. The three Englishmen watched with enjoyment. Stella brought out her beautiful cake. Because it had been planned for a much smaller number of guests, she gave three big pieces to the soldiers and the rest was divided into much smaller portions for the others. What there was no lack of, however, was the wine that flowed freely from the flasks that were put on the table.

George's radio gave off a signal: George answered and from the other end came the order to return to the company. The three soldiers said good-bye in high spirits. They hugged Jim and Dina, whom they now considered to be one of them, and promised to come back as soon as they could. Leaping on their cycles, they disappeared rapidly the way they had come.

The guests were not interested in leaving. They wanted to stay in the farmyard and talk about the gifts the Englishmen had brought. They kept sniffing the coffee, chocolate, tea—thrilling odors they had not smelled for years.

They went away in dribs and drabs and when we were finally alone, we went over what had happened. Bista had not lost his habitual calm and was busy with his old pipe he had filled with the tobacco the soldiers brought. Jim and I discussed what would be the best thing to do. I was determined to put myself at the disposal of the 8th Army for whatever kind of job they wanted to give me. I told Jim I would do it when the first patrol and the first officer arrived. Jim was torn between his sense of duty and his fear of leaving Dina, even if temporarily. His sense of duty prevailed and he decided it would be right to go to the first British commander and explain the situation. Anyway, before he could get married he would have to return to Birmingham to prepare the necessary documents.

Our minds were now turned toward the future. We had closed the adventurous and risky chapter of two fugitives and opened a new one full of hope and optimism, signaling a decisive turn for our future.

It would be difficult to leave Bista, Stella, and Delia. I was bound to them by a very deep affection and felt like I was betraying them by leaving to return to Florence. I encouraged myself not to look too far into the future and to try to take one step at a time; in the meantime I would stay at Consuma and try to make myself useful to the English army. I would have a way to earn some money and could begin to pay Bista back at least for my keep and hospitality for my months with him. I would never be able to repay him and Stella properly for risking their lives to hide me in their house.

Delia was melancholy. She was a passive spectator of the excitement going on around her. In the end, with the return to normality, she would be left alone, without Dina, without Jim, and without Enrico. She would have to give up too many things at once. We had become good friends, and I felt she depended on me. She was very sweet to me, trying in every way to show me her affection with special attention. I let her know she was the preferred member of the family, but I gave myself definite limits, knowing that one day everything had to end. I was sorry to see her so unhappy and detached from what was going on.

CHAPTER 17

Freedom!

For two days we saw no more of George and his friends. Evidently the Allies were getting ready for a forward push. We climbed up the observation hill and saw that the roads between Montevarchi and Florence were congested with trucks and military vehicles that were not German. The 8th Army had moved north of Montevarchi and we could consider ourselves liberated for all intents and purposes. We also saw a long column of soldiers who were not English. They were German prisoners marching slowly southward, escorted by English soldiers armed with machine guns. Finally the situation was reversed, and those who until a few days earlier had terrorized us were now reduced to a herd of desperate individuals going toward their destiny of defeat.

I started running toward that disheveled crowd. I would not have missed that sight for anything in the world. I burned to yell at them: "Look at me, you sons of bitches, I'm a Jew! And I'm still alive!" I ran down to the road where they would pass and began to wait. First to arrive was a jeep with three English soldiers, moving at a snail's pace. The Germans were close behind. They were in miserable shape. Their uniforms were dirty and many of them wore only pants and undershirts. They must have been walking for hours, dragging their feet in exhaustion. They stared ahead dully, as if they did not realize what was happening. On their faces you could read the tragedy that had befallen Germany.

What good would it do to taunt them? Either they would not understand what

I was saying or would be indifferent. I gave up the idea and was satisfied to enjoy that sight, which more than anything else gave me the physical sensation of Germany's collapse, crushed by the horror of its cruelty and wickedness against the Jews. I felt vindicated for all my suffering and for the death of so many of my unfortunate brothers. Finally the Germans were finding out, even if in a small way, what it means to be a fugitive and to have to submit to the humiliation of defeat.

My only response was to make the victory sign. The English escort smiled and waved. It was wonderful finally to be able to express what I felt in my heart, without fear. This was finally the freedom on which the true Western democracies are based: the freedom to profess one's own faith, the freedom to express one's own ideas, the freedom from oppression of a totalitarian regime.

I did not move until the column was far away; I would never forget that scene. Slowly I returned to the family who had watched the prisoners from a distance with the same happy sensations and feeling it as a thankful herald of peace. I told Bista I was going to Montevarchi the next morning to feel out the situation since the British army had arrived. He said he would go with me. Then we put back all the food we had hidden from the Germans. We needed to feel normal again, to reestablish things as they were before.

I took care of the two oxen with a meticulousness that came from knowing I would not be doing it much longer. I changed their bed of straw, filled their trough with fresh food, and stayed to talk and caress them for a quarter of an hour.

I got up early the next morning, shaved, and put on my best clothes. I was certainly not Beau Brummel, but I did the best I could. Bista was ready, and after we had a quick breakfast with real coffee, we left the house for a fast walk to Montevarchi.

This was a new road to me, so I was curious about everything I saw. Occasionally we would pass a house scarred with bullet holes from the recent shellings. People were already starting to repair the war damage.

We met up with some English tanks heading north at top speed, making an infernal clanging racket. It was incredible how fast they could go. An English soldier stood in each open turret wearing a leather helmet and dark goggles. The jeeps that shot ahead of the tanks seemed like small toys in comparison.

Montevarchi was in the throes of mass confusion. Military trucks, tanks, self-propelled guns, ambulances, and whatever else made up the British war machine filled every street and piazza. The inhabitants wandered around looking at and touching everything. Some were talking with the soldiers who offered them cigarettes and chocolate.

It all had the aspect of a grand event, such as celebrations of the patron saint or important national holidays. We headed toward the city hall piazza. A large sign above the door of the government building read: ALLIED MILITARY GOVERNMENT OF OCCUPIED TERRITORIES—AMGOT. I decided that was the place for me to introduce myself.

I asked Bista to go in with me. In English I inquired where I would find the commander of the AMGOT, and the sentry pointed to stairs going to the second floor. We were stopped by another sentry and I explained the reason for my visit. From him I learned that the commander was actually the Military Governor of the area, an American army captain. He had us sit down and wait.

After a few minutes we were introduced. The governor was a tall, thin officer around 40 years old. His name was Connelly and he was from Dayton, Ohio. I introduced myself and Bista and told him my story very briefly, explaining that Bista was the last of the farmers I had lived with, and that he had saved my life. He seemed happy to meet us and shook Bista's hand warmly, congratulating him for what he had done.

He asked what he could do for me and I told him I wanted to make myself useful to the Allies in any way he thought best. He thanked me for my offer, and with the simple concreteness typical of Americans, told me that from eight o'clock the next morning I could be his interpreter and follow him wherever he went. The sentry outside his office would get me a pair of army trousers and a khaki shirt, in order to give me the appearance of belonging to the Allied armed forces, but without military rank or status. I would be a simple civilian at the service of the United States, with a salary we could discuss at our leisure the following day. The work schedule would be eight hours a day, with a one-hour break for lunch. I could go to the military mess. Sunday was my day off.

I was elated and thanked the captain for the honor of being named his personal interpreter. I assured him I would be at work on time. We shook hands. Slapping me on the back, he said: "You're a fine young man."

"Thank you very much," I replied and left his office with Bista, who of course had understood nothing of what the captain and I had said.

We stopped by the sentry, who took me into an office with stacks of cardboard boxes. He opened one of them and pulled out some American army cotton shirts and trousers and told me to pick out two pair in my size. I stripped down, found my size, and soon left proudly with my paramilitary outfits under my arm.

On the street I explained to Bista everything that had transpired so quickly. "I'm sorry," I added, "I cannot continue working for you as I have in the past."

"Don't worry, Enrico. The important thing is that we have all come out of this big mess safe and sound."

We went to pay our respects to his friend, the marshal of Public Security, who welcomed us warmly and expressed his delight over our safety and restored freedom. I told him about the appointment I had received from the American governor and he congratulated me for being chosen. He said we would have the opportunity to collaborate because his office was directly responsible to the Allied Military Government.

While we were wandering around Montevarchi I wanted to have a look at the two factories belonging to Donati and Loria. Of course they had been confiscated by the Fascists and both had been damaged in the Allied bombing.

When everyone back at the house heard what had transpired they were happy for me, but sorry I would be away from Consuma from Monday to Saturday each week. I put on my new work clothes, and for the first time I could look in the mirror and see myself in decent clothes. I liked wearing that uniform that made me look like a soldier. It made me feel complete and involved in something that would satisfy my aspirations for a few months at least. I decided that from now on I would shave every morning. I wanted to look neat; Captain Connelly was impeccably groomed and certainly would expect the same of me.

It would be useful to have the bicycle I left Florence with, which was now with Santi at Duro. I would try to borrow one from someone at Montevarchi; it would make it much easier to go back and forth from Consuma to Montevarchi's city hall.

The day passed quickly. We ate in a merry mood, and I went to bed early because the next morning I had to get up early to be at work at eight. When Jim came to bed later I was already fast asleep. Before going to sleep, I lay thinking in the dark. I made a mental list of all the things I wanted to do after I was working as an interpreter. I had to track down and get in touch with papa, mamma, and Liliana. In my search I would take advantage of my new role. Because the telephone lines were not up yet I would get a message to them through the army communications system.

The second thing I wanted to do was find out about my friends and relatives, beginning with my brother Franco who, as far as we knew, had had to stay in Malta. I was also anxious to find out about Gianna, whom I knew was in Casentino, not far from where my family was staying.

The third thing was go to Florence as soon as it was liberated and find out what was left of our house and its contents. Unfortunately the marshal had already given me some unhappy prospects in that regard.

Those were the pressing things. I just hoped the captain would help me get them done quickly. He seemed like a sensitive and kindhearted person.

Bista woke me at six. I got up quietly so Jim could continue sleeping and went into the kitchen to shave and wash. After a breakfast with real coffee, I dressed in my new clothes, and with a martial step as behooves an almost-soldier, I started off for Montevarchi.

People seemed to look at me curiously, unsure whether I were a real soldier or not. I pretended not to notice and walked quickly like a man going about his business.

I reached the city hall at eight sharp. When I introduced myself to the sentry, who had already been informed about me, he gave me a badge with "Interpreter" printed on it, which I attached to my shirt above the pocket.

I went up to the second floor and the sentry said to wait in the hall, but it was a short wait because the governor arrived in five minutes. I jumped up quickly, and not knowing how to greet him, I made an awkward attempt at something resembling a military salute. He smiled and said: "Don't bother with that stuff. Just say 'good morning, sir.'"

"All right," I replied, and stood stiffly waiting for him to give me something to do. He went into his office and closed the door behind him. I guessed that meant there was nothing for me to do but wait, so I sat back down. In the meantime the sentry had me fill out a questionnaire about myself. I noticed there was no mention of "race," as was customary with the dear Fascists. However, the form asked what kind of identity papers I possessed. Under the circumstances in which I left Florence to go to Chianti I had taken no papers that would identify me as a Jew. I left that space blank, gave everything to the sentry, and sat back down to wait.

After a time the captain came out of his office and invited me to follow him. We got into a jeep, the captain gave the driver an address, and we took off rapidly, with me in the back seat. Connelly turned to me and explained that we were going to Arezzo to meet with the chief of police to discuss the question of the Republican

Fascists who were still at liberty and should be in jail. They represented a dangerous element to the security of the Allied soldiers, in addition to being liable for regular criminal trials for the crimes they had committed before liberation.

I was pleased that one of the first missions of the Allied government was to capture these delinquents. It was an outstanding debt I would gladly help the captain collect as soon as possible.

The meeting with the police chief was dispatched quickly. He gave us a long list of the Republican Fascists in the province of Arezzo. We had to select those who lived in our territorial jurisdiction and bring them in for questioning one by one. A military office had been set aside for this purpose.

We returned to Montevarchi and with a sergeant of the Military Police (the famous "M.P."). I set about patiently making a list of the Fascists in our territory. There were many, and I wondered how much time it would take to interrogate them, make a dossier of their accusations, and institute proceedings for trials. The answer I received was that because it was a state of war and everything was in the hands of the Military Government, the procedure would be short work. The important thing was to get the most dangerous and compromising elements out of circulation fast. They would have to stay in jail until all the testimony concerning their accusations could be collected. There was no hurry to let them out.

I would be present as interpreter at the first summary interrogations. It was of great interest to me. The list of people to question was given to the local police who had the responsibility of bringing them in. In the meantime I continued going around with the captain, checking everything that pertained to the public offices in the area: the hospital, aqueduct, electric and gas centers, train station, and so forth.

My work as interpreter was fairly easy, but what bothered Connelly the most was that while his questions were concise, to the point, and clear, the answers he received from his various interlocutors were a mixture of meandering, hard-to-understand, and verbose discourses that I had to translate word for word, making us lose valuable time. It made me realize the enormous difference between American and Italian ways of thinking and acting. I preferred the American a million times over.

In the end, Connelly and I decided that instead of my translating the Italians' wordy responses word for word, I would just translate the gist of it. This plan made it all faster and less tiresome.

Many requests came in for material necessities that had been lacking for many months, especially in the health sector. The captain took note of everything and sent in requests for what he considered really necessary. He had admirable skill in defining a problem, reducing even the most difficult one to a simple formula, and making rapid and irreversible decisions. This was the only way to deal with the problems, and for good reason: there was still a war going on.

I liked my work. It gave me the opportunity to learn how public agencies are managed, and my contacts with the various officials were cordial. Naturally everyone was totally receptive to the Allied government that for a certain period would take the place of the Italian government still to come. Only on a very few occasions was an official hostile or uncooperative. On such occasions the captain set things straight very quickly by removing the individual from his post.

I went about trying to find something resembling a bicycle. One of the sentries had some unknown person lend me one. I signed a receipt obligating me to return the velocipede at the end of my work as interpreter. Having a bike to get around on gave me a greater sense of freedom.

I attended some of the interesting summary interrogations of the Fascists. Everyone, except for some rare exceptions of so-called "pure" Fascists, denied belonging to the Republic of Salò on principle. In fact, they had always been fanatical anti-Fascists! The brazen way some of them lied was quite incredible. But the play always had a short run. Each one of them had a short "curriculum" so that, after their first sickening lies, the interrogation took a less farcical turn and, after a few objections by the person conducting the interrogation, those abominable souls gradually began to admit some "marginal" responsibility, insisting they followed orders from on high and therefore were not responsible for the evil of others. They had simply followed unavoidable orders. Poor innocent lambs. . .

On the other hand, the "pure" Fascists had a proud and arrogant attitude. They were proud of belonging to the Republic of Salò and of following their Duce after the Germans had put him back in charge. They despised their comrades (and here they were right) who denied their Fascist past to save their skin. They called them "traitors." The interrogations of the "pure" were very expeditious. They admitted their responsibility and therefore were sent to jail to meditate about their misdeeds. In time a proper trial would be held.

One of those interrogated was particularly interesting. The man being investigated was around 60, well known in Montevarchi as a fanatical Fascist. His academic title was "doctor." In the United States "doctor" usually refers to a medical doctor. So when the captain saw that title, he hesitated a moment. In fact, there was a great need for physicians to keep the health situation under control. Speaking in English to the noncommissioned officer conducting the interrogation, Connelly pointed out that because he was a doctor, perhaps it was advisable to postpone his immediate arrest.

Evidently the man caught on to what was happening and when asked if he were a medical doctor, he said he was. I knew very well he was lying and suggested the captain ask which hospital he worked in and what was his specialization. He tried to keep up the deception, muttering something about his "practice" and poor patients. But after some even more stringent questioning, he did not have the nerve to continue and admitted he was a "doctor," but not in medicine: his doctorate was in business: straight to jail with the aggravating circumstance of false statement.

The days sailed by. The captain seemed satisfied with my work as interpreter and a cordial friendship grew between us. I did everything possible to keep on top of the situation and often, in the heat of the captain's conversation with others, when their responses were blatant rubbish or disrespectful toward the captain, instead of translating what they said I would give a sharp answer, saying what I knew the captain would say. In effect, I went beyond my role of interpreter, and Connelly let me know it courteously, but with military firmness. I apologized, and the conversation peacefully continued its course.

One day he said my salary would be 2,000 lire a week. This seemed an enormous amount compared to what I had earned the preceding year. I thanked him and said that with that money I could reimburse Bista for part of my expenses.

Life at Consuma flowed along pleasantly, with a continual stream of English soldiers with whom Jim or I had come into contact. They always brought presents for the family and the house was overflowing with nice things. The Nepis had become the envy of all their neighbors. Such a thing happened in no other farmer's house. It was only right that they be recognized for what they had done for Jim and me.

The time came for Jim to report to the command of the British 8th Army. One morning he went to Montevarchi and asked to speak with an English officer. The meeting was basically a formality of a purely military-administrative nature. Jim had to give all the information about the detachment he belonged to and an account of all that had happened from the moment he was taken prisoner by the Germans to the present day. Military regulations required that he be immediately reinstated into his detachment, but first he had to go to England for an unspecified time. No exception was possible. The news, even if less severe than it could have been, threw Jim and Dina into a panic. Their only hope was that upon his return to England Jim could find the way to persuade the military authorities to give him preferential treatment, because he wanted to marry the daughter of those who had saved his life. Facing this possible, but uncertain, prospect, he had to present himself to the English command, which had him immediately repatriated.

The atmosphere in the Nepi household after Jim's departure was less joyful. We were all sad and missed him. Dina especially was depressed and fearful about her future with Jim. I tried to make her see reason and convince her that the war would be over soon and that she and Jim would be married soon afterward.

I was sorry to see everyone so dejected; actually nothing tragic had happened. It was a matter of having a little patience. I tried to lighten the atmosphere by telling what I had done during the day and bringing some small gifts that the soldiers I worked with had given me.

I decided the time had come to try to get in contact with my parents. While I had begun to talk about it with Captain Connelly, one morning the sentry on duty at the city hall said a captain from the 8th Army, a cousin of mine, had asked to see me. I was dumbfounded and asked him to tell me more about him. I finally figured out he was my cousin Douglas Tayar from Malta, who had enlisted in the 8th Army with an Indian detachment. He was going through Montevarchi on his way to Florence, when, stopping by the Allied command, he had learned that a Tayar was interpreter for the American governor of the zone. He left a message for me because he could not stay, having to continue on his mission to Florence.

CHAPTER 18

Return to Florence

Finally we met. It was a very happy meeting, given the exuberant nature of Douggie (as he called himself). He told me that from the moment he landed in Italy his only thought had been to get in contact with us. In fact, a few days earlier he had gone to Florence on his motorcycle, without realizing that the city still had not been liberated by the Allied troops. He had gone directly to our house on Via della Cernaia 6 to ask about us. When they saw an English officer everyone thought Florence was liberated, but it was not at all. Douggie just had time to find out that no one had had any news of us for almost a year, and because Florence was still in German hands, he turned on his heels and sped back to whence he had come!

Franco had stayed in Malta for a long time as an enlistee in the English army, attached to an anti-aircraft battery that brought down Italian planes bombing the island every day. When the situation in England became very critical, because of the continual German bombardments, he was transferred to London, where he was also attached to the anti-aircraft defense. He was very well and was just waiting for the war to end so he could return to Florence.

I told Douggie what had happened since my family and I left Florence, of my several meetings with Liliana, and of my own adventures and misadventures. I gave him papa and mamma's last address in Casentino and asked him to go there and give them my good news. He promised to do it and keep me informed.

A few days later, to my great surprise, I saw Liliana arrive in Montevarchi. Douggie had tracked them down and told them everything. Thank heavens they were also well, and after going through so much unavoidable anxiety they had reached the day of liberation safe and sound. They could not wait to see me. We still had no word about Franco, except what Douggie had told us.

I asked the captain for a day off to be with Liliana. I took her to Consuma to meet the Nepi family. Liliana's arrival restored the happy family atmosphere. There was a great overlapping of conversations. Everyone wanted to know everything. Papa and mamma had come through the worst period of the war with flying colors. Even in Casentino there had been ugly clashes between the partisans, Fascists, and Germans. Gianna and her family were well and sent their greetings. As was to be expected, Bista invited Liliana to stay a couple of days so we could spend some time together.

I told Liliana about Jim and his engagement to Dina and about Carlone's brief appearance. Looking back was like watching an old adventure film. So many things had happened in such a short time. Liliana and I took turns talking about our respective experiences. My work as interpreter for the governor interested her a great deal. As soon as she went back to Florence she would look for a similar position.

We were immersed in our accounts when the news arrived that Florence had been liberated—news that put us in an immediate state of anxiety. We wanted to return to our home at once to see what condition it was in, but access to the city was absolutely prohibited for civilians: only military vehicles with special permission could circulate. The city was under the strict control of the Allied Military Government.

However, we had an overriding need to renew contact with the ties of our life before our flight. We wanted to close the parenthesis of our secret lives and resume normal lives. Through Douggie, who was stationed in our vicinity, we were able to make a deal with a young captain of the Indian battalion of the 8th Army, himself an Indian. He had to go to Florence the next day for a brief assignment and come back to Montevarchi the same afternoon. It was ideal for us. We begged him to take us with him. He thought it over. It was a big risk for him to take two civilians to Florence while the total prohibition was in effect. Douggie put on pressure and in the end the captain gave in.

He drove the army "half-truck" himself. For the entire trip we had to stay hidden in the back where equipment was generally carried. The truck was entirely covered with rainproof canvas. That posed no problem for us, since the trip from Monte-varchi to Florence, between checkpoints and other stops, would not last more than 40 minutes. However, they were 40 minutes of great tension. Five or six checks had to be made along the road. Luckily for us no one thought to look in the back of the truck.

At various times we were able to establish where we were through a tear in the canvas. Finally we reached Nave a Rovezzano. We were home! Through a little window behind the driver's seat we were able to direct the captain to Via della Cernaia. He stopped at number 6. We got out after first making sure no one was around to see us.

We agreed to meet there at three in the afternoon, and the captain went on about his business. We looked around for a minute from the sidewalk. Nothing seemed different about our building or the little house papa had built, except for pockmarks on the facade from shell explosions.

There was complete silence everywhere. The street was deserted. We went into the lobby and rang for the concierge. Rosita came to open the glass partition, and when she saw us her mouth and eyes flew open as though she had seen two ghosts.

"Signorini Tayar!" she screamed. "You've finally come home," and she covered her tearful face with her hands. We hugged her, happy to see her. We asked about her daughter who had married a man who lived not far from Montevarchi. She told us about the police marshal who had come to inquire about our house. Our apartment had been stripped of everything, and she did not even have a key.

On our door was a notice that the apartment had been requisitioned by the OF-FICE FOR DISPLACED PERSONS and that access was forbidden to everyone.

The blood ran to my head. I tore the notice off the door. With a pencil I scratched through what had been written, turned it over, and wrote in large letters: THE OWN-ERS OF THIS APARTMENT ARE JEWS AND ENGLISH CITIZENS. FROM THIS DATE THEY HAVE TAKEN LEGITIMATE POSSESSION. WHOEVER DARES SET FOOT IN THIS APARTMENT WILL BE REPORTED TO THE ALLIED MILITARY GOVERNOR FOR HOUSEBREAKING AND TRIED ACCORDINGLY. Liliana and I signed it.

I was furious. I got some glue from Rosita and reattached the paper to the door. I told Rosita we would hold her responsible if she let anyone in our house. We would come back to Florence as soon as possible. The poor woman was terrorized by the way I yelled at her. I had really lost control. I was so furious when I saw that the Fascists had taken our things. Rosita said it was a Fascist of the Republic of Salò, a certain Califano, who looted our things. I made a note of the name and promised myself to make a complaint at the right time.

I apologized to Rosita for speaking to her so rudely. It had nothing to do with her. I was mad at the Fascists who had persecuted us for so many years and now I could finally vent my feelings and had the right once again to say how I felt without fear of being slapped in jail. Rosita calmed down and we left on friendly terms.

We had some hours at our disposal before meeting our Indian friend, so we decided to walk around Florence to get an idea of the general conditions of the city. Rosita had told us that the Germans had blown up the bridges over the Arno in an attempt to delay the Allied advance. They had spared Ponte Vecchio, but to block access to it, they destroyed all the buildings near it within a radius of hundreds of meters on either side.

We went to have a look. It was devastating. Mountains of debris were at both ends of the bridge. Occasionally we saw an isolated wall still standing; on one a small painting was still hanging. I would never have imagined that the destructive madness of the Germans could have reached such a point. It would have been much better to demolish the Ponte Vecchio, which had little artistic merit, than to destroy so many homes of such poor people who were not even given time to take away the most essential things.

Via Por Santa Maria no longer existed, only mountains of ruins in its place. The same for Via Guicciardini almost as far as Piazza Pitti. Even Via dei Bardi and Borgo S. Jacopo were blown up. Lungarno Acciaioli was a mountain of debris for a good distance.

At the risk of hurting ourselves, we climbed up a pile of debris to get a view of the Arno from the Ponte Vecchio on down: the other bridges were gone. Of that marvel of a bridge, Santa Trinita, only two broken pillars remained, and the engineers of the 8th Armoured Division were already building a Bailey bridge in its place. It was almost finished and would be a vital passageway for moving Allied troops from south to north. Other Bailey bridges were being built above and below Santa Trinita.

It was a desolate sight to see the remains of those beautiful bridges sunk so miserably in the river. Pieces of iron or cement thrust out of the water and pointed to the sky as though invoking a vendetta.

We walked through the streets of the center. If possible, we wanted to find out something about our relatives and Jewish friends. We headed toward the temple on Via Farini. The offices of the community center were closed. Only the non-Jewish custodian was there, who had remained in his little community apartment during all those months. We asked what had happened to the Jews in Florence and learned that many—more than 200—had been deported to German extermination camps and no one knew what had happened to them. The hope that they might still be alive was very slight. Who in particular had been deported he had no idea.

The Germans had seriously damaged our synagogue before they left. They had tried unsuccessfully to force open the doors where the *sefarim* are kept. Many of them had already been removed by some courageous Jews and buried somewhere. Not satisfied, the Germans had blown up some columns that supported the women's gallery, part of which collapsed along with the columns. We were not allowed to go into the temple, but the custodian said it was very badly damaged.

We went away very depressed because of the enormous number of deported Jews and because of the destruction that the damned Germans had done to the temple. And this was only the beginning of what had been feared.

The telephones were not working after the Germans kindly had the foresight to blow the central office to smithereens. Therefore there was no way to contact anyone who could tell us anything. I did not feel like going around knocking on the doors of our relatives and friends. I was afraid of what other bitter surprises might greet me.

We continued to wander around the streets of Florence, slowly working our way back to Via della Cernaia. We found a bar open and went in for a cappuccino. We had some sandwiches that Stella had thoughtfully prepared for us. The bar man laughed when we asked for a cappuccino. He had no electricity or gas and the espresso machine did not work. Besides that he had no milk or coffee! The only thing he could serve us was a warm orange soda. We made the best of it and ate our sandwiches with a glass of warm orange soda that was like drinking a purgative.

We reached Via della Cernaia ahead of time and talked with Rosita, describing the disaster we had seen, things she had only heard about. I was pleased to see she had calmed down. She told us that after we left that morning she had told everyone in the building about our coming back in good health. Many of them had read the notice I had stuck on our door and were glad I had done it.

The Indian captain arrived punctually. Without letting anyone see us, we quickly climbed into the truck and stayed hidden until we reached Montevarchi. During the trip Liliana and I could talk of nothing but what we had seen and heard. We were still in shock from the damage the Germans left, which had deeply wounded one of Florence's most noble and ancient areas. We discussed our moving back to Florence. The building was standing, but our apartment was completely empty, including the beds. Going to a hotel or *pensione* for any length of time was out of the question. Papa's depleted finances would not allow it. Perhaps we could ask our friends and relatives to put us up, staying at several homes until we could furnish our house well enough for all four of us to sleep there.

The first thing to do was to move our parents closer to Consuma for a few weeks, to bring them closer to Florence. However, we could not do that until we had permits from the military authorities. Surely Captain Connelly would help me get them.

We reached Montevarchi and got out on a deserted little street. We thanked our Indian friend and walked the rest of the way to Consuma. Only Stella and grandmother were in the house; Bista and the girls were out in the fields, and I went to call them. When we were together we told them what we had seen and done that day. They were all very sorry to hear about the destruction of Florence and how our house had been robbed of everything.

I asked Bista's advice about where we might put up our parents for a few weeks near Consuma, while waiting to return to Florence. There was a little *pensione* in Montevarchi where they could stay relatively inexpensively. Stella could provide their food. Naturally I wanted to make it clear that all this would be adequately compensated. Papa and mamma could spend the day at Consuma, in pleasant and comfortable surroundings with Liliana, while I continued my work as interpreter and so contribute to the finances in part.

Now it was a matter of going to Casentino and bringing our parents back to Montevarchi. I asked Liliana to do it because I did not want to take more time off work.

Liliana left the same day, after we went to Montevarchi to reserve two rooms in the *pensione* Bista had mentioned. It was in a very small house, but quiet and sunny. The rooms were spartan, but they had the great advantage of being moderately priced. I begged Liliana to be careful when she told our parents about our visit to the house. I was worried about papa's reaction, but not mamma's, considering her strong character.

When I returned to work I felt it my duty to apprise the captain of my plans for the immediate future. I did not want him to suddenly find himself without an interpreter.

He appreciated my honesty and left it up to me to find a substitute. That would not be so easy because in that area not many knew even how to speak correct Italian. I put out the word wherever my work took me.

Gradually the problems with the normal functioning of the public offices were resolved and the governor could keep abreast of things without going from place to place as he had had to in the beginning. This kept me in the city hall many hours a day without much to do. It was still not possible to communicate by telephone, so I had no idea when my parents would arrive at Montevarchi.

I was not worried because Liliana had warned me that papa might need to do everything calmly and quietly, "without rushing the events," as he often said. However, I stayed in constant contact with the *pensione* where they would be staying, and I told Liliana to look for me at the city hall during work hours to tell me when they arrived. I wanted to see them as soon as possible without wasting time.

This is the way it happened: I was busy translating a newspaper article for the captain when the sentry came to say that a Miss Tayar wanted to see me. I ran from my room to embrace my sister, but before going to the *pensione* with her, I asked the captain's permission, which he gave at once.

We ran to the *pensione*. My heart was in my throat with the excitement of seeing my parents again. We ran up the stairs two at a time and literally burst into the small room where papa was sitting and mamma was unpacking their two suitcases. I held both of them in a silent, deeply heartfelt embrace. As I held them close I relived those moments 11 months ago when I had embraced them before leaving, not knowing what the future might bring.

Now, thank heavens, I could hold them again safe and sound. These were intensely joyful moments for all of us. Papa was still as thin as when I had left him. He was wearing the same suit, which showed obvious signs of being worn well past its prime. He was wearing his customary shirt and tie, which matched the condition of his suit. Mamma had lost weight, but she looked well. Her hair was much whiter than when I last saw her. With her eyes full of happy tears she could not stop stroking my face and murmuring: "My Enzo, my Enzo." It had been a long time since I had heard anyone call me by my real name. To hear mother say it with such gentleness gave me goose bumps.

Papa tried to control his emotions, but from his trembling voice I could tell his happiness at seeing me again was too powerful. Poor papa always wanted to be in complete control of himself without ever letting go. I remember whenever one of us, for whatever reason, went to him or mother to be cuddled, he would say we were a bunch of "sissies." We talked a blue streak while mamma continued putting things in drawers and in the wardrobe; she stopped every so often if my story touched on something she wanted to hear.

Liliana mostly listened; it was better for our parents to talk and ask questions. They told me about their last move before coming to Montevarchi. Events had not transpired as quickly in the Casentino as they had in the Valdarno. There were some pockets of resistance where the Germans were hanging about and this made the situation more precarious. They had not wanted to prolong their stay at Poppi, so late one evening, with the help of Marcello, a young man of the family where they were staying, they began to walk over the mountains and woods to reach a small town called Vanna, where they knew an Indian attachment of the 8th Army had just arrived. That walk was particularly hard on my father because of his weak eyesight.

Marcello then returned to Poppi and led Liliana to our parents. Together they went to the command of the Indian battalion and requested a ride to Montevarchi in a military vehicle. This request precipitated a problem, because the various military commands were instructed to take any "displaced person," that is, a refugee, immediately to one of the detention camps readied for that purpose, which meant going even farther away.

When they related their particular story, a noncommissioned officer said: "There is a Captain Tayar in our regiment. Are you related to him?"

Neither my parents nor Liliana could imagine what Tayar this was. They thought of Franco, but it did not seem possible he could have become a captain. It turned out to be Douggie. They sent for him, and thanks to him they not only avoided being sent to the detention camp but also were able to be moved swiftly to Montevarchi in a military truck.

After about an hour of constant talk I felt light-headed and needed to return to reality. We had had all the time we needed to talk, and now it was time to make plans. We wanted news of Franco, which had to come from Douggie and his contacts through military channels. It was time for me to return to work, so we made a date for dinner at a little trattoria. I thanked the captain for giving me the time off and told him about meeting my parents. He was very understanding and did everything he could to make my life easier.

That afternoon I interviewed a woman about 50 years old who had been brought to my attention by an official of the city hall. A few months ago she had come to Montevarchi from northern Italy, to escape the bombardments, and would be there until the north was liberated.

She spoke English rather well and was interested in working as an interpreter. I thought she seemed the right person to work for Captain Connelly, and he agreed. It was established that I would call her three days before my departure and give her all the necessary instructions. I was pleased to have everything arranged so favorably. Bit by bit my life was inching toward new horizons that seemed more serene and promising each and every day.

Finally we all had a meal together in the small trattoria. There was not a wide choice of food, but none of us had much appetite after all the excitement of the morning. I told them about my stay at Consuma, and described each member of the family one by one. I wanted them to know all about the Nepis before they met.

The next day was Sunday and I was able to devote all my time to my family. I went to get them early in the morning for the walk to Consuma while it was still cool. I was pleased to see how well both papa and mamma managed the walk without becoming too tired. It would not be a problem for them to do it twice a day.

The meeting with the Nepis was festive and warm, with an immediate mutual fondness. Stella invited them to sit in the kitchen where she had prepared a very delicious breakfast, with real coffee (which papa and mamma had not tasted for years), bread, honey, and butter. While we were at the big table happily eating and talking, I whispered to mamma that I wanted her to come with me to my room for a minute.

We excused ourselves and she followed me. I closed the door and had her sit on the only available chair, while from a drawer I took the old pair of trousers I had worn the day I left Florence. I had tried not to wear them too often, for fear they might wear out and I would have to throw them away. They were too precious!

I handed them to mamma and said: "Now, thank heaven, you can take back the diamond you sewed in the seams before I left. As you see I did not have to use it. But just knowing I had it in case of extreme need made me feel more secure. Now you can put it back in your ring, and I can wear your *Shadai* again that I kept with the diamond."

Mamma slowly took my trousers. The diamond and *Shadai* came out of hiding. Holding me tightly, she said, "The Lord has loved our family and saved us from the tragic end of so many of our brothers. You must be grateful to Him for the rest of your life." We remained in that embrace, our eyes glistening with tender feelings. When we returned to the kitchen everyone was curious about our red eyes. I briefly told them the story of the diamond and *Shadai* and changed the subject, because talking about it made me relive past torments, and I wanted to put sadness behind me.

From a little leather jewel sack in her handbag mamma extracted the thin gold chain to go around my neck with the *Shadai*. From that moment I have never been without that little gold medallion with my mother's name and date of birth on the back.

After we had finished breakfast, I invited mamma, Liliana, and Bista to take a walk around the farm. Papa made himself comfortable in a deck chair outside, under the shade of a linden tree.

We wandered around the farm far and wide. I showed her exactly where I met Jim when he was escaping from the Germans, and naturally I told the story of his happy engagement with Dina. I pointed out all the land I had plowed, and the rows of vines with beautiful bunches of nearly ripe grapes. I was thinking: "When the grapes are harvested I'll be in Florence," and I was sorry, because that was work I would be very happy to do alongside the Nepis.

We found papa sleeping tranquilly under the linden tree, and mamma and Liliana began to talk with Stella and Bista. I took Dina and Delia by the arm and walked them to the cool woods. I wanted to talk with them alone and tell them my plans, and most of all I wanted to discuss Dina's plans with Jim.

The first part of the discourse was a little painful, especially for Delia. When I said that in a few weeks my family and I would be returning to Florence to take up our old life, Delia's face grew dark and she grew silent. My return to Florence was a subject she could not accept; the events of the last few days had happened too quickly and she had not got used to the idea that I would not be with her and her family any longer.

I promised her I would come back to Consuma as often as possible, even after I returned to Florence, and that I would try to spend some days with them in September for the grape harvest. This promise seemed to reassure her some. However, it did not do away with the basic problem.

Dina was also sorry I was leaving. She would also be left completely alone, with Jim gone. We talked about her wedding plans. She had had only one brief message from Jim: he had arrived safely and was getting all the papers in order. Dina said she wanted to get married before the end of the year, even if Stella and Bista preferred they wait until their son Dino returned from the military prison camp.

I told Dina and Delia about the absolute necessity for me to recoup the time I had lost over the past six years, between persecutions, forced labor, and dodging the Fascists. A young man of my age should already have a university degree or at least a clear idea of the profession he wanted to follow. I was exactly where I had been in 1938, when I had to quit school. I urgently needed to begin some kind of productive work earning a salary.

I could not thank the girls enough for all the Nepi family had done for me and for saving my life, but above all for their affection that had sustained me at the most crucial times. For this I would do everything in my power to show my gratitude in a concrete way. All I had to give Dina and Delia were words, but I was determined to follow them with deeds.

In the afternoon Liliana and I had a long talk with our parents. We wanted to plan exactly what we would do for the next few days. I was charged with obtaining from the governor four permits to return to Florence as soon as possible. When we were there, we would stay at Pensione Bellettini or another economical *pensione* for a few days. We would try to furnish our empty house as well as we could: four beds, a couple of chests of drawers, a table and four chairs would be enough for a start. We would do everything we could to recover what the Fascists had stolen, and after we made it livable, Liliana and I would look for work with the Allied Government of Florence. I would ask Captain Connelly to write me a letter of recommendation to his American colleagues in Florence.

With the little savings papa had been able to hold onto, and with Liliana's and my earnings we could get along for a few months. In the meantime papa would try to get back with his old company of before the war, and that would be the road I would take for my future.

The plan seemed right and possible to implement. Now it was up to us. After this clarification I could see that papa was very encouraged and had recovered his positive and optimistic attitude. Mamma, with her usual equanimity, was sure we would reach all our goals and she contributed her wealth of boundless confidence, of which we had great need.

I kept a daily check on the situation in Florence, where there was total confusion and lack of everything. The Allied Military Government worked industriously to get such an important city back on its feet, a city gravely crippled by Nazi ferocity. They needed strong young people to contribute to the renaissance of Florence. Anyone unable to give assistance had better stay out of the way.

I laid out our plans to the governor, telling him that Liliana and I had decided to make ourselves available to the governor of Florence and that we would be grateful if he would send our request directly to him. He promised to do it and in fact after about a week he received a positive reply: we would be able to return to Florence and we would be employed by the Military Government of the city. We set the date of our return and got the four permits for that day and, even more important, a military vehicle that would take us to Florence with all our baggage.

Bista and Stella were sad to see me go, but happy for me because I could finally begin a new life. I told them it was not a matter of "farewell," but only of "see you soon," and I wanted to come back often. The good-byes were affectionate, as is appropriate with people who love each other.

We left Montevarchi in the early morning in a "half-truck." Our parents sat in front with the driver, and Liliana and I sat on our baggage in the back of the little truck. This time we did not have to hide so we left the canvas open in order to enjoy the view.

An incredible number of military vehicles were coming and going on the road. In less than an hour we were at Via della Cernaia, with our baggage unloaded and waiting at the door. We rang Rosita's bell, who came at once and gave papa and mother a very emotional welcome. My notice was still on the door. I asked if anything important had happened. Nothing except comments of satisfaction on the part of the other families in the building that we were still alive. That was something.

Mother still had the keys to our apartment. We went in and found it as empty as an old shoe box. Dust was everywhere. Mother checked to see if the water, electricity, and gas were in working order. There was light and water, and this was already something positive. Rosita offered to help clean the house and mother accepted before hearing the end of her sentence.

I got an idea: our only relatives in Florence were the Bemporads and the Archivoltis. Why not borrow some furniture from them?

The driver of the military truck was willing to take me to Via Fiume where the Bemporads lived, if I showed him the way. We drove down the length of Via Nazionale and in a few minutes were at Via Fiume. When Beppina, Vittorio's wife, opened the door we embraced happily. They were all well, and although they had had their share of misery, they were now safe. Unfortunately, she could not say the same of Silvia and Gilda Coen, her mother and sister, who had been taken away by the Germans to an extermination camp. This news was very sad. How much more news of that kind would I hear?

I explained our situation to Beppina and asked if they had any furniture they could lend us so we would not have the expense of a *pensione*. Sadly, what they had was Silvia and Gilda Coen's furniture, which was not being used any more. They could also give us other things we would need, such as sheets, blankets, and kitchen utensils.

I wanted to make the most of having a military truck at my disposal, so I asked Beppina if I could take everything right then and there. Of course, as long as the driver and I did the work. No problem!

We dismounted and loaded onto the truck everything it would hold. This took some time, but in the end we had the necessary things to get started. I would go back with Liliana the next day to pick up other small items. I hugged Beppina and thanked her for such providential help.

We returned to the house with that precious cargo and rang the doorbell. Liliana ran to the window to see who it was and could not believe her eyes when she saw the things we had loaded on the truck. Rosita gave us a hand unloading things as quickly as possible, because the driver had to get back to his unit, and I had taken too much advantage of his kindness.

Everything was piled inside the building entrance. I thanked the young soldier and gave him a tip for his trouble. I asked him to thank the governor for all his help, and he quickly left.

Bit by bit we carried upstairs the furniture and other things Beppina had lent us. Mamma and papa were happy to be able to stay in the house without having the expense of a *pensione* for who knows how many days. Unfortunately, I had to tell papa that we had been able to get all these good things because the Germans had deported Silvia Coen, papa's aunt, and Gilda Coen, his cousin, to concentration camps. They were fragile and old and there was little hope of their being able to escape the gas chambers. Papa was deeply saddened by it, naturally, and there was little I could say to console him. It was an extremely bitter first awakening to a reality I had unconsciously suppressed over the last few years.

We worked quickly to set up the little bit of furniture and furnishings. I put a small bed in the middle of the room that had been Franco's and mine. Nothing else. The room seemed like a metaphysical painting with a little bed in the middle of that large, deserted area.

Papa and mamma fixed up their room with two beds and a dresser, and Liliana had only a bed to furnish her room. In the living room we put the table with four chairs, and the kitchen was furnished with some cabinets and a stove.

It certainly did not seem like the house we had left so hastily a year ago, but we were happy just the same because we had finally returned safe and sound and had replanted our roots in the same place we had fled. We had our whole life ahead of us to build the future.

While mother worked to put the house in order, Liliana and I went to Piazza della Vittoria to buy something to eat from our usual suppliers. We were disappointed with what little the stores had and did not buy much. On the other hand, we were gratified by the warm welcome all the store owners gave us when they saw us come in. They had all given us up for dead because of our sudden disappearance. We had to repeat our story in a telegraphic way to each one, promising to fill in the details later on.

The most moving encounter was with the dairy owner on Via Vittorio Emanuele. He had been like a brother to us throughout the time of the persecutions. He had always put an additional portion of milk aside for us that I would pick up at the back door after closing hours. As soon as he saw us, that fine, lanky man, with a slightly bent back, ran to us and hugged us both affectionately. "I'd given you up as lost," he said with a voice broken from emotion. "I've wondered so many times what happened and no one could tell me anything about you." We filled him in with more details of our adventures and said good-bye after he had given us some milk and butter, refusing to let us pay.

We went back home with a nearly empty shopping bag, but luckily we had the food Stella had given us when we left. We told our parents of the warm welcome from the various shopkeepers and we all sat down for the first meal in our house. With Bista's wine we made a toast to the family's health and to a serene and happy future.

The following morning papa, mamma, and Liliana went to thank Beppina for all she had done for us and to give her their condolences for the loss of Silvia and Gilda. I had made an appointment for mother with the chief of police on Via Zara to file a complaint against Califano for robbing our house. This same office had a long list of receivers of stolen goods and secondhand dealers, and they could help us get our things back.

The police deputy received us courteously. It was obvious that everyone was prepared to do everything they could to help us and to compensate us for what we had to suffer and lose because of the Fascists.

A police agent was put at our disposal without time limitations. He would go with us to all the shops, storerooms, or houses where stolen things were known to be hidden. For every object we recognized as ours, they would draw up a report of confiscation and formally accuse the possessor of receiving or purchasing stolen goods. It would be immediately returned to us and transported to our house at the receiver's expense.

For a number of days mother and I made the rounds looking for our things. The results were not always positive. Inevitably we found an attitude of great surprise wherever we went: "Jews?" "Fascists?" "Persecutions?" Who had ever heard of them? It seemed like a joke, but it was true.

The presence of a policeman with rather insistent and brusque ways refreshed their poor memories and, "Yes, now I remember. Maybe I have a little something in the house." We would go to his house, and I can tell you we found more than a little something!

In the house of one secondhand dealer, we found in a sideboard all my parents' silverware they had received as a wedding present, engraved with the initial *T.* The policeman asked him why he had that initial on his silverware, when his last name began with *F,* which he could not answer satisfactorily. Immediate sequester.

We found nearly 60 percent of what had been stolen. Almost a miracle, I thought. Certainly the main reason we found it was the speed with which we were able to implement the investigations. If we had waited a few more weeks perhaps the various "fences" would have made everything of doubtful provenance disappear. We interrupted our search because for the moment we had recovered enough to allow us to lead an almost normal life.

We went to thank the deputy for his cooperation and said that we would return as soon as we had finished some urgent business.

Papa went to the bank to see what had happened to the things in his safe deposit box and found it empty. Everything had been taken by the Fascist thieves. This disheartened him a great deal, but all he could do was file a complaint against an unknown person, the same as forgetting about it forever.

After we had recovered a good part of our furniture we returned nearly everything that Beppina had lent us. It might help some other relative or friend.

A whirlwind of sad and happy events swirled around us. The sad ones were the discovery of friends and acquaintances who had died in concentration camps or on battlefields. Gianfranco Sarfatti's death, who died fighting with the partisans, was a deep blow. Giuliano Treves, who returned to Florence immediately after the liberation, was shot by a Fascist sniper on Piazza S. Spirito. We had been very close during that miserable time of forced labor at Sesto Fiorentino, and it was hard to accept the fact that both were gone. In hindsight, I am sure that if I had had to choose between death as a Jew in an extermination camp or death as a partisan, I would have chosen the latter.

It was very difficult to get news of my other Jewish friends, because the telephones still were not working and I had too many pressing things to think about. I postponed the investigation for a few days. The first thing I had to do was to go to the Palazzo Vecchio, where the Allied Military Government of Florence had its offices, and ask to see the secretary of the Military Governor, General Hume of the American 5th Armored Division. After a long wait I was ushered into one of the many stupendous frescoed halls of the Palazzo Vecchio, near the Salone dei Cinquecento. General Hume's secretary was a young American sergeant by the name of Berkowitz. He was a handsome man, more preoccupied with his looks than with the work he had to do in the course of the day.

I introduced myself and asked if by chance he had received a message from Captain Connelly regarding me. He searched through a pile of papers on his table and finally pulled out the right one. He read it carefully and asked: "Are you Jewish?"

To which I replied: "Of course I am. Why do you think I was hiding?"

As I had understood at once from his unmistakable last name, he was also Jewish, and this made our dialogue much more cordial and positive.

He asked me many particulars about my family, about what happened during the period of persecutions, about my political leanings, and many other details that had to do with questions of military security, because I would be working in an area where "secret" clearance was required. I understood the reason for the questions and answered them as precisely and patiently as possible.

Finally he seemed satisfied and told me he would check everything with the "local police," that is, the carabinieri, and if everything was in order, he would call me.

When the official part of the colloquium was over, I thought to broach a less official one, of equal importance to me, however. It was September and the holidays of Rosh Hashanah and Yom Kippur were coming. Unfortunately it was not possible to use our temple because of the destruction caused by the Germans, but I asked Berkowitz if he thought there were enough Jews in the American 5th Army who might want to commemorate these important holidays with the Jewish community of Florence. He replied that he personally would be very happy to, and there certainly would be a few hundred Jewish soldiers of the same mind. However, given his rank of sergeant, even though he was General Hume's secretary, he did not have the authority to organize it.

He made a telephone call to one of his superiors, explaining our conversation, and hanging up the receiver, he said: "Come with me. I'll have you meet Major Bertrand Goldsmith." We crossed a large entrance hall and entered another stupendous frescoed hall that was normally the personal office of the mayor of Florence.

Berkowitz introduced me to Major Goldsmith, who gave me a cordial handshake and a smile: we three belonged to the same "parish." We came rapidly to the point of the visit: Goldsmith was very interested in organizing religious services for all the American and English Jewish soldiers in Florence and surrounding areas, along with the Florence Jewish community, if possible. He asked about our temple, and I had to tell him it was not usable. However, services could be held in a theater or movie house in Florence large enough to hold several hundred people.

The major was all for the idea and said that when a suitable place was found he would try to find a rabbi among the military chaplains who would conduct the religious services for both holidays. He would also see that it was publicized so that the Florentine Jews would also know about it. I gave him the address of the offices of our community center in case he needed something.

So it came about that we could serenely celebrate our first New Year after the liberation from Nazi-Fascist terror in the largest movie house in Florence, the Rex, which, though no architectural jewel, was the only place that could hold the large number of Jewish soldiers. Never before in Florence was a religious service celebrated for such a large number of Jews.

All the Florentine Jews were present who by the grace of God had escaped capture and who were in the city. The American Jews were in the majority, but the biggest surprise for all of us was the participation of members of the 178th Company and the Palestine Water Tank Unit, both sections of the newly formed Jewish Brigade within the British 8th Army. All the soldiers in the Brigade were Jews and came from what at that time was still called Palestine. I had not been aware of this special unit, but I could see that many Florentine Jews had already met and made friends with them.

I went with my parents and Liliana to take part in the deeply moving experience. This also gave me the opportunity to see those friends of mine I had not seen for so many months, and I was pleased so many of them were still alive and flourishing. I hoped that those who were not there were in some other part of Italy and in good health.

At Yom Kippur there was a commemoration for the dead, especially for those unfortunate Jews who died in German concentration camps. I was very touched, especially by the prayer of thanksgiving to the Lord for allowing those Jews present to survive. The atmosphere was mystical. It seemed to be reliving the experience of the people that Moses led across the Red Sea to escape the Egyptians.

In that large crowd filling the movie/temple, there were three well-defined groups: the first was composed of Florentine Jews only recently freed from the nightmare of persecution, many of whom were mourning relatives and friends who died in concentration camps. These Jews still had an expression of shock and disbelief on their faces at finding themselves reunited, after such a long time, to pray to and thank the Lord who had saved them.

The second group was composed of American Jewish soldiers who in their laundry-fresh uniforms and tanned and smiling faces brought a breath of great well-being and optimism. They were the symbol of restored freedom and the radiant future awaiting us.

The third group was composed of soldiers of the Jewish Brigade, who were a combination of the first two groups: each one carrying on his shoulders a very recent story of suffering that had made him emigrate from European countries to Palestine. But they also represented the future of world Judaism. They were the pioneers who, with the sad memory of the Holocaust, would establish the State of Israel, a country for all of us Jews of the Diaspora. Never in my life would I ever celebrate a Rosh Hashanah and Yom Kippur so full of emotion and meaning.

I saw Federico again and we exchanged the same exuberant greetings as always. His family was well and after they left Chianti they had hidden in Florence with some non-Jewish friends.

Among the many friends I saw again was Gianna. We gave each other a big hug, and I told her how much I had thought about her and how I had missed her. She was very kind, but perhaps less thrilled than I. I did not let it bother me.

I was able to embrace almost all my partners from the dirt-shoveling days. Some of them had decided to leave Italy for Palestine. Luciano Servi and Umberto Calò were among these. I knew that the soldiers of the Jewish Brigade were working hard to encourage Florentine Jews to emigrate to Palestine. I believed that anyone who felt like it should follow their advice. Only with a massive counter-exodus of young people would a new State of Israel be possible.

As for me, I had other plans for my future, but this did not keep me from thinking of the future of world Judaism, and how vital it would be for all of us to have a Jewish state, our point of reference. I would do whatever I could to help my brothers reach this objective.

After the holidays ended I went to Major Goldsmith to thank him for how well he had organized everything at the Rex movie house. I also brought him greetings and thanks from my Florentine Jewish friends and could see he was pleased. While I was speaking with him, Sergeant Berkowitz came into his office to tell me that the carabinieri's report had arrived and everything was in order. I could become a part of the Allied Military Government of Florence.

Goldsmith, who did not know I had applied for work, seized the opportunity to ask me if I wanted to work in his office. He needed a young man with my qualifications.

I accepted on the spot. He called his assistant, Sergeant Arthur Epstein (another American Jew), and asked him to get all the necessary documents ready. I would collaborate with him in whatever work he assigned me.

I felt at ease and happy to have found a job so quickly. I went home to give everyone the news. Now we had to find something for Liliana. She had put in her application at the Palazzo Vecchio, but so far had received no reply. I spoke to Epstein who promised me he would look into it. In a week Liliana had a good job with Major Richardson, head of the engineering office, an American, but not a Jew.

Now that we were both employed we could bring a fair amount of money home to help our parents keep "the boat afloat" (as our father said).

The work gave me the opportunity to get a picture of the many things involved with the administration of Tuscany. I was in contact with many people in the Florentine society of a high cultural level and this was very stimulating.

Speaking with Epstein one day, I told him about my idea to get the Allied Military Government involved with a Florentine charitable organization. I thought it would be a fine gesture for them to donate an ambulance to the Confraternita della Misericordia of Florence. Epstein agreed, but the money had to come from somewhere. I remembered an American army officer I had recently met: Rock Ferris, a very nice young man and an excellent piano player. I suggested to Epstein a concert at the Pergola theater, which had not been damaged and was probably available. A grand piano could be supplied by the Ceccherini store of Florence.

Rock Ferris was enthusiastic about the idea. However, he needed a couple of weeks to limber up his fingers and practice the pieces he would play. Epstein spoke with Major Goldsmith, who approved everything and made me responsible for organizing it. It was the first time I had tried to do something with all the apparatus of a military organization at my disposal. All I had to do was ask for something and it was done. I learned what it means to have the "power" in one's hands, even on a limited basis. I had tickets printed, posters put on the walls, and an article written for the local paper, *La Nazione,* which publicized the initiative of the Allied Military Government and its charitable goal.

The tickets all sold in a few days. The concert was an outstanding success and we were able to buy the ambulance for the ancient Confraternita della Misericordia.

Papa and mamma and Liliana were my guests. Major Goldsmith did the honors at the Pergola theater and thanked me for my good job of organizing.

In spite of all these activities piling one on top of another, I did not forget for even a second my promise to Stella and Bista to return for a visit. The system of public transportation between cities was still nonexistent. Getting permission to travel between Florence and Montevarchi was easy, but getting there was the problem. I managed it with a small dilapidated truck from a transport company that shuttled between Florence and Montevarchi. They were always overloaded and I would have to ride with boxes and sacks of food. No problem—that is, until the truck was so packed that I indeed had to make the whole trip from Florence to Montevarchi sitting on the big canvas covering all the merchandise. It was an adventure with the wind blowing over me and the truck banking sharply on the curves, which forced me to hang on tight to keep from being hurled onto the road. In the end, I caught a cold.

The Nepis welcomed me like a son and brother. They wanted to hear about everything I had done in Florence since I left. I told them everything without leaving out a single detail. That evening after supper we all sat around the big fireplace and I talked and talked while they listened in silence.

I realized I was talking about things totally removed from their way of life. I was talking about a world unknown to them, where in the course of one day many things can happen that might not happen in a year of a farmer's life.

I felt nostalgic for that simple existence and for the deep and true friendship I had established with them. Being in their company around the fireplace took me back to the pleasant times when I worked in the fields, ate sitting in the shade with Delia keeping me company, or slept in my hiding place in the woods.

I told them about my work in the Allied Military Government, about my relations with my superiors, about the splendid offices in the Palazzo Vecchio, and I wondered if they were envying me or, perhaps, pitying me. When I told about my encounters with all my old friends from the dirt-shoveling days, I could see Delia was hurt. She understood that I was now reestablished in my old world and consequently I had left the world she belonged to. It hurt me to see her like that.

I brought gifts for everyone, including grandmother. I gave Bista an envelope with some money toward what I owed him for my keep. He did not want to take it, but gave in to my insistence. They were happy with the gifts I bought at the American PX with Major Goldsmith's permission. I stayed overnight so I could spend Sunday with them, sleeping in "my" bed among familiar smells and sounds.

Jim managed to get word to them regularly. He was waiting to be discharged from the army before he could marry. Dina could not wait to get married and in the meanwhile was putting together her trousseau. They still did not know when their son Dino would be back, but they knew he was all right.

The next morning I walked around the farm with Bista and Delia. The grape harvest had begun and I was sorry I could not take part in it, but promised to come back for the harvest celebration supper.

I visited the two oxen. As always they were chewing away without interruption. From my caresses they immediately recognized their old friend. Nothing had changed in the rhythm of country life. Week followed on week and the seasons brought with them their specific duties with implacable regularity. Mother Nature regulated the farmers' calendar. The only imponderable was the weather that could determine a good harvest or a bad one.

The war went on. In August, General De Gaulle triumphantly entered a liberated Paris. The Germans continued to withdraw from territories they had so easily occupied at the beginning of the war. In Italy they pulled their troops back as far as the Tosco-Emilian Apennines, where they had prepared a defensive line, the "Gothic Line," in an attempt to defend themselves during winter.

Nevertheless, their destiny was sealed and nothing in the world could stop the Allied offensive. Now that our freedom was restored, there was no problem getting news about the events of the war on all the chessboards of the world. We heard more details about the Jews in the German concentration camps that were gradually being liberated by the Allied troops. Particularly hair-raising were the stories coming from the few survivors, and the number of Jews slaughtered in gas chambers grew every day.

I went to our community center offices to get the latest about the Florentine Jews who still had not returned to their homes. The information was very sketchy, because nothing was yet known about the many Jews who fled to Switzerland or the United States. Otherwise they already had the names of more than a hundred Jews from Florence who were certain to have ended up in the monstrous camps of the Nazis.

While I was there, an officer from the Jewish Brigade arrived. He wanted the names of the Jews in Florence he could contact in an attempt to create ties with the soldiers of his unit. This seemed like something that would be welcome and I encouraged the secretary of the community to do what the officer requested. In time this initiative had a positive outcome. Meetings were planned between the soldiers and Florentine Jews that worked out so well that many of our young women fell in love and became engaged to young soldiers of the Jewish Brigade, going to live in Palestine after they were married. The extroverted and impulsive natures of the young soldiers were undoubtedly more interesting than my rather reserved and timid ways with the gentle sex. Besides, after I came back to Florence I had thrown myself body and soul into my work and had little free time to spend with my friends as I had before I left. With the phones not working well it was difficult to make contact and I could not pursue a relationship with frequent personal visits.

Our family life proceeded calmly and serenely. Mamma had taken full charge of running the household and everything ran perfectly. With what Liliana and I earned we could allow ourselves the luxury of hiring a maid for a few hours two or three times a week to free mamma from the heavier housework. This pleased her and gave her time to devote to helping the fugitive Jews who passed through Florence on their way home.

Papa was impatient with his forced inactivity. There was nothing he could do yet as long as the United States was involved in war with the Germans and the Japanese. The latter, in fact, were giving the most trouble because of the enormous distance between the United States and Asia.

As for me, I had become one of the small cogwheels in the Allied Military Government machine. I was still under the direct and cordial supervision of Major Goldsmith and Arthur Epstein in the same magnificent office in Palazzo Vecchio. It was very pleasant going from one office to another, through those magnificent frescoed halls full of stupendous sculptures and antique furniture. These were the halls where the Medici plotted their intrigues and governed Florence. Speaking English eight hours a day was good for me because it made me comfortable with the language, something that would stand me in good stead in my future work.

For getting around town I got my old bicycle back through Federico. I had left it with his tenant farmer at Radda in Chianti, who had kept it and returned it intact. Now I could move around freely and get more done, both for myself and mamma.

On the Gothic Line front to the north of Florence things were at a standstill. Winter passed. The Germans tried a desperate counteroffensive in the Ardennes that failed miserably. In February there was a meeting in Yalta between Roosevelt,

Churchill, and Stalin where they planned the final attack on the German troops that would put an end to the fighting in Europe. On April 25, 1945, Italy was at last completely liberated by the Allies. On April 27, Mussolini was shot on Piazzale Loreto in Milan along with his mistress, Clara Petacci. On April 30, Hitler committed suicide with his lover, Eva Braun, whom he had married several hours earlier, in his Berlin bunker.

With these dramatic episodes the curtain fell on the reign of terror that those two madmen had started in Europe. Germany was occupied partly by the Allied army and partly by the dictator Stalin's soldiers. It was reduced to rubble by the bombardments, and who knows if the German people realized all the crimes committed from 1939 on. Hitler's collaborators and accomplices were about to face their Nuremberg judges who would condemn them in the name of humanity.

Every day the tragedy of the Holocaust assumed greater unimaginable and horrible proportions. There were millions and millions of innocent victims. The films and photographs made by the Allied troops when they entered the various concentration camps showed scenes of unspeakable atrocity. The world was horrified when it found out how much blood dripped from the hands of the German murderers.

The blood of Florentine Jews also flowed. The names of 248 of these martyrs is written on a marble memorial that the Jewish Community of Florence put at one side of the temple. Every Yom Kippur the rabbi blesses this memorial in their names. Each time I pass this memorial to enter the temple of Florence my eyes rest on those names and I always feel the suffering of my people. My heart weeps for those who had to undergo, in the name of the Lord, this supreme test. I know that we, often surviving thanks to the generosity and goodness of people who risked their lives for ours, remain in the world by the will of the Supreme Being so that the Holocaust might be remembered forever, passed down from generation to generation until the end of time, so that the barbarities are not repeated and the wolf cannot spill the blood of the lamb with impunity.

EPILOGUE

A fter our return to Florence, my father and I reopened the Italian office of the Roditi Company. My brother, Frank, who had served in the British army throughout the war, joined us in this commercial venture when he was demobilized a few months after V-E Day.

In 1946, while on my very first trip to New York, I met Vicki Fornari, a young Italian woman who had left Italy with her family at the outbreak of the Fascist persecution of the Jews. We married in 1950, and had four children: Peggy, Jane, Michael, and Pamela.

In 1949, Frank and I started our own export business, representing several major American and Canadian retailers and wholesalers in connection with their purchases on the Italian market. We eventually opened a similar office in Tel Aviv.

In 1973, Vicki and I divorced. Two years later, I married Marika, a lovely Jewish Hungarian girl whom I had met in Israel. We have a son, Richard.

Frank married Lilla, a cousin from Malta, and they had two daughters. After Lilla died at the age of 50, Frank married Vittoria, a first cousin of my first wife, with whom he had two more daughters.

My sister, Liliana, moved to New York in 1950. She married Melvin Levison, a professor of education at Brooklyn College, and they have two daughters and a son.

My parents continued to live in Florence, surrounded by their children and grandchildren. My father was 79 years old when he passed away, and my mother died at the age of 91.

Now retired, Marika and I divide our time among Florence, New York, and San Moritz, Switzerland. We are proud of our children and derive great satisfaction from their accomplishments.

As the shadows and occasional ghosts of the war years recede into the past, they seem almost surreal. They still inhabit my memory, remain an integral part of my consciousness. I was blessed with a fate far kinder than the vast majority of European Jews who were brutally oppressed, tortured, and murdered. But my experiences and those of my family and friends are part of the history of the Holocaust, and I have recorded them here to bear witness as best I could to the days of rain.